S0-BLI-042

Universities and Business: Partnering for the Knowledge Society

Published by Economica Ltd,
9 Wimpole Street
London W1M 8LB

© *Economica Ltd, 2006*

All rights reserved

First published 2006

Printed in France

Luc E. Weber and James J. Duderstadt
Universities and Business:
Partnering for the Knowledge Society

ISBN 2-7178-5190-9

Universities and Business: Partnering for the Knowledge Society

Edited by

Luc E. Weber

James J. Duderstadt

ECONOMICA

London • Paris • Genève

Titles in the Series

To Frank H. T. Rhodes
A guiding force in founding the Glion
Colloquium and shaping these important
conversations
among university, industry and government lea-
ders from Europe and North America.

His insight, wisdom and leadership
have been essential to their success and impact.

His colleagues dedicate this book to him
with admiration and gratitude.

CONTENTS

PREFACE

The Glion Colloquia were begun in 1998 to bring together university leaders from Europe and North America to compare perspectives concerning the challenges and opportunities facing higher education. These meetings have usually been held in Glion, near Montreux, Switzerland, although the second meeting in 2000 was held in La Jolla, California. Each meeting has had a particular theme, such as the global forces driving change in higher education, university governance, the interaction between universities and society, and the rapidly changing nature of research universities.

The fifth Glion Colloquium, held from June 18 to 21, 2005, in Switzerland, concerned the key relationship between research universities and the business sector. Participants included university leaders from Europe and the United States, along with senior officers of several global corporations, including Hewlett Packard, Dupont, Nestlé, Hoffman-La Roche, Daimler Chrysler, the Fraunhofer Institutes, and the Bank of England.

The emergence of a global, knowledge-driven economy has created an ever-greater dependence of society, business and industry on research universities for advanced education (particularly in science and engineering), research and development, innovation and entrepreneurial activities. From San Diego to Dublin, Helsinki to Shanghai, there is a growing recognition throughout the world that economic prosperity and social well-being in a global, knowledge-driven economy require significant public and private investment in knowledge resources such as universities and corporate R & D laboratories, as well as strong relationships between business and higher education.

The Glion V meeting began with an overview of the impact of the global knowledge economy on business, higher education, and government policies in Europe and the United States (Weber, Duderstadt, Newby and Frost, Gourley and Brennan, and Van Vught). Participants discussed the efforts of the European Community to develop a framework to position Europe for the knowledge economy through major strategies such as the Lisbon agenda, including efforts to better integrate learning and research among European universities through the Bologna process and the European Research Area. This was contrasted with the long-standing partnership in the United States among government, universities and business, although it was also acknowledged that there were numerous worrisome trends including the decline in federal research funding in the physical sciences and engineering, the erosion of basic research activities in industry, and the waning student interest in science and engineering careers that concerned U.S. participants. Yet, while the importance of universities to the knowledge economy was a primary focus of the Glion V meeting, participants were reminded of the broader public purpose of higher education that sometimes did not align well with a market orientation.

Subsequent sessions of the meeting concerned the differing perspectives on the relationship between universities and business, contrasting the views of business and university leaders, as well as those of participants from Europe and the United States. The first of these sessions concerned the changing nature of knowledge transfer from the campus to industry (Andersson, A. Jones, Johnson, Brody, Tsichritzis and Kreysel), noting the differences among the physical sciences, biomedical sciences, and engineering. Here there was considerable discussion of changing paradigms of technology transfer, driven by the growing importance of both innovation and entrepreneurial activities, as well as by the changing nature of the faculty and the needs of the business community.

The sessions concerned with the European perspective on university-business relationships (Lebret, Manson and Aebischer, Harryson and Lorange, Lambert, Soboll and Mueller) and the American experience (Fox, Faulkner, Johnson, Connelly) had similar themes. Several business leaders expressed the increasing frustration of industry about the complex negotiations involving intellectual property rights, although they also noted the growing dependence of industry on university basic research as financial pressures shifted corporate R & D more towards product development. Both business and university leaders stressed the need for a more strategic approach to these relationships — less as a philanthropic relationship in which industry provides financial support to universities, and more in the form of a strategic alliance, much as would exist between industrial partners.

There was one particularly notable difference between the European and American perspectives from university leaders. While European leaders tended to give most attention to the interaction between universities and large companies, the American universities, drawing from the successful efforts in high-tech economic development in regions such as Silicon Valley, Boston, Austin, and San Diego, tended to place a premium on technology transfer through the start-up of new companies spinning off from campus research activities. In a sense, several of the American university leaders suggested that their universities could serve society best by creating new companies and new industry, rather than serving established companies. Since the ownership of intellectual property was critical to attracting the investment capital necessary for the start-up of these new companies, it was understandable that American universities have become more tenacious in the negotiation of intellectual property rights.

The final session of the Glion V meeting focused on the increasing concerns about human capital, particularly in key areas of science and engineering (Winckler and Fieder, Johnson and Jones, Wulf and Vest). A combination of waning student interest in such careers, coupled with restrictions on immigration in the wake of the terrorist attacks in September 2001, posed the possibility of significant shortfalls in the availability of scientists and engineers in the United States. While this was not yet considered a serious problem in Europe, the rapid emergence of large science and engineering workforces in developing nations such as India and China posed a considerable threat to economic competitiveness in a technology-driven knowledge economy.

As in earlier Glion V meetings, the opportunity to compare the differing perspectives of university leaders from Europe and the United States proved both stimulating and valuable in considering the evolution of these important social institutions. Business leaders provided particularly valuable insight as to how the university could best serve society in an ever more competitive global knowledge economy. Academic leaders acknowledged, in turn, that significant changes were necessary in the structure of the university to facilitate these important partnerships. This book includes both the papers presented in the conference, as well as a summary of the discussions at the various working sessions and the text of the dinner talk given to the participants by Peter Brabeck-Lamarthe, CEO and President of Nestlé.

* *
*

The organizers of the Glion V Colloquium wish to thank the numerous sponsors of this important event and this subsequent publication. We are particularly grateful to Hewlett Packard Corporation in the United States and Europe, as well as in Switzerland, the State Secretary for Education and Research in Bern, for their generous financial support, without which the Fifth Colloquium would not have been possible, as well as the production and the distribution of this book. We also warmly thank the Board of the Swiss Federal Institutes of Technology in Zurich and Lausanne, Nestlé in Vevey and the Credit Suisse in Zurich for their financial support. Finally, we want also to extend special thanks to the University of Geneva for its patronage of the meeting and financial support.

Finally, we are particularly pleased to thank those who directly or indirectly contributed to the production of this book. We are very grateful to Gerry Taggart from the Higher Education Funding Council for England who took extensive notes of the debates and made useful proposals for the issues addressed in the summary of this book. We also thank very warmly Mr. Edmund Doogue in Geneva, who provided rigorous editorial assistance. Finally, we thank Ms Martina Trucco, University relations manager for Latin America at Hewlett Packard, and Dr. David Maradan, lecturer at the University of Geneva, for their very kind and efficient help in making the colloquium run smoothly.

Luc E. Weber   James J. Duderstadt
University of Geneva   *University of Michigan*

CONTRIBUTORS
AND
PARTICIPANTS

CONTRIBUTORS

Patrick AEBISCHER

Professor Patrick Aebischer was trained as an MD (1980) and a Neuroscientist (1983) at the University of Geneva and Fribourg in Switzerland. From 1984 to 1992, he worked at Brown University in Providence (Rhode Island, U.S.) as an Assistant and then Associate Professor of Medical Sciences. In 1991, he became the chairman of the Section of Artificial Organs, Biomaterials and Cellular Technology of the Division of Biology and Medicine of Brown University. In the fall of 1992, he returned to Switzerland as a Professor and Director of the Surgical Research Division and Gene Therapy Center at the Centre Hospitalier Universitaire Vaudois (CHUV) in Lausanne. In 1999, Patrick Aebischer was nominated President of the Swiss Federal Institute of Technology in Lausanne (EPFL) by the Swiss Federal Council. He took office on 17 March, 2000. He is a member of numerous professional societies, both in Europe and America. He is a fellow of the American Institute for Medical and Biological Engineering and a fellow of the Swiss Academy of Medicine. Patrick Aebischer is also a founder of two biotechnology companies: CytoTherapeutics (today Stem Cell In) and Modex Therapeutics (today IsoTis). His current research focuses on the development of cell and gene transfer approaches for the treatment of neurodegenerative diseases.

Bertil ANDERSSON

Bertil Andersson is a biochemist who has focused on molecular aspects of plants, especially the structure, function and regulation of photosynthesis. He is the Chief Executive of the European Science Foundation (ESF), based in Strasbourg, having taken up this post in January 2004. He was previously Rector of Linköping University, Sweden, and, prior to that, Professor of Biochemistry at Stockholm University. He is also a Visiting Professor and Fellow of Imperial College, London. He is a member of the Nobel Foundation, having also served as a member of the Nobel Committee for Chemistry (including serving as its Chair). He is also Vice-President of the European Research Advisory Board (EURAB).

Peter BRABECK-LETMATHE

Born in 1944 in Austria, Peter Brabeck-Letmathe graduated from the University of World Trade in Vienna with a degree in Economics. After joining the Nestlé Group in 1968, he spent a significant part of his career in Latin America, moving from sales manager and marketing director in Chile, to head of market, first in Ecuador and then in Venezuela. Transferred to the international headquarters in Vevey, he was appointed Executive Vice-President in 1992, and Chief Executive Officer in 1997. Peter Brabeck-Letmathe has been Chairman and CEO of Nestlé since April 2005.

John BRENNAN

John Brennan is Professor of Higher Education Research at the Open University, where he is also the Director of the Centre for Higher Education Research and Information. A sociologist by training, prior to joining the Open University in 1992, he was Director of Quality Support at the U.K. Council for National Academic Awards. He has written several books and many articles on different aspects of the relationship between higher education and social change. He has directed several national and international projects on the same theme, including an international study of the role of universities in the transformation of societies. Other international projects have focused on quality assurance in higher education and on the labour-market experiences of graduates.

William R. BRODY

William R. Brody became the 13th president of the Johns Hopkins University on 1 September, 1996. Previously, he had been provost for Health Sciences at the University of Minnesota and, from 1987 to 1994, director of the Department of Radiology at Johns Hopkins University. Dr. Brody received his B.S. and M.S. degrees in electrical engineering from the Massachusetts Institute of Technology, and his M.D. and Ph.D., also in electrical engineering, from Stanford University. Dr. Brody previously served as professor of radiology and electrical engineering at Stanford University (1977-1986). He has been a co-founder of three medical device companies, and has made contributions in medical acoustics, computed tomography, digital radiography and magnetic resonance imaging.

Thomas CONNELLY

Thomas Connelly is Senior Vice-President, Chief Science and Technology Officer of the DuPont Company. He also leads DuPont's Corporate Plans in Biobased Materials business and DuPont Ventures. At DuPont he has directed research labs in the U.S. and Europe. He has led DuPont Businesses including Engineering Polymers, Kevlar k and Fluoroproducts. Dr. Connelly studied Chemical Engineering and Economics at Princeton. He received his doctorate in Chemical Engineering from Cambridge.

James J. DUDERSTADT

Dr. James J. Duderstadt is President Emeritus and University Professor of Science and Engineering at the University of Michigan. A graduate of Yale and Caltech, Dr. Duderstadt's teaching and research areas include nuclear science and engineering, applied physics, computer simulation, and science policy. He has served as chair of numerous national Academy and federal commissions, including the National Science Board.

Larry R. FAULKNER

Larry R. Faulkner serves as president of the University of Texas at Austin, after prior appointments as provost, dean of the arts and sciences, and head of the department of chemistry at the University of Illinois. His research includes electrochemistry and analytical chemistry. Among many scientific awards and distinctions (Edward Goodrich Acheson Award from the Electrochemical Society, the American Chemical Society Award in Analytical Chemistry, U.S. Dept. of Energy Award, Charles N. Reilley Award from the Society for Electroanalytical Chemistry) he was elected to the American Academy of Arts and Sciences.

Martin FIEDER

Martin Fieder studied biology and behavioural biology at the University of Vienna, obtaining his Ph.D. in 1998. His research was supported by a grant in 1991 from Chiba University in Tokyo, and from 1994-98 he was a research fellow at the Institute of Zoology and the Institute of Anthropology of the University of Vienna. Among his recent publications, Dr Fieder has co-authored several articles on human reproduction and related subjects. Since

2000 he has been employed in the Strategic Planning section of the Rector's office at the University of Vienna.

Marye Anne FOX

Marye Anne Fox, physical organic chemist, is Chancellor and Professor of Chemistry at the University of California, San Diego. Previously, she was Chancellor of North Carolina State University and Distinguished University Professor of Chemistry. She has received many national and international awards for her contributions to science and science policy, and has held more than 50 endowed lectureships at universities around the world. She currently serves on the U.S. President's Council of Advisors on Science and Technology, on the National Academy of Sciences Committee on Science and Engineering Policy, and as chair of the National Research Council's Government-University-Industry Research Roundtable.

Alice FROST

Alice Frost is currently Projects Consultant at the Higher Education Funding Council for England working on major projects. She has previously held a number of policy positions at the Council, including Head of Research Policy and Head of Learning and Teaching, and is due to take up post as Head of Business and Community Policy in April 2006. Alice Frost has had a varied career in the U.K. in national public policy (including in the Department for Education, Cabinet Office and House of Commons), higher education policy (Universities U.K. and the charitable sector), and in the regions. She studied politics at undergraduate and postgraduate levels at Oxford University.

Brenda M. GOURLEY

Professor Brenda Gourley joined The Open University as Vice-Chancellor in January 2002 from the University of Natal, where she had been Vice-Chancellor since 1994 and previously Dean of the Faculty of Accounting and Management and Deputy Vice-Chancellor. She is a member of the British Council's Education and Training Advisory Committee and on the Board of the International Association of Universities. Professor Gourley has continuing academics interests in Strategies and Systems Thinking, Leadership and Ethics, and was awarded an honorary degree by the University of Nottingham in 1997 for her contribution to Higher Education.

Sigvald J. HARRYSON

Dr. Sigvald Harryson holds a Master of International Business (1991) from Lund University; a Doctoral degree (1995) from St. Gallen University, and a Ph.D. (2002) from Göteborg University. He is currently Director of the Growth

Through Innovation Program at the Baltic Business School in Sweden, and the Managing Director of Harryson Consulting GmbH in Switzerland. Dr. Harryson started his career as a development engineer in five countries within the Tetra Pak Group — primarily working within the fastest-growing business: Tetra Brik Aseptic in Carton. He also spent 10 years in management consulting: working as a Consultant at BCG, a Principal of Booz Allen Hamilton, and a Partner of Arthur D. Little, where he was in charge of the Technology and Innovation Management (TIM) practice. Dr. Harryson has published in several leading journals, including *HBR*, *Journal of Product Innovation Management* and the *International Journal of Technology Management*. One of his Edward Elgar books on TIM was recently published in Chinese by Peking University Press.

Wayne JOHNSON

Wayne Johnson is Vice-President for University Relations Worldwide at Hewlett Packard in Palo Alto. He is responsible for higher education programmes in research, marketing and sales, recruitment, continuing education, public affairs and philanthropy. During his career, he has gathered significant management experience across a diversified set of business operations, including university relations management, engineering management, programme management, international training and logistics, research, international business development and commercial business development, mainly with Raytheon in different locations, as well as with Microsoft Research. He has an M.B.A. from Boston College Carroll School, and a B.A. from Colgate University. He is a board member of Anita Borg Institute for Women and Technology (ABIWT), Government-University-Industrial Research Roundtable (GUIRR), Accreditation Board for Engineering and Technology (ABET) and Alliance for Science and Technology Research for America (ASTRA).

Anita K. JONES

Professor Jones is a University Professor at the University of Virginia. She served as the Director of Defense Research and Engineering for the U.S. Department of Defense in the 1990s. More recently, she has served as a member of the two Boards that oversee the U.S. National Science Foundation and Science Foundation Ireland. Professor Jones is a member of the National Academy of Engineering. She received the Augusta Ada Lovelace Award from the Association of Women in Computing in 2004.

Russel C. JONES

Russel Jones is a private consultant, working through World Expertise LLC to offer services in engineering education in the international arena. Prior to that, he had a long career in education: as faculty member at MIT, department chair in civil engineering at Ohio State University, dean of engineering at University of Massachusetts, academic vice president at Boston University, and President at University of Delaware.

Michael-Alexander KREYSEL

Michael-Alexander Kreysel is Executive Assistant to the Senior Vice President of the Fraunhofer-Gesellschaft, Germany. In addition, he is currently involved in the German innovation initiative launched by the German Chancellor. He received his degrees in business administration and entrepreneurial finance from the University of Cologne (diploma, 1999) and the Technical University of Dresden (Ph.D., 2005). He specialised in the field of venture capital, entrepreneurship and innovation management.

Richard LAMBERT

Richard Lambert was appointed as an external member of the Monetary Policy Committee in England with effect from 1 June 2003. The MPC is responsible for setting interest rates to meet the government's inflation target. In December 2003 he completed a review on behalf of the government of the relationship between business and universities in the U.K. Richard Lambert started working at the *Financial Times* in 1966 as a trainee and retired as Editor in 2001. During the intervening years he edited the "Lex" column (74-79), was New York Bureau chief (82-83) and Deputy Editor (83-91).

Hervé LEBRET

Dr. Hervé Lebret graduated from the Ecole Polytechnique, France, in 1987, SupAero in 1989 and obtained an MS from Stanford University in 1990. After two years of project management for the French department of defence, he went back to academia to obtain his Ph.D. in electrical engineering from Université de Rennes in 1994 (with another year spent at Stanford University). He stayed in academia from 1994 to 1997 as dean of studies of the ENSTA (Paris) and a researcher at Onera (Palaiseau, France). His domain was the development and application of convex optimization algorithms in signal processing, antenna design and finance. In 1997, he began a new career in venture capital with Index Ventures in Geneva, Switzerland. Index has successfully invested in companies such as Virata, Numerical Technologies, Skype, and more recently in EPFL spin-offs BeamExpress and Innovative Silicon. He left Index to work at EPFL in 2004 in technology transfer and support to innovation; he currently runs the INNOGRANTS, a new grant mechanism assisting EPFL innovators.

Peter LORANGE

Dr. Peter Lorange has been President of IMD since 1 July, 1993. He is Professor of Strategy and holds the Nestlé Chair. He was formerly President of the

Norwegian School of Management in Oslo. His areas of special interests are strategy, global strategic management, strategic planning, strategic alliances and strategic control. In management education, Dr. Lorange was affiliated with the Wharton School, University of Pennsylvania, for more than a decade. Dr. Lorange has written or edited 18 books and over 130 articles. He has conducted extensive research on multinational management, strategic planning processes, strategic control and strategic alliances. He received his undergraduate education from the Norwegian School of Economics and Business, was awarded a Master of Art degree in Operations Management from Yale University, and his Doctor of Business Administration degree from Harvard University.

Jan-Anders E. MANSON

Professor Jan-Anders E. Månson obtained his Ph.D. from Chalmers University of Technology, Gothenburg, Sweden, in 1981. Following some years as Technical Director of Konstruktions-Bakelit AB, Sweden, he was appointed Professor at University of Washington (Chemical Engineering), Seattle, and later at the Royal Institute of Technology (Polymer Technology), Stockholm, in the field of Composite Materials. In 1990 he joined the Swiss Federal Institute of Technology in Lausanne (EPFL) as Professor and Director of the Composite and Polymer Laboratory, and in year 2000 as Director of the Institute of Material Science. His research is focused on the next generation materials and processes for the fast-growing polymer and composite field related to aerospace and automotive, as well as to sport and medical applications. He has coordinated several large school-wide projects such as the EPFL — Alinghi America's Cup collaboration and the Bertrand Piccard Solar Impulse project. He is member of the Swiss Academy of Engineering Science (SATW), and the Royal Swedish Academy of Engineering Sciences (IVA). Since 2004 Jan-Anders Månson has been Vice-president of EPFL, responsible for Innovation and Technology Transfer.

Klaus MUELLER

Klaus Müller is an organic chemist by training (ETH Zurich; 1970, Ph.D. with Prof Albert Eschenmoser), but also got involved in theoretical and physical organic as well as biostructural chemistry. In 1982, he joined F. Hoffmann-La Roche AG, Basel, where he set up and further developed molecular modelling, biostructural research, bioinformatics, and was involved in the development of automated and miniaturized key technologies in discovery research. Since 1998, he has been head of Science & Technology Relations, acting as liaison person to both academic and non-academic external groups, as well as internally between different discovery research disciplines. He is a board member and acts as Secretary-General of the Roche Research Foundation and is on the board of several other scientific foundations. Since 1990 he has been extraordinary professor at the University of Basel, teaching structural chemistry as well as chemistry- and bio-informatics.

Sir Howard NEWBY

Sir Howard Newby joined the Higher Education Funding Council for England as Chief Executive in October 2001. Prior to that he was Vice-Chancellor of the University of Southampton from 1994 to 2001. His earlier posts include Chairman (1988-94) and Chief Executive (1994) of the Economic and Social Research Council, Professor of Sociology at the University of Essex (1983-88) and Professor of Sociology and Rural sociology of the University of Wisconsin, Madison (1980-83). He has also held visiting appointments in Australia and elsewhere. Professor Newby has published many books and articles on social change in rural England and was for eight years a Rural Development Commissioner, a member of the government body responsible for the economic and social regeneration of rural England. From 1983-88 he was Director of the ESRC Data Archive, a national facility for storing and disseminating computerised datasets for use by researchers in the public and private sectors. From 1999 to 2001, he was President of Universities U.K., the U.K. body which represents the University sector. He was also President of the British Association for the Advancement of Science for 2001-02. Professor Newby was awarded a CBE in 1995 for his services to social science and a knighthood in 2000 for his services to higher education.

Horst SOBOLL

Horst Soboll studied physics at the University of Giessen in Germany and was awarded a doctorate in 1973. He held various management positions at CONTROL DATA Corporation in Frankfurt and Hamburg from 1973-1989. In 1989 he joined DaimlerChrysler Research as a Project Manager of Information and communication Technology. In 1995 he was named Director of Technology Policy, and in 2002 he became Director of Research Policy and Communications. Since 2005 he has been working as an independent Consultant for Research, Technology and Innovation for various European initiatives. He is engaged in several European Research Committees including (as Chair or ViceChair) EIRMA, EURAB and UNICE.

Dennis TSICHRITZIS

Dennis Tsichritzis is Senior Vice-President of the Fraunhofer-Gesellschaft, Germany. He received his degrees in electrical engineering and computer science from Athens University (diploma 1965) and Princeton (Ph.D., 1968). From 1968 to 1985, he was professor of computer science at the University of Toronto. He was also professor at the University of Crete and director of the

Institute of Computer Science. From 1985 to 2002, he was professor of computer science at the University of Geneva, and, from 1991 to 2001, he was also Chairman of the Board of the GMD (German National Research Centre for Information Technology). He has worked in several fields of computer science, including theory, operating systems, database management, office automation object-oriented systems, and multimedia.

Frans van VUGHT

Frans van Vught (1950) is a member of the high-level Group of Policy Advisors presided by the president of the European Commission. In addition he is a member of the Executive Board of the European University Association (EUA), president of the European Centre for Strategic Management of Universities (ESMU), a member of the German "Akkreditierungsrat" and of the University Grants Committee of Hong Kong. Professor van Vught was President and Rector of the University of Twente, the Netherlands, from 1997 to 2005. Before that he was the founding director of the Center for Higher Education Policy Studies (CHEPS). Prof. van Vught is a member of the Dutch national Innovation Platform, the Dutch national Social-Economic Council and the Dutch national Council on Education. He has published widely in higher education and has worked with many governments and several international organizations (OECD, UNESCO, World Bank).

Charles M. VEST

Charles M. Vest served as president of the Massachusetts Institute of Technology from 1990-2004. A professor of mechanical engineering at MIT, and formerly at the University of Michigan, he is a member of the National Academy of Engineering, has served on the U.S. President's Council of Advisors on Science and Technology since 1994, and has chaired the President's Committee on the Redesign of the Space Station and the Secretary of Energy's Task force on the Future of Science at DOE. He recently served as a member of the Commission on the Intelligence Capabilities of the United States regarding weapons of mass destruction. He is a director of IBM and DuPont, holds eight honorary doctorates, and was vice chair of the U.S. Council on Competitiveness for seven years.

Luc E. WEBER

Educated in the fields of economics and political science, Luc Weber has been Professor of Public Economics at the University of Geneva since 1975. As an economist, he serves as an adviser to Switzerland's federal government, as well as to cantonal governments, and has been a member of the "Swiss Council of Economic Advisers" for three years. Since 1982, Prof. Weber has been deeply involved in university management and higher education policy, first as vice-rector, then as rector of the University of Geneva, as well as Chairman and, subsequently, Consul for international affairs of the Swiss Rectors' Conference. He is also the co-founder, with Werner Hirsch, of the Glion Colloquium and a funding Board Member of the European University Association (EUA). At present he is chair of the Steering Committee for Higher Education and Research of the Council of Europe and vice-president of the International Association of Universities (IAU). He has been awarded an honorary doctorate by the Catholic University of Louvain-la-Neuve for his contribution to Higher Education.

Georg WINCKLER

Georg Winckler studied at Princeton University and the University of Vienna, and was appointed Full Professor of Economics at the University of Vienna in 1978. He has been Visiting Scholar at the International Monetary Fund (1990-1991), Visiting Professor at Georgetown University (Fall 1995) and at other universities, and Rector of the University of Vienna since 1999. He was President of the Austrian Rectors' Conference (2000-2005), Vice-President of the European University Association (2001-2005) and President since March 2005. He has been a member of the European Research Advisory Board since 2004.

Wm. A. WULF

Elected in 1997, Dr. Wulf is currently on leave from the University of Virginia to be President of the U.S. National Academy of Engineering. He previously served as Assistant Director of the National Science Foundation, and founded and was CEO of a software company, Tartan Laboratories. He is a Fellow of five professional societies, and a foreign member of seven Academies. He has written over 100 papers and three books, and holds two US Patents.

PARTICIPANTS

The following leading academics, business representative and political figures participated at the Fifth Glion colloquium and contributed comments and statements to the revision of the papers collected here and to the conclusion.

Michel BENARD, Director, HP University Relations Technology Programs.

Ernst BUSHOR, Vice-President of the ETH Board and former Minister of Education of the Canton of Zurich.

Carles SOLA, Minister of Higher Education, Research and technology of the Government of Catalonia and former Rector of the Autonomous University of Barcelona.

Peter Van BLADEREN, Director of the Nestlé Research Centre, Lausanne, Switzerland.

Paul WELLINGS, Vice-Chancellor of Lancaster University, U.K.

PART I

••••••••••••••

The Role of Universities,
Business and Government
in Meeting the Needs
of Society

CHAPTER 1

European Strategy to promote the Knowledge Society as a Source of renewed economic Dynamism and of social Cohesion

Luc E. Weber [1]

PREAMBLE

S ince the 1950s, Europe has been engaged in an ambitious political and economic integration process which received a new boost with the fall of the Berlin wall in 1999 and, soon afterwards, the collapse of the communist USSR. Twenty-five countries now make up the enlarged European Union, soon to be 27, with more expected to join later. Few people doubt that this free market of 450 million people is beneficial to the citizens of Europe. Nevertheless, Western Europe, and in particular the countries which adopted the Euro, is suffering from a slowdown in economic growth, as well as high unemployment and a rapidly ageing population. At the same time, the economies of the East European countries which recently joined the E.U. are taking off, the United States is benefiting from more than 15 years of solid economic growth, and many Asian countries, in particular China, India and South Korea, are becoming major economic powers, as peasant societies and models of mass production transform themselves into genuinely innovatory producers. Figures 1 to 3 below illustrate some of these facts. (see also OECD, 2005a & b)

1 I am very grateful to Dr. David Maradan, of the Department of Economics at the University of Geneva, who collected the data and prepared figures 1 to 4.

Figure 1: Average annual growth rate of GNP in selected countries

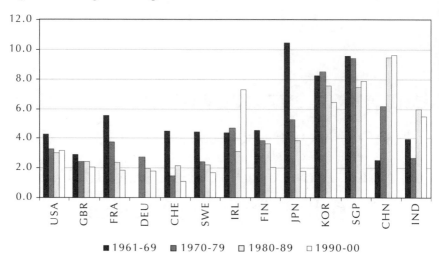

Source: World Bank

Figure 2: Unemployment in several European countries

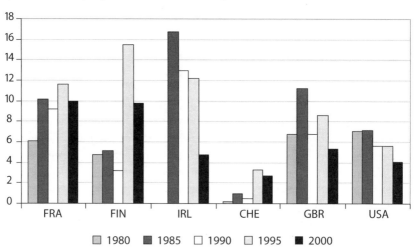

Source: Eurostat

It is highly unlikely that Western Europe will be able to maintain its high living standards, envied by many, if it does not take action to revive economic growth. Most experts agree that Western Europe has four possible options:

Figure 3: Evolution of median age in several European countries and in the U.S.

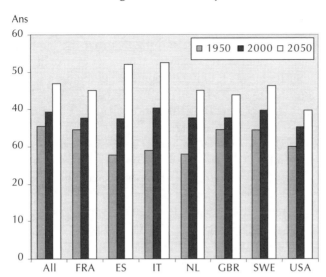

Source: Algave & Plane, 2004

a) encourage immigration by many young, preferably qualified, individuals, a measure which would certainly prompt strong opposition among the general public; b) ensure that the relatively generous social welfare system remains "sustainable" in a period in which population is ageing and economic growth is slowing down, thus presenting a major challenge; c) increase economic growth by eliminating the numerous barriers to competition; and d) investing more in the knowledge society as a source of economic dynamism.

In this introductory contribution to the theme of the fifth Glion collo-quium, written from a European perspective, I shall focus on the fourth pillar of regained economic dynamism, the development of the knowledge society. This action was launched politically at the 2000 Council of the Heads of State of the European Union in Lisbon (Lisbon European Council — President's conclusion, 2000) — henceforth referred to as the "Lisbon agenda" — with the following statement: "To become the most competitive and dynamic knowledge-based economy in the world, capable of sustainable economic growth with more and better jobs and greater social cohesion". Inspired by the development of the European Higher Education Area (EHEA) — better known under the name "Bologna process", the strategy was to create, for research, the European Research Area (ERA) (Commission of the European Communities, 2000) and to raise investment in research to an average of 3% of GNP (for more details, see, for example, Weber & Zgaga, 2004).

Five years later, at mid-term, it appears that the European Union is not on track to reach the ambitious political goal set for 2010. This is due to at least two reasons: weak economic growth in the larger European nations, creating major obstacles in public finances; and the fact that the implementation of the goals set at the level of the European Union relies strongly on the efforts of member countries and on industry. Some, in particular the Scandinavian countries, continue to invest heavily in higher education and research, and some, like the U.K., are increasing their efforts, but the situation is in general getting worse in most other countries.

Conscious of this programme failure, the new European Commission, in office since November 2004, is trying to restart the process. It has just published a Communication, "Working together for growth and jobs, a new start for the Lisbon Strategy" (2005a), addressed to the spring 2005 European Council. Although this communication suggests action in a variety of domains, it appears as if Higher Education and Research (HE/R) had never been so high on the European Commission's agenda. The speech that President Barroso addressed to 600 university leaders meeting in Glasgow for their biannual convention speaks for itself: the title was "Strong universities for Europe". Moreover, the Commission has just published a new communication aimed at universities, with the title "Mobilizing the brainpower of Europe: enabling universities to make their full contribution to the Lisbon Strategy" (2005b), and is going to publish later another communication on the role of universities in research. Will these new initiatives be more successful than the previous one? At this stage, it is difficult to say, as it depends on so many actors and factors and, in particular, on the policies implemented in the members countries, as well as in European countries that are not members of the European Union.

This introductory contribution begins by showing that Europe's investments in higher education and research are lagging behind. Then, it briefly examines the main articulations of the policies put in place over the last five years or about to be launched to restart the "Lisbon agenda". It finishes with a few comments and a set of questions addressed to the colloquium.

EUROPE AND THE KNOWLEDGE SOCIETY: THE PRESENT SITUATION

Higher education and research (HE/R), economic growth, employment and quality of life

Education has numerous functions in modern societies: intellectual and democratic training, acquisition of professional skills, knowledge production, etc (Cohen, 2005). It is a rational strategy for individuals to invest in their human capital as it increases their productivity, which means higher salaries, and it reduces the risk of long-term unemployment. The investment in human capital is also an excellent policy for society as a whole, as it contributes to economic growth and development (Aghion & Cohen, 2005). Recent studies have shown that the closer a country is to the "technology frontier", the more profitable it is to invest in knowledge through higher education and research. For a country far from the technology frontier, it is more profitable to grow by adapting technology from the most advanced countries and therefore to invest in primary and secondary education. When a country approaches the technology frontier, the possibilities of imitation become more limited and it then becomes more profitable to invest in higher education (Cohen, 2005).

HE/R and a society based on knowledge are also necessary conditions — but not sufficient — for the promotion of democratic values, social cohesion, cultural development and individual security and well-being.

It is therefore obvious that for individuals and society as a whole, expenditures in HE/R have to be considered as investment and not as consumption expenditures.

European investment in Higher Education and Research is lagging behind

At first sight, in the light of Europe's standard of living and quality and sophistication of industrial products and services, one could get the impression that the European level of investment in HE/R is sufficient. However, as Mora (2005) and Cohen (2005) have shown at a conference organized by the European Commission in February 2005, "total expenditure on higher education in Europe has not increased in proportion to the growth in the number of students. A substantial gap has opened up with the U.S. and other developed countries" (Mora, 2005). In 2004, while Korea, the U.S. and Canada spent more than 2.5% of GNP on higher education, this ratio lies between 0.9% and 1.8% in European countries, with France, Germany and the U.K. spending just a bit more than 1% (see figure 4 for an overview). This gap is also confirmed if we consider expenditures per inhabitant. Perhaps the most striking fact is that the source of this considerable variance is to be found overwhelmingly in private investment — students' fees and private funding provided by the business sector and foundations, as well as from the endowment funds in research universities. Whereas private funding accounts for two thirds of the total funding in American universities, in most European universities that proportion is around 10% (Mora, 2005; Commission staff working paper, 2005a).

The situation is very similar for research. In 2004, Europe's total investment in research amounted to 1.97% of GDP, whereas the U.S. invested 2.76% and Japan 3.12% (Commission staff working paper, 2005a). The gap

Figure 4: Total Investment in tertiary Education as a Percentage of GDP, 2001

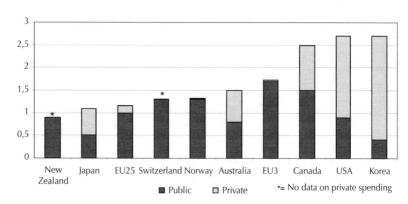

Source: European commission, Staff working paper, Annex to the Communication *Mobilising the brainpower of Europe* (2005a). (EU3=Denmark, Finland and Sweden, the three best performing countries).

with the U.S. in research investment is estimated by the European commission to be €130 billion a year and might be widening. However, when analysing the origin of the gap, it is important to keep in mind that 57% of the U.S. Federal Government Research and development funding is appropriated to national defence research (Morgan, 2005).

When analysing these figures, we must be aware that we are considering input figures, which leads us to assume that the efficiency of the system is the same. However, even if it was possible to prove that the European HE/R systems were more efficient than those of the leading countries — though we do not have any strong evidence supporting it — the gap is obviously important and the theory shows that, in any case, higher investment would contribute to higher economic growth and employment.

These global figures do not reflect the important regional disparity between countries. For research, in particular, the overwhelming volume of fundamental and applied research is carried out in a triangle located in North-West Europe, whose origin lies somewhere around Vienna. The ranking of the best European research universities proves this unambiguously. If we believe that university education must be based on research, we can also extrapolate that the content of teaching is better in this part of Europe than in the rest of the continent.

European diversity and economic development

Europe is a conglomerate of nearly 50 States, some very small, with a total population of 800 million inhabitants. They all have their specificity regarding standards of living, history, culture, traditions, language, education systems, governmental and administrative, as well as economic systems. This diversity is a great asset and strength if there is people's mobility and permeability to ideas and practices from other countries. But it is also a burden because it makes cross-border relationships more costly and because the multiplication of systems — basically to resolve similar problems — imposes higher transaction and efficiency costs.

EUROPEAN POLICIES TO PROMOTE THE KNOWLEDGE SOCIETY

Tendencies in the 1980s and 1990s

Considering any development in Europe, policies conducted by countries within and outside the EU are determinant, despite the growing importance of the European Union. Globally, it is fair to say that HE/R have not been a priority of governmental policy in recent decades in the great majority of countries, with the consequence that the investment per head in higher education decreased significantly in most countries due to the massification of student numbers. Moreover, in many countries, doubts about the efficiency of the sector are at the origin of increased political pressures. Apart from Ireland and Finland in particular, which believed in HE/R as an engine of economic development, most of the impetus came from the European Union. The two flagship programmes are the "research framework programmes" launched in the early 1980s to stimulate joint research programmes between university and industry as well as institutions from various countries, and the "Erasmus program" established in 1987 to encourage student and staff mobility between participating countries for 1-2 semesters. Although quite successful if we consider that more than 1.2 million students have benefited from it, the Erasmus program concerns only a small proportion of the total number of European students. The research framework programmes in their early versions were focused on applied research and development — therefore being mainly of interest for industry and applied science higher education institutions.

The emergence of Higher education and research as a factor of prosperity

The turn of the millennium has witnessed the launch of two very important initiatives aiming at creating a European area of higher education and another one for research (see, for example, Weber & Zgaga, 2004).

The European Higher Education Area (EHEA). The initiative to introduce the European Higher Education Area (EHEA) was launched in 1998 by the Ministers of Education of France, United Kingdom, Germany and Italy at the celebration of the 700th anniversary of La Sorbonne in Paris — independently of the European Union — and confirmed a year later in Bologna (Italy) where 29 countries signed a declaration aimed at creating a European Higher Education Area (EHEA) without borders by 2010. The central idea of the so-called "Bologna process" is to promote student and staff cross-border mobility thanks to the adoption by participating countries of a system of "Bachelors" and "Masters", and to the introduction of a harmonized credit system (European credits transfer system or ECTS).

In order to take stock of the progress made and to give new impetus to the process, the ministers in charge of higher education meet every two years to evaluate progress made (Prague in 2001, Berlin in 2003, Bergen in 2005 and London in 2007) on which occasions they adopted new members (45 out of the 48 European countries are now participating in the process) and new pillars, the most important one being to add in 2003 doctoral studies as a third higher education cycle, in order to secure the link with the European research area (for more information, see the Bologna secretariat 2005-2007 website).

At mid-term of the process, it is amazing to observe that all but three European countries, including Russia, have decided to participate in this large-scale exercise of transparency, but also to see that the implementation is well underway (see for ex. Reichert & Tauch, 2005). This implies a gigantic — some call it revolutionary — reorganization of the study programmes in approximately 4,000 higher education institutions, universities and professional/vocational colleges. Moreover, to guarantee the necessary trust between institutions to make sure they will accept students who have acquired a certain number of credits in another institution, particularly in another country, the quality of institutions and its audit, as well as the recognition of degrees, have moved to the centre of preoccupations in European countries.

Moreover, the discussion about quality as well as the necessity for institutions to adapt more rapidly to a changing environment helped to reveal that the governance of higher-education systems at national or regional levels and of nearly all European institutions was not favourable to decision-making, certainly rapid decisions, encouraging a few countries and institutions to adapt their system to 21st century requirements.

With the first groups of students to receive the new "bachelor" presently graduating, it is much too early to judge if the process will deliver its promises regarding students and staff mobility, which have become a necessity to secure that the European diversity is an asset, as well as to promote the transparency and readability of the European higher education system, a necessary condition for its attractiveness to non-European students. Although the European higher education system will remain quite diversified, the Bologna process acts presently as a strong engine of change and of adaptation to the climate of increasing competition in a globalized world.

The European research Area (ERA): Well aware that knowledge is the essential engine of economic development and that Europe is not investing as much as countries like the U.S. or Japan in the development of new knowledge, the Heads of State of the European Union decided in 2000 in Lisbon to increase their national and common (through the budget of the European Union) investments in research and technology development in order to become "the most competitive and dynamic knowledge-based economy of the World by 2010" (Lisbon European Council – President's conclusion, 2000). The strategy proposed was to create the "European Research Area" (Commission of the European Communities, 2000) in better integrating national efforts by encouraging researchers to work together at the European Union level, by promoting cooperation between university and industry and by lowering administrative and political barriers to that cooperation (Weber & Zgaga, 2004). Two years later, the European Commission issued a communication, "More research for Europe, Towards 3% of GDP" (2002), stating that the only way to reach the ambitious target set in Lisbon in 2000 was to increase the general effort made in research to reach 3% of GDP and that two thirds of this effort should be made by private industry (Weber & Zgaga, 2004). In order to reach this 3% objective by 2010, the public sector and companies should increase their expenditure on research by an ambitious 6.5% and 9.5% respectively on average each year and the number of new researchers in Europe should increase by 700,000 persons or approximately 70%!

Considering the extremely high ambitions of the Lisbon agenda, it is not really surprising that the European Union is, at mid-term, far from its 2000 objective, in particular because the implementation of reforms in Member States has been quite scarce and the additional financing has been provided neither by the public sector, nor by companies (Kok, 2004). The hard truth is that the gap in research investment between Europe and its main competitors — traditionally the U.S. and increasingly from Asia — is actually increasing. Obviously, self-persuasion is not sufficient, and the European Union, as the promoter of a renewal of the conditions for economic growth in Europe, cannot produce a miracle with its own very limited budget, particularly as the Union has also difficulties in materializing these future-orientated priorities in its own budget.

A new start for the 'Lisbon Strategy'?

In view of the fact that in the face of international competition and an ageing population, economic growth could soon decrease to 1% per year (less than half today's growth rate), the much valued social and environmental European model will become unaffordable. This hard reality, described by the Sapir (2003) and Kok (2004) reports, encouraged the new European Commission put in place in November 2004 under the presidency of Barroso to take the necessary initiatives to initiate a new start to the "Lisbon Strategy". In a new communication to the spring European Council (2005a) the Commission is proposing to establish a new kind of partnership with Member States and to focus efforts on productivity and employment.

Observed by a university leader, never have HE/R been so high on the agenda of the European Commission! Following a renewed action plan focused on the contribution of Higher education and research to the knowledge society, the Directorate general for Education and culture drafted a communication to boost the role of higher education and research in developing the knowledge society, "Mobilising the brainpower of Europe" (2005b), proposing an action plan to reinforce European universities, which followed another communication "The role of universities in the Europe of knowledge" (2003). The Directorate General for Research, Science and Society organized last year an important conference in Liege on "Europe of knowledge 2020" (2004), then created a Forum on university-based research which published the report "European Universities: enhancing Europe's Research base" (2005), and is presently drafting another communication on the topic. The change of policy, if accepted by the European Council and Parliament, should produce a doubling of the part of the EU budget allocated to policies aimed at increasing growth and employment, at supporting innovation and spreading knowledge through high quality education. However, it is all but certain that the means to reach this ambitious European goal will be set aside, in particular thanks to a decrease of the share allocated to the European common agricultural policy.

Regarding research more specifically, the European Commission is proposing to double the budget allocated to the seventh framework programme for the period 2007-2013. The proposed new programme (Commission, 2005c) will basically be a continuation of the previous programme with support for cooperation between researchers from different origins, university and industry, a form of direct support to researchers and infrastructures. However the programme includes a very important and interesting innovation for research-intensive universities, the creation of a European Research Council (ERC). This council will, exclusively on the basis of merit, allocate grants to young researchers and new groups as well as established teams active in the most promising and productive areas of research, within and across disciplines, including engineering and social sciences and the humanities. The Commission also promises to simplify the appropriation procedures, which rightly have a reputation for being very bureaucratic and using more often lump-sum financing or grants (Commission staff working document, 2005b).

Among other initiatives, we note that the Commission (2005a) will propose the creation of a "European Institute of technology", which, according to early discussions, could take the form of a network of leading universities in science and applied science. We also observe a genuine interest in the statutes of researchers. Moreover, the improvement of technology transfer remains a very challenging issue for European university and industry.

The policies regarding higher education are largely a continuation of the policy launched in 1999 in Bologna. Although important politically, the enlargement of the Bologna signatories to 45 countries at the Bergen summit (Communiqué, 2005) is significant for the contribution of higher education to the "Lisbon agenda", in particular the decision to introduce doctorate studies in the Bologna process in Berlin in 2003, thus making sure that the EHEA and ERA will be strongly linked together through the doctorate studies. This has stimulated an intensive collective inquiry on how to make doctorate studies attractive, not only for those looking for academic positions, and how to best organize them. Some other positive benefits are also the intensifying discussion about the organization of joint degrees — masters and doctorates — between two institutions, quality assurance and audit, governance, funding and the link between higher education and research.

CONCLUSION

Despite its great potential due to its cultural diversity, good education and huge market, Europe is not doing well economically: economic growth is moderate and the trend is decreasing, the population is rapidly ageing, and the social system that Europe is proud of is not sustainable under these conditions. Moreover, high employment rates in many countries cast a shadow over the quality of its social model and of its environment.

Most countries, in particular in the west, are struggling to put courageous policies in place, but governments have difficulties obtaining a majority because individuals and organizations attach increasing weight to their own interests.

The European Union, whose budget is less than 1.5% of GNP, tries to initiate pro-active policies of change thanks to analysis, suggestions and exhortations. However, it cannot act as a real European government would do without strong, even unanimous, support from the member States and the majority of the European parliament. Moreover, the European Union must make a great effort to support the development of the poorer regions of Europe, mainly in the South and now in the East in the ten — soon 12 — countries which just joined the Union.

The importance of HE/R has grown over time, but it is only quite recently that it has been considered as a key instrument to make sure Europe becomes again very competitive in order to financially support its developed social system and to challenge the good economic performance of the U.S. and rapid development of many Asian countries.

Two important initiatives have been taken at the turn of the millennium: the creation by 2010 of the European higher education area which now concerns the whole of Europe (apart from three countries) and the launch of the "Lisbon agenda" of regained competitiveness thanks to a massive investment in knowledge, with a strong effort on research.

The simple fact that so many countries have agreed to work together to eliminate the multiple barriers which till recently made the idea of a European higher education area just a dream and to join forces in research is remarkable and, no doubt, will have very positive effects in the future.

However, it would wrong to neglect the level of ambition and complexity of the task. Regarding higher education, there will still be for many years nearly 50 countries with different systems and rules. Obviously, everyone will have adapted their system by 2010 according to their interpretation of the Bologna objectives and their capacity to manoeuvre, but there will still be differences or even new differences will be created, which will constitute obstacles to mobility. Moreover, the quality level of institutions will remain very different, which means that it would be wrong to expect that good institutions will accept those students coming from lower level institutions without special requirements. Considering the financial barriers to mobility and the still strong tendency for students to study first in their regional university, it would be too ambitious to imagine that all students or even a majority of students will take advantage of the enrichment of spending study time abroad or even complete their studies by visiting two or three universities. On a more optimistic note, I believe that the incitation to offer joint programmes between two or more universities will improve the quality of the teaching programmes offered jointly. Due to the relatively small size of European universities, networking is a necessity, all the more so as they can be a first step towards merging. Finally, the broad effort put on quality education and institutions is generally welcome, provided the bureaucratic tendencies of some quality agencies do not take over systems which are owned by the institutions themselves.

Regarding research, the increased budget devoted to research and the creation of the European research council at the European Union level are also generally welcome developments. However, I do not see how many Member State governments can increase their budget for HE/R considering the disequilibrium of their public finances and the fact that social tasks like old-age pensions and health will be increasingly demanding with the ageing population. More than that, I am wondering how (on the basis of which analysis) the objective that European countries should on average invest 3% of GNP for research has been fixed. Probably, it is because it corresponds to the level of the U.S. investment. However, to believe that 3% is a correct target because it is the U.S. level of investment implies that we assume that the efficiency of research spending in the U.S. and in Europe is similar. Is it? Perhaps, but nobody knows.

In the matter of financing, there are two sources of funding which are still not really exploited in Europe, in particular the individual financial participation to higher education and donations from companies as well as foundations. Although this topic was traditionally a taboo in most European countries, the atmosphere is changing in the sense that it is now possible to raise the issue in most circles. However, few countries are ready to introduce substantial students' fees (for example, covering 25% of the average study costs). Moreover, universities are not yet ready to launch fund-raising campaigns within their alumni as very few institutions keep in touch with them.

Finally, perhaps the biggest weakness of the European system compared with the U.S. one lies with the governance/leadership of European universities. Presently, in nearly all institutions, it is extremely difficult to make substantial changes due to internal resistances and blockages. Most leaders do not have the competence and are also probably too near in their status to the deans and professors to take a real leadership role. Moreover, too many leaders do not have enough professional training to lead a huge institution like a university. Europe would be well advised to work on that too.

REFERENCES

Aghion, Ph. & Cohen, E. (2004), *Education et croissance*, La documentation française, Paris.

Algave, E. & Plane, M. (2004). *Vieillissement et protection sociale en Europe et aux Etats-Unis*. Etudes et Résultats No. 355.

Barroso, J. M. (2005a). *Europe 2010: a European renewal*, speech at the World Economic Forum plenary session. Davos, 29 January.

Barroso, J. M. (2005b). *Strong Universities for Europe*, speech at the Convention of the European University Association. Glasgow, 2 April.

Bologna secretariat website (2005-2007). http://www.dfes.gov.uk/bologna/

Cohen, E. (2005). "Funding Strategies to increase/improve investment", Conference *Enabling European Higher education to make its full contribution to the knowledge economy and society*, Brussels, 10 February. http://europa.eu.int/comm/education/policies/2010/doc/conference2005/plenary_1_cohen_paper.pdf

Communiqué of the Conference of European Ministers responsible for Higher Education. (2005). *The European Higher Education Area – Achieving the Goals*. Bergen 19-20 May.

Bologna Declaration. (1999). *Joint declaration of the European Ministers of Education*. http://www.bologna-bergen2005.no/Docs/00-Main_doc/990719BOLOGNA_DECLARATION.PDF

Commission of the European Communities. (2000). Communication from the Commission to the Council, the European Parliament, the Economic and Social committee and the committee of the regions, *Toward a European research area*. COM (2000) 6 final. http://europa.eu.int/eur-lex/lex/LexUriServ/site/en/com/2000/com2000_0006en01.pdf

Commission of the European Communities. (2002). Communication from the Commission, *More Research for Europe, Towards 3% of GDP*, COM (2002) 499 final, Brussels. http://europa.eu.int/eur-lex/lex/LexUriServ/site/en/com/2002/com2002_0499en01.pdf

Commission of the European Communities — Communication from the commission. (2003). *The role of universities in the Europe of knowledge*. http://europa.eu.int/eur-lex/lex/LexUriServ/site/en/com/2003/com2003_0058en01.pdf

Commission of the European Communities. (2005a). Communication to the spring European council, *Working together for growth and jobs, a new start for the Lisbon Strategy*, COM (2005) 24, Brussels.

Commission of the European Communities. (2005b). Communication from the commission, *Mobilising the brainpower of Europe: enabling universities to make their full contribution to the Lisbon strategy*. COM (2005) 152 final.

Commission of the European Communities. (2005c). *Proposal for a decision of the European parliament and of the council concerning the seventh framework programme of the European community for research, technological development and demonstration activities (2007-2013)*. COM (2005) 119 final, Brussels.

Commission staff working paper. (2005a). *Annex to the Communication from the commission: Mobilising the brainpower of Europe: enabling universities to make their full contribution to the Lisbon Strategy, European Higher Education in a Worldwide Perspective*. SEC (2005) 518, Brussels. http://europa.eu.int/comm/education/policies/2010/doc/workuniversity2005_en.pdf

Commission staff working paper. (2005b). *Simplification in the 7th Framework Programme*. SEC (2005) 431. http://europa.eu.int/comm/research/future/pdf/ec_2005_0431_1_en.pdf

Directorate General Research. (2004). *The Europe of Knowledge 2020: a Vision of University-Based Research and Innovation; Conference proceedings*. European Commission, Brussels.

Europe (the) of Knowledge 2020. (2004). *A vision for University based Research and Innovation*. Liège, April 2004. http://europa.eu.int/comm/research/conferences/2004/univ/index_en.html

Forum on University-based Research. (2005). *European Universities: enhancing Europe's Research Base*. European Commission, DG for Research Science and Society, Brussels.

Kok, W. (2004). Report from the High Level Group chaired by Wim Kok, *Facing the Challenge, The Lisbon strategy for growth and employment*. Brussels. http://europa.eu.int/growthandjobs/pdf/kok_report_en.pdf

Lisbon European Council. (2000). *Presidency conclusions*. 23-24 March. http://ue.eu.int/ueDocs/cms_Data/docs/pressData/en/ec/00100-r1.en0.htm

Mora, J. G. (2005). *"Mobilising funding for increased investment"*, Conference *Enabling European Higher education to make its full contribution to the knowledge economy and society*. Brussels, 10 February. http://europa.eu.int/comm/education/policies/2010/doc/conference2005/workshop_1_jose-gines-mora_paper.pdf

Morgan, A. W. (2005). *"Funding University Research in the USA at National and State Levels"*, contribution at the *4th Symposium of the Russian Higher Education Program*. Salzburg Seminar, 9-13 April.

OECD. (2005a). *Economic policy reforms, growing for growth*, press conference, London, 1 March 2005.

OECD. (2005b). *Economic policy reforms, going for Growth, Structural Policy Indicators and Priorities in OECD Countries*. OECD, Paris.

Reichert, S. & Tauch, Ch. (2005). *Trends IV: European Universities Implementing Bologna*. European University Association, Brussels.

Sapir, A. (2003). Report of an Independent High-Level Study Group established on the initiative of the European commission, *An agenda for a growing Europe, Making the EU economic system Deliver*, Brussels. http://www.euractiv.com/ndbtext/innovation/sapirreport.pdf

Sorbonne Joint Declaration. (1998). *Joint declaration on harmonization of the architecture of the European higher education system*. http://www.bologna-bergen2005.no/Docs/00-Main_doc/980525SORBONNE_DECLARATION.PDF

Van Vugth, F. A. (2004). "Closing the European Knowledge Gap? Challenges for the European Universities of the 21st Century", in Weber & Duderstadt (eds), *Reinventing the Research University*, Economica, Paris, pp. 89-106.

Weber, L. & Zgaga, P. (2004). "Reinventing the European Higher Education and Research sector: The Challenge for Research Universities", in Weber & Duderstadt (eds), *Reinventing the Research University*, Economica, Paris, pp 29-49.

CHAPTER 2

University-Industry-Government Partnerships for a 21st century Global, Knowledge-Driven Economy: An American Perspective

James J. Duderstadt

The powerful forces driving change in our world today — demographics, globalization, technology — are also demanding change in the role, character and relationship of knowledge organizations such as research universities, corporate R & D organizations, federal laboratories, and government. A radically new system for creating wealth has evolved that depends upon the creation and application of new knowledge. We are shifting from an emphasis on creating and transporting physical objects such as materials and energy to knowledge itself; from atoms to bits; from societies based upon the geopolitics of the nation-state to those based on diverse cultures and local traditions; and from a dependence on government policy to an increasing confidence in the marketplace to establish public priorities.

The American system of research and advanced education, relying on a partnership between universities, industry and government, has been highly successful over the past half-century in addressing priorities such as national defence and health care. However today's hypercompetitive, global, knowledge-driven economy, characterized by trends such as the outsourcing of production, services and perhaps even innovation, coupled with the off-shoring of knowledge workers, will demand a substantial restructuring of our economies, while raising serious questions about the relevance of our current research and educational paradigms. More specifically, the shift in national priorities from "guns" (the Cold War) to "pills" (the health care needs of an ageing population) and now to "butter" (the innovation necessary to compete in a global, knowledge-driven economy) raises serious questions about the adequacy of our current knowledge infrastructure.

For example, in an increasingly competitive global marketplace, innovation both in the creation of new products, systems and services, and the management of global enterprises has become more important than conventional assets such as financial capital, natural resources and unskilled labour – at least for developed nations. And innovation requires new knowledge (through research), human capital (through education), infrastructure (both physical and cyber) and new policies (intellectual property, anti-trust, tax), all of which depend both on public and private investment and upon the capacity of knowledge institutions such as research universities, corporate R & D, and national laboratories.

This paper will consider the current status, challenges and concerns characterizing the American system for the conduct of research and advanced education, drawn heavily from several recent studies by the National Academies of Science, Engineering and Medicine.

THE AMERICAN KNOWLEDGE INFRASTRUCTURE

The character of today's American research university was shaped some 50 years ago by the seminal report, *Science, the Endless Frontier*, produced by a World War II study group chaired by Vannevar Bush (Bush, 1945). The central theme of the document was that the nation's health, economy and military security required continual deployment of new scientific knowledge; hence the federal government was obligated in the national interest to ensure basic scientific progress and the production of high-quality scientists and engineers.

Rather than attempting to build separate research institutes or academies, the Bush report recommended instead a partnership among universities, industry and the federal government. The federal government would provide research grants to university faculty investigators through a competitive, peer-reviewed system to conduct basic research on the campus, along with contracts to industrial R & D laboratories for more applied research and development aimed at specific objectives (e.g. national defence). Federal support was channelled through an array of federal agencies: basic research agencies such as the National Science Foundation and the National Institutes of Health; mission agencies such as the Department of Defense, the Department of Energy, the National Aeronautics and Space Administration and the Department of Agriculture; and an assortment of other federal agencies such as the Departments of Commerce, Transportation and Labor. Research universities and corporate R & D laboratories were augmented by a number of national research laboratories with specific missions, such as atomic energy or defence research.

Industrial R & D activities, including cutting-edge basic research, were strongly supported by corporate leadership and the investment community who recognized the importance of research to long-term product development and profitability. Additional federal policies were developed to strengthen further this partnership among universities, industry and the federal government, such as the Bayh-Dole Act, which gave universities ownership of the intellectual property developed through federally sponsored research, thereby stimulating the transfer of knowledge from campuses into the marketplace.

Clearly this research partnership among universities, industry and government has been remarkably successful. Federally supported academic research programs on the campuses have greatly strengthened the scientific prestige and quality of American research universities, many of which now rank among the world's best. Furthermore, by combining research with advanced training, it has produced the well-trained scientists, engineers and other professionals capable of applying this new knowledge. The university-industry-government partnership has not only provided leadership in the pursuit of knowledge in the fundamental academic disciplines, but through the conduct of more applied mission- and product-focused research, it has addressed national priorities such as health care, environmental sustainability, economic competitiveness, and national defence. It has laid the technological foundations for entirely new industries such as microelectronics, biotechnology and information technology (National Academy of Engineering, 2003).

Today most current measures of technological leadership, such as the percentage of GDP invested in R & D, the number and productivity of researchers, and the volume of high-tech production and exports, still favour the United States. Yet worrisome trends are appearing that cast doubt over its longer-term scientific and technological leadership. The accelerating pace of discovery and application of new technologies, investments by other nations in R & D and the education of a technical workforce, and an increasingly competitive global economy are challenging U.S. technological leadership and, with it, future U.S. prosperity and security.

SIGNS OF CONCERN

Despite record levels of federal funding for research, most of the increases over the past 25 years have been focused on a single area — biomedical research — that currently accounts for 62% of all federal research funding flowing to university campuses (with 45% to medical schools). In contrast, federal funding for research in the physical sciences and engineering has been relatively stagnant or declining over the same period. Put another way, 30 years ago federal funding of research in physical science, engineering and biomedical research was roughly comparable at $5 billion a year each. Today, physical science and engineering continue to receive $5b. a year and $8b. a year respectively, while biomedical research has ballooned to $28b. a year (U.S. Department of Energy, 2003). While some growth in the latter area is justified both by the research opportunities in life sciences and by the health care needs of an ageing population, there has clearly been a very serious distortion in the federal research portfolio that is driving similar distortion on the campuses in areas such as priorities for investment in capital facilities and student interest — particularly at the graduate and post-doctoral level.

There has been a similar shift in funding by industry and federal mission agencies such as the Department of Defense away from long-term basic research to short-term applied research and product development. The market conditions that once supported industrial investment in basic research at pre-eminent laboratories at AT&T (Bell Labs), IBM, RCA, GE and other giants of corporate America have been replaced by the demands of institutional investors for cost-cutting and near-term profitability. Ironically this shift has occurred at a time when the federal share of the nation's R & D activity has declined from 75% to less than 25%, implying that the increased emphasis on applied R & D is coming at the expense of fundamental long-term research.

The pressures on discretionary spending associated with a growing federal budget deficit pose a further challenge. Although the federal 2006 Fiscal Year (FY) R & D budget will amount to $132b., the majority of these expenditures (and all of the growth) will be for defence and homeland security, consisting primarily of advanced development in areas such as weapons systems and counter-terrorism measures. In fact, the magnitude of federal investment in R & D that actually creates new knowledge has been stagnant at roughly $60b. for the past three years. This federal funding is likely to decline still further as the administration seeks deep cuts in the research accounts of mission agencies such as the DOD, DOE and NASA (except for manned spaceflight) over the next several years. Of course, this is occurring at a time when many of our economic competitors are ratcheting up their investments in research capacity and graduate education.

The availability of adequate human resources — particularly scientists and engineers — is also a growing concern (National Academy of Engineering, 2004). While there is always an ebb and flow in college enrolment in various disciplines, there has been a noticeable decline in student interest in careers in science and engineering over the past two decades. In the United States, engineering graduates dropped from 85,000 per year in 1985 to 65,000 in the mid-1990s, recovering only recently to 75,000 (National Science Board, 2004). To put this in context, the United States currently accounts for less than 8% of the new engineers produced globally each year, while China and India are each currently producing roughly 200,000 engineers per year. In the United States, only 4.5% of college students major in engineering; in Europe, this rises to 12%; but in Asia, over 40% of college students major in engineering, which, when combined with the dramatic increase in college enrolments in countries such as China and India, implies that the U.S. is currently producing less than 5% of the world's scientists and engineers. (Wulf, 2004).

In the past the United States has compensated for this shortfall in scientists and engineers to some degree by attracting talented students from around the world. But post 9/11 constraints on immigration policies and an increasingly cynical view of American foreign policy have cut deeply into the flow of international students into our universities and industry (Committee on Science, Engineering and Public Policy, 2005). This situation is compounded by our nation's inability to address the relatively low participation of women and under-represented ethnic minorities in science and engineering. As presidential science advisor, John Marburger, concluded: "The future strength of the U.S. science and engineering workforce is imperilled by two long-term trends: First the global competition for science and engineering talent is intensifying, such that the U.S. may not be able to rely on the international science and engineering labour market for its unmet skill needs. Second, the number of native-born science and engineering graduates entering the workforce is likely to decline unless the nation intervenes to improve success in educating S & E students from all demographic groups, especially those that have been under-represented in science and engineering careers."

THE LAW OF UNINTENDED CONSEQUENCES

So how did this happen? Why, at a time when many other nations are investing heavily in building their research and education capacity in science and engineering, is investment in new knowledge and human capital largely stagnant or even declining in the United States? To some degree, it was a consequence of the well-known law of unintended consequences.

For example, although the United States has rarely had a top-down R & D policy successfully proposed and achieved at the presidential level (perhaps with the exception of the Apollo mission to the moon), its democratic system of government is generally responsive to the will of the electorate, at least over the long term. In one sense, then, it is not surprising that as national priorities shifted from the Cold War to the health of an ageing population, there should be a corresponding shift of federal R & D priorities from the disciplines key to national defence such as physical science and engineering to the biomedical sciences. Using this argument, one might also anticipate that as national priorities are focusing increasingly on economic competitiveness in a global economy – perhaps momentarily disrupted by the 9/11 attack – there would be a corresponding shift to funding those disciplines critical to technological innovation such as information technology and systems engineering.

However, the current process for appropriating federal dollars, both in the administration and in Congress, is distributed among a complex array of constituencies and committees that can be easily hijacked by special interest groups and susceptible to lobbying from powerful interests such as the pharmaceutical industry. This highly political approach to federal investment in science and technology is aggravated by the rampant growth of earmarks to the appropriation bills by aggressive institutions aided by skillful lobbyists and sympathetic Congressional representatives that bypass competitive peer review and erode research funding still further (e.g. over $3b. in FY2005 alone).

Yet another example of unintended consequences is provided by the antitrust rulings that led to the breakup of monopolies such as AT&T, thereby subjecting important national research assets such as Bell Laboratories to serious decline in the face of the demands of shareholders more focused on short-term profits than long-term competitiveness. This erosion in the capacity of industry to conduct long-term research will only be aggravated by the accountability demanded by legislation such as the Sarbanes-Oxley Act in the wake of the Enron scandal.

Federal agencies and national laboratories have experienced similar pressures to shift away from basic research toward more short-term development activities. Even DOD's Defense Advanced Research Projects Agencies (DARPA), which supported much of the long-term basic research in electronics, computers and networking that led to technologies such as the Internet, are now constrained to 18-month project cycles. Many national laboratories long ago lost their primary missions (e.g. nuclear power development) and are today drifting without compelling priorities, sustained only by the political pressures of their "marching armies" (e.g. the thousands of scientists and engineers they employ).

Another concern arises from the remarkable success of the Bayh-Dole Act of 1980, designed to stimulate the transfer of intellectual property arising from federally sponsored research into the commercial marketplace. Prior to Bayh-Dole, fewer than 250 patents were issued to universities each year; in 2003, 3,629 patents were issues to U.S. universities, yielding over $1b. in licensing income and 248 start-ups with very positive economic consequences for the nation. (National Science Board, 2004).

Yet this strong incentive to transfer technology from campus research into the marketplace has also infected the research university with the profit objectives of a business, as both institutions and individual faculty members attempt to profit from the commercial value of the products of their research and instructional activities. Universities have adopted aggressive commercialization policies and invested heavily in technology transfer offices to encourage the development and ownership of intellectual property rather than its traditional open sharing with the broader scholarly community. They have hired teams of lawyers to defend their ownership of the intellectual property derived from their research and instruction. On occasions some institutions and faculty members have set aside the most fundamental values of the university, such as openness, academic freedom and a willingness to challenge the status quo, in order to accommodate this growing commercial role of the research university (Press and Washburn, 2000) (Stein, 2004).

Ironically, the complex cacophony of intellectual property licensing negotiations, which vary not only from university to university, but even from company to company, has created a backlash of frustration on the part of American industry. Many major companies are now beginning to outsource their R & D activities along with their university relations to other nations with more attractive and coherent licensing policies.

Yet this is just one example of an even more basic economic transformation likely to reshape in very significant ways the relationship between universities, industry, and government: global sourcing. A new commercial ecosystem is evolving where enterprises will distribute not only production but also creative activities such as design, R & D, and innovation across global networks. As the recent report of the National Intelligence Council's 2020 Project has concluded: "The very magnitude and speed of change resulting from a globalizing world – apart from its precise character – will be a defining feature of the world out to 2020. During this period, China's GNP will exceed that of all other Western economic powers except for the United States, with a projected population of 1.4b. India and Brazil will also likely surpass most of the European nations. Globalization – growing interconnectedness reflected in the expanded flows of information, technology, capital, goods, services, and people throughout the world – will become an overarching mega-trend, a force so ubiquitous that it will substantially shape all other major trends in the world of 2020." (National Intelligence Council, 2005).

Of course, developed nations have long experienced the outsourcing of production and low-skill jobs to other nations with lower labour costs. But today we see the off-shoring of high-skill, knowledge-intensive service jobs to nations like India and China, characterized by both low wages and, perhaps more importantly, an increasingly skilled technical workforce, stimulated by major investments in science and engineering education. Activities such as product design and R & D, which used to be critical components of a company's core competency, are now distributed across global networks. In fact, even innovation itself, long considered the most significant asset of the American business culture, is also being off-shored by many companies. There are growing concerns that such global sourcing, driven not only by low cost but as well technological leadership, could lead to the erosion of the capacity of our nation to add any true value in the business enterprise, beyond financial gymnastics. (Friedman, 2005).

In a global, knowledge driven economy the keys to economic success are a well-education workforce, technological capability, capital investment and entrepreneurial zeal — a message well-understood by developed and developing nations alike throughout the world that are investing in the necessary human capital and knowledge infrastructure.

WHAT TO DO?

So, where is the United States headed? Will we face the same decline and fall that have characterized other brief hegemonies, as we outsource and offshore all of the value-added needed by our economy — at least until China and others stop buying dollars. Or will our concern in the wake of 9/11 drive us inwardly toward the Fortress America characterizing the early 20th century. Or perhaps even more frightening (at least to many), will the United States embark on a "democratize the world" mission. Perhaps we will go to Mars...

Whatever our national priorities and future visions, it is becoming painfully clear that our current partnerships, programs and policies for the conduct of research and advanced education are sorely in need of overhaul. Study after study — from our National Academies, from federal organizations such as the National Science Board and the President's Council of Advisors on Science and Technology, from scientific organizations such as the American Association for the Advancement of Science, from industrial groups such as the Council on Competitiveness and from the media itself — have raised a cacophony of concerns about the possible erosion of U.S. science and technology, now converging into a strong chorus demanding both transformation of and reinvestment in this important enterprise.

Ironically, almost a decade ago, a National Academy of Sciences study suggested a blueprint that addresses many of the concerns today. The report, *Allocating Federal Funds for Science and Technology* (Committee on Criteria for Federal Support of R&D, 1995), aimed at making the research funding process more coherent, systematic and comprehensive; ensuring that funds were allocated to the best people and the best projects; ensuring that sound scientific and technical advice guided the allocation process; and improving the federal management of R & D activities. The report recommended, as a guide to federal research policy, that the nation should achieve and maintain absolute leadership in research areas of key strategic interest to the nation (e.g. those directly affecting national security or economic competitiveness), and should furthermore be among the leaders in all other scientific and technological areas to ensure that rapid progress could be made in any area in the event of technological surprises ("ready to pounce"). According to this principle, for example, it is clear that the nation should strive to be the absolute leader in areas of strategic importance such as biotechnology, nanotechnology and information technology. However it need only be among the leaders in an area like high-energy physics (implying, of course, that the United States should be prepared to build expensive accelerators through international alliances rather than alone as in the ill-fated Superconducting Supercollider).

This report also recommended the use of an alternative to the federal "R & D" budget category that more accurately measured spending on the generation of new knowledge: The Federal Science and Technology (FS&T) budget was designed to reflect the true federal investment in the creation of new knowledge and technologies by excluding activities such as hardware procurement and the testing and evaluation of new weapons systems. In contrast to the federal R & D budget, roughly $130b. today, the FS&T budget amounts to roughly $60b., and has remained relatively stagnant or declining for many years, strong evidence of the erosion in federal investment in true knowledge-generating research (Committee on Science, Engineering and Public Policy, 2002). From these perspectives, it is clear that the current U.S. research portfolio neither provides the magnitude of investment or disciplinary balance necessary to address the nation's key priorities — national security, public health, environmental sustainability, or economic competitiveness.

There is a deeper concern: maintaining the nation's leadership in technological innovation. As the source of new products and services, innovation is directly responsible for the most dynamic sectors of the U.S. economy (Council on Competitiveness, 2004). Here our nation has a great competitive advantage, since our society is based on a highly diverse population, democratic values, and free-market practices. These factors provide an unusually fertile environment for technological innovation. However, history has also shown that significant public investment is necessary to produce the essential ingredients for innovation to flourish: new knowledge (research), human capital (education), infrastructure (facilities, laboratories, communications networks), and policies (tax, intellectual property). Other nations are beginning to reap the benefits of such investments aimed at stimulating and exploiting technological innovation, creating serious competitive challenges to American industry and business both in the conventional marketplace (e.g., Toyota) and through new paradigms such as the off-shoring of knowledge-intensive services (e.g. Bangalore).

A recent National Academy of Engineering study on the capacity of U.S. engineering research summarizes the challenges facing our nation:

"U.S. leadership in technological innovation seems certain to be seriously eroded unless current trends are reversed. The accelerating pace of discovery and application of new technologies, investments by other nations in research and development (R & D) and the education of a technical workforce, and an increasingly competitive global economy are challenging U.S. technological leadership and, with it, future U.S. prosperity and security. Although many current measures of technological leadership — percentage of gross domestic product invested in R & D, number of researchers, productivity level, volume of high-technology production and exports — still favor the United States, worrisome trends are already adversely affecting the U.S. capacity for innovation. These trends include: (1) a large and growing imbalance in federal research funding between the engineering and physical sciences on the one hand and biomedical and life sciences on the other; (2) increased emphasis on applied R & D in industry and government-funded research at the expense of fundamental long-term research; (3) erosion of the engineering research infrastructure due to inadequate investment over many years; (4) declining interest of American students in engineering, science, and other technical fields; and (5) growing uncertainty about the ability of the United States to attract and retain gifted engineering and science students from abroad at a time when foreign nationals constitute a large and productive component of the U.S. R & D workforce." (National Academy of Engineering Committee, 2005, p. 1).

The report concludes: "The United States is at a crossroads. We can either continue on our current course — living on incremental improvements to past technical developments and buying new, breakthrough technologies from abroad — or we can take control of our destiny and conduct the necessary research, capture the intellectual property, commercialize and manufacture the products and processes, and create the high-skill, high-value jobs that define a prosperous and secure nation."

The world and the structure of academic research have changed greatly since Vannevar Bush first proposed the partnership among government, universities and industry that has been so effective in the United States. As Friedman stresses, today "intellectual work and intellectual capital can be delivered from anywhere — disaggregated, delivered, distributed, produced and put back together again. The playing field is level. The world is flat! Globalization has collapsed time and distance and raised the notion that someone anywhere on earth can do your job, more cheaply." (Friedman, 2005). Yet the basic principles undergirding the research partnership among government, universities and industry remain just as compelling as they did half a century ago: national interests and global competitiveness require investment in creating a highly educated and skilled workforce as well as an environment that stimulates creativity, innovation and entrepreneurial behaviour as the key assets of a knowledge economy.

REFERENCES

Bush, V., (1945). *Science, the Endless Frontier, A Report to the President on a Program for Postwar Scientific Research* (Office of Scientific Research and Development, July 1945), reprinted by the National Science Foundation, Washington, D.C., p. 192.

Committee on Criteria for Federal Support of Research and Development, (1995). *Allocating Federal Funds for Science and Technology*, National Academy Press, Washington, D.C.

Committee on Science, Engineering and Public Policy, (2003). *Observations on the President's Fiscal Year 2003.* Federal Science and Technology Budget, National Academy Press, Washington, D.C.

Committee on Science, Engineering and Public Policy, (2005). *Policy Implications of International Graduate Students and Postdoctoral Scholars in the United States,* National Academy Press, Washington, D.C.

Council on Competitiveness, (2004). Innovate America, Washington, D.C. Available online at: http://www.compete.org/pdf/NII_Final_Report.pdf

Friedman, Thomas, (2005). *The World is Flat: A Brief History of the 21st century,* Farrar, Strauss, and Giroux, New York.

National Academy of Engineering, (2003). *The Impact of Academic Research on Industrial Performance,* National Academy Press, Washington, D.C.

National Academy of Engineering, (2004). *The Engineer of 2020: Visions of Engineering in the New Century,* National Academy Press, Washington, D.C.

National Academy of Engineering Committee to Assess the Capacity of the U.S. Engineering Research Enterprise. Duderstadt, J. J. (chair), (2005). *Engineering Research and America's Future: Meeting the Challenges of a Global Economy,* National Academy Press, Washington, D.C.

National Intelligence Council, (2005). *Project 2020,* United States Printing Office, Washington, D.C.

National Science Board, (2004). *Science and Engineering Indicators 2004,* Washington, D.C., chapter 5.

Press, E. & Washburn, J., (2000). "The Kept University", *The Atlantic Monthly,* pp. 39-54.

Stein, D. Ed., (2004). *Buying in or Selling Out: the Commercialization of the American Research University,* Rutgers University Press, Piscataway, New York.

U.S. Department of Energy, (2003). *Critical Choices: Sciences, Energy, and Security,* Final Report of the Secretary of Energy Advisory Board Task Force on the Future of Science Programs at the Department of Energy, Washington, D.C.

Wulf, W., (2004). *National Academy of Engineering 2004 Annual Meeting, President's Remarks.* National Academy of Engineering, Washington, D.C.

CHAPTER

War and peace:
how did we get here
in HE-business relations?

Alice Frost and Howard Newby

INTRODUCTION

Wars have had a major impact on research in the 20th century: the century of technological discovery as a motor for economic development. The First World War produced a major impetus for the investment by governments of developed countries into science, and also produced significant spin-offs in terms of domestic use (for example, mauvene in WW1 uniforms as founding for modern chemistry, similarly, from WW2, new developments in electronics, aviation, atomic energy etc). And, following WW2, governments invested into higher education as a source of transformation of modern industry and economy. To quote from the Universities Grants Committee of the UK in 1948 (Quoted in Becher & Kogan, 1992): "There has emerged from the war a new and sustained public interest in the universities and a strong realization of the unique contribution they had to offer to the national well being, whether in peace or war... A heightened sense of social justice generated by the war has opened the door more widely than before".

The relationship between defence science and technology and fundamental research is an interesting case of the inter-play between use and discovery. The need to solve real world problems provided an impetus to discovery, and new discoveries provided opportunities for new solutions to real world problems. And governments have sought to use that relationship to deliver public goods, such as defence, but also increasingly to pursue economic goals. (And that inter-play is reflected in policy thrusts such as seeking secondary domestic and economic uses out of new defence technologies.)

THE 'THIRD STREAM'

In the U.K., there has been increasing interest in recent years in "third stream" as a mission direction in HE, additional to those of teaching and research (as the first and second streams). This links with academic debate on the forms and nature of scholarship, including scholarships of discovery, integration, teaching — and *application*. And the last, scholarship of application, is described, for example, in the following extract from Ernest Boyer's *Scholarship Reconsidered* (Boyer, 1990): "The scholarship of application, as we define it here, is not a one-way street. Indeed, the term itself may be misleading if it suggests that knowledge is first "discovered" and then "applied". The process we have in mind is far more dynamic. New intellectual understandings can arise out of the very act of application — whether in medical diagnosis, serving clients in psychotherapy, shaping public policy, creating an architectural design, or working with the public schools."

So the third stream agenda focuses specifically on how higher education impacts on the economy and society and vice versa. Much of the underlying activity to the third stream is specifically either "pieces" of research or of teaching. But there is nevertheless an important added value in looking at these through the prism of their interplay or engagement with the world. And that creates a specific policy and strategic focus which is distinct from those largely of research and teaching, in considering how we can make the third stream work most effectively to the benefit of both HE and the world of its use.

Much of the early policy interest in the U.K. in third stream, following U.S. examples in the 1960s and 1970s, addressed "technology transfer", with the focus on science and engineering, on transmission from HE research into exploitation and on achieving economic and commercial goals. So the policy debate was couched in fairly technocratic and mechanical concepts — legal regulations such as Intellectual Property regimes, commercial regulations such as spin-off companies and "hard-edged" and use-focussed disciplinary references such as "new technologies". But even in the early days, there were always some broader, more organic strands within the development of policy in the U.K., linking it to interactive, communicative and flow models, greater disciplinary ranges and to more wide-ranging conceptions of public benefit than wealth creation.

Just as third stream has become a more powerful policy and strategic emphasis in the U.K., so too has the question of mission specialisation or differentiation. The experience of higher education in the U.K., as in the developed world more generally, is of increasing success as a major societal function, which accelerates its pace rapidly in the 20th century. From origins in scholarship, higher education begins to play a dominant role in the basic research enterprise, in the early development of the professions, in initial vocational education — and then in continuing professional and skill development, in social and economic regeneration, in the development and production of culture and the arts, and so on.

Just as the functions of higher education have expanded, so the scale of delivery has also accelerated. Over the 20th century, the contribution of higher education, and the university sector more specifically, has changed from a relatively small and specialist system, producing the elite cadre needed to support the "professions", to a mass system widening its doors to an increasing diversity of entrants and serving much broader education and training needs. The transition from elite to mass higher education (from 8% participation of the population in HE in the first half of the 20th century to 42% today) has probably been the major challenge to the HE sector and to national governments in the latter part of the last century.

While the third stream, as conceptualised as knowledge **transfer**, has largely been about the relationship between research and use, in a broader modern notion of third stream as knowledge **exchange**, we can also look at the relationship between teaching and use. Obviously, a lot of this can be subsumed within the issue of engagement between higher education teaching and the employers of graduates and postgraduates. The job of higher education has historically largely been about the production of graduates prepared for entry into the professions, which included the profession of scholar. But the teaching contribution of higher education has broadened considerably in the context of lifelong learning as a component of a knowledge-based economy. The exchange between users and HE teaching may then include a great diversity of components — the initial preparation of highly qualified people and entry into professions, meeting the needs of professional updating (CPD), the development and exchange of skills, the exchange of people-embodied tacit knowledge, and the definition of professional competence and knowledge domains as part of workforce development and definition of professional standards. And as part of this trend toward lifelong learning, higher education qualifications, skills, knowledge, etc, are likely to become important to an increasing range of sectors of the economy.

In the U.K., possibly uniquely, the reaction to the expanding potential of the HE sector in the latter part of the 20th century has been successively to break down different legislative or statutory frameworks which compartmentalise or channel different parts of the sector to play specific roles. This has been combined with an increase in the use of market or quasi-market forces as a means to drive quality, efficiency — and diversity. And this in turn has led to greater attention to the issue of institutional management and leadership, since public funds are now riding on the performance of institutional managers in the context of a more private-sector type market environment in which there may be winners and losers.

This trend toward the unleashing of market forces in HE will become stronger in the U.K. in the next year with the introduction of variable fees for undergraduate provision in England, and hence this will prompt even greater market attention from institutional leaders. Of course, university leaders in the U.K., as in U.S. or Australia, have been engaged for some time in concern over their performance in the expanding, but competitive global market for HE itself, with attention, in teaching, to their international brands and overseas student recruitment, and, in research, to their access to global knowledge networks and performance in the global knowledge-based economy. But, at the same time, there has also been increasing attention to the local and regional aspects of third stream and knowledge exchange, with a greater trend (but from a low base) in the U.K. toward regionalisation and devolution as a component of economic and social development. This provides a very challenging environment for institutional leaders to define their sources of comparative advantage when they may participate in local, regional, national and global markets. And far from being isolated in "ivory towers", universities find themselves at the vanguard of economic and social development, but also operating themselves increasingly as a marketized commodity in a cut-throat global market.

There are very present today concerns that HE leaders may converge in their strategies, particularly when there are both prestige and funding influences that make some strategic choices much more attractive than others. This particularly applies to the research mission, with the access it provides to international prestige, brand and peer networks, as well as to highly competitive and substantial funding. If institutional strategies converge, then nations as a whole may lose out on a sufficiently diverse range of HE offerings to meet public interest needs. (And, from an efficiency point of view, given the complexity of functions and potential local, regional, national and global markets, it seems unlikely that many institutions could operate successfully in all.) The national system needs then to ensure that there is a sufficiently diverse and nuanced range of influences and funds that can help institutional leaders play to particular strengths, but which is flexible to evolving HE roles and to the need to unite activities and disciplines in unpredictable combinations. And probably the greatest challenge to the future is achieving, in any national system, the right balance between differentiation to achieve diversity, and connection and collaboration to achieve innovation in "novel" (interdisciplinary) ways. The U.S. super-universities of scale are a means to achieve both, but it is less clear how the European systems with a greater range of smaller institutions can achieve both. This points toward the need for more sophisticated future debate on the scale of institutions, but also on the different purposes and advantages of collaborations, strategic alliances, etc.

The Higher Education Funding Council for England (HEFCE) has taken a leading role in the development of third-stream policy, working with other national partners. In particular, HEFCE has taken forward the creation of a specific fund to support engagement between HE and "users" (the Higher Education Innovation Fund — HEIF) working with government departments, regional bodies etc. While once we talked of technology transfer, the new language of HEIF expresses itself largely in terms of knowledge exchange. So it embraces an interactive relationship between HE and users, a broader conception of those users (businesses, to public services, to social enterprises or not-for-profits), a greater subject range transitioning from "technology" to "knowledge" and a breadth of engagement across teaching and research.

NEW STRATEGIC DIRECTIONS

At this time, the HEFCE is developing its next Strategic Plan for 2006-11 (November 2005 http://www.hefce.ac.uk/aboutus/straplan.asp). In our draft plan we propose new developments to open up of our conception of the potential points of contact between HE and the world, of the possible benefits to HE and users from knowledge exchange and the sophistication of our models for achieving deep engagement. In particular we are beginning to focus on:

- **The new context for engagement between HE and users in this century.** We can anticipate increased global economic competition as some of the differences between developed and developing nations break down in terms of their sources of comparative advantage. And as part of this, global firms or organisations may become increasingly promiscuous in where they base themselves, to migrate to the most flexible regulatory regimes, best labour markets, best sources of capital, and indeed highest quality HE knowledge base. And a source of competitiveness for any country may be to attract these global players to their shores. These global players may be drawn into countries by factors that go beyond the economic, to the quality and life, cultural stimulation, lack of threat etc provided by any country, which can provide an attractive environment for the highest quality people. But, at the same time, in a post-modern dynamic, we may expect more attention by domestic governments to the economic and social disparities within their territories, with a view to ensuring productive and vital communities that deliver quality of life to their electorates, provide a basis for economic competitiveness and reduce the need for public expenditure on health, crime etc. Beyond the global economic dynamic, we may also anticipate that there will be a need for more intensive promotion of civic and community engagement, at global, national, regional and local levels, to achieve a fairer, sustainable and more peaceful world. At the heart of both agendas could be a critical role for HE, in third stream mode, as a source and inspiration for rational and innovative problem-solving.

- **Expanding opportunities in third stream.** In the context of this much larger agenda for third stream, we can envisage that the contribution from HE will continue to move rapidly beyond the historic focus on business and wealth creation, on the science and engineering disciplines, and on research and development as the privileged conduit for engagement. This will then provide greater opportunities for a wider range of HE disciplines to play a part in third stream, and in inter-, intra- and multi- disciplinary modes.

- **Change in HE teaching and third stream.** Specifically, in terms of HE teaching, we will also continue to move rapidly beyond traditional conceptions of "professional" education (medicine, law etc) as the dominant mode in which HE teaching connects with engagement with employers. The dynamic will continue toward new roles in skill development, CPD, workforce development and vocational progression routes appropriate to new business sectors that historically have not engaged with HE.

As a result of these forces, HEFCE is proposing in its draft strategic plan that the broadening conception of third stream, together with the increasing emphasis and requirement for mission specialisation, may open up possibilities for a new mission descriptor or brand for a **"third stream intensive institution"**. Such an institution will put engagement at its heart. It will embrace strong business, public service or social enterprise representation in its governing arrangements, and its top management will make a priority of their interactions with critical business and community organisations. The senior management of the organisation will provide a strong focus and deep expertise in the third stream mission, and will have in place structures below to ensure that third stream work is strategically and effectively promoted and managed. The impact of institutional activity on the performance of "client" businesses, public services and charities will be a key measurable in driving strategy and investment decision-making within the institution. User impact will provide the same kind of driver for staff in this kind of institution that publication in a peer-reviewed journal might in an institution with a research mission focus.

We will have to present any such mission opportunity as a positive addition to the choices open to universities in England. The dynamic in the U.K. has been to break down compartmentalisation or stratifications of the HE sector, and we cannot swim against the tide. We will need to be sensitive to the natural dynamic within the U.K. HE system, and to provide an opportunity that is forward- not backward-looking. As part of this, we will need to make it clear that the potential for knowledge exchange from research remains very important and such research is highly user-relevant.

CONCLUSION

If the third stream is to fulfil its potential we will need some vision at the national level to enable such new types of mission to flourish, and to keep the HE system evolving to a new place in its engagement with the 21st-century world. A lot of the national debate will inevitably continue to be around wealth creation and the economic competitiveness of our nation, since wealth provides a foundation for other things. But we have stressed — and indeed in our title — that we also need to highlight the potential of HE to contribute toward realisation of the values of peace, civilisation and civic and community spirit in our country and globally (not least as a way of inspiring the more idealistic young people of the present day as budding social entrepreneurs). So HEFCE has also proposed in its plan that we should embark upon the development and implementation of an explicit "civic, cultural and community engagement strategy".

Who knows whether any government will ever put the same investment it has into war and wealth into peace and a sense of love and vitality in our society? Probably not, but this kind of investment is nevertheless something that becomes even more relevant year to year. We face greater challenges — and opportunities — to live in a peaceful, and intellectually and culturally stimulating world. We live in a globally connected world, but we often still struggle to understand and enjoy the diversity of people, as well as the multiculturalism in our own nation. HE campuses themselves, staff and students, are mini-microcosms of this diversity of backgrounds and nations. So we believe we do not celebrate enough the civilising contribution that HE can make to a more complex, social environment. And we do not trumpet enough to governments and to the public that HE prepares people for participation in civic life, and provides the expertise to support innovative rational problem-solving. And we do not shout enough about how HE provides resources for intellectual and cultural enrichment that make this a more exciting and vital world in which to live. But we should.

REFERENCES

Becher, T & Kogan, M. (1992). *Process and Structure in Higher Education*, Routledge, London.

Boyer, Ernest L. (1990). *Scholarship Reconsidered: Priorities of the Professoriate*, Carnegie Foundation for the Advancement of Teaching, Stanford CA.

HEFCE. (2005). *Strategic Plan 2006-11: draft for consultation* (November 2005), HEFCE, Bristol. http://www.hefce.ac.uk/aboutus/straplan.asp)

Howells, J., Nedeva M., & Georghiou, L. (1998). *Industry-Academic Links in the UK*, HEFCE, Bristol.

Lambert, R. (2003). *Review of Business-University Collaboration* (December 2003), HM Treasury, London.

Porter, Michael E. & Ketels, Christian. (2003). "U.K. Competitiveness — moving to the next stage", *DTI Economics paper No 3 (DTI/ESRC)*, May.

U.K. Government. (2004). *The ten-year Science and Innovation Investment Framework*. (July 2004), HM Treasury/Department of Trade and Industry/Department for Education and Science.

CHAPTER

Strategic Alliances between Universities and their Communities

By Brenda M. Gourley and John Brennan

INTRODUCTION

O rganizations are changed and shaped by the alliances that they make. This paper examines the potential impact on universities of their community alliances. This article draws on the experiences of two universities, in different settings, and their alliances with communities — alliances which fundamentally changed many important aspects of how those universities conducted their core functions. Alliances are particularly important in situations where community "development" is needed to help create a climate in which conventional business can thrive. They are often funded by the business community — sometimes under the banner of "corporate responsibility". The experiences of these two universities are set within a wider consideration of universities' roles in social transformation and of the nature of their relationships to their host and other societies.

The two universities are those where one author served as Vice-Chancellor and Principal; each university unique in its way, operating in different parts of the world: one, the University of Natal (now KwaZulu-Natal), situated on the east coast of South Africa — a traditional, residential university, multi-campus, offering a full range of disciplines, with 30,000 students — a university that survived and thrived through historic times in the struggle for freedom — and did so largely because it engaged so thoroughly with its communities. It was, by necessity, required to reconceptualize its role in the new South Africa and earn its credibility in a very diverse and newly democratised society.

Indeed that process continues; transformation is hardly an event, much more a process.

The second university is The Open University in the United Kingdom — one of the great inventions of the 20th century, one specifically designed to reach communities and people who had not had the opportunities made possible by higher education. It is a university conceived as one where there are no entry qualifications, only tough exit standards — a university that also had to earn its credibility; a university which is essentially "distance" in concept, yet one that offers a great deal of local student support; a university which has grasped the opportunities offered by the wonders of technology and whose reach is now global in nature; a university which has a very large, "networked", virtual community of over 200,000 students. It is also, of course, a university which offers a model for reaching the many millions of people who need higher education in this knowledge society of ours and for whom society would never be able to afford provision using the conventional model.

WHO DEFINES 'COMMUNITIES'?

Universities operate in a variety of settings, and cater for a variety of students. Some cater mostly for a local higher education need; others draw students from all over their country and even the world. Some are located in societies which are very multicultural in nature, others in societies which are culturally rather homogeneous. All are experiencing the forces of globalization, while at the same time recognizing the various identities (culture, ethnicity, religion and more) that people bring with them to higher education. Technology and the possibilities of the "network society" introduce different issues and possibilities. Thus, issues of where boundaries are drawn, which identities are recognized and catered for, which cultures dominate, are all delicate and contested. Under such circumstances, "engaging with the community" is a very complicated exercise.

It was Manuel Castells who introduced the concept of a network society (Castells, 2000) and, indeed, in a university such as The Open University, community has many of the attributes of such a society. Certainly "community" has come to mean more than one thing. We all know that it is now common for people to live in areas remote from their work, to be very mobile and to have allegiances in many areas. Indeed the knowledge society is fostering increasing numbers of "stateless" individuals who migrate to follow work or interest without regard for boundaries. Yet we also know that the majority of the peoples of the world are not that mobile or sophisticated and do look to their geographically local university for their higher education. Not only that, but we know that the forces of globalization are themselves feeding a need that people have for identity — usually expressed in terms of culture, ethnicity, religion or whatever. As our societies become more complex, people have multiple identities: occupations, disciplines, football teams and more. Thomas Friedman expressed this very well in his book *The Lexus and the Olive Tree* (Friedman, 2000). In a "knowledge" network society, the nature of the university experience and what localness means, what "community" or "the public" mean, which particular identities are recognized and catered for, where boundaries are drawn, all these are particularly important to debates about curricula, research and the very purposes of universities.

It is instructive to bear in mind that it is not only universities that grapple with these terms and try to act on their interpretations. Anyone who works in the public-policy arena has similar issues. In a recent published lecture, Janet Newman, a professor of public policy, talks about how difficult it is "to speak about a public domain, and to think about how we should act in it; indeed the language of public domain, public sphere, public realm, public sector, all imply a rather spatial metaphor that fails to capture the mobile, elusive and problematic character of publicness." (Newman, 2005, p. 2) She gives examples of "how the boundary between public and private is culturally contested, but also raises issues about who can speak about — and for — particular publics; who has a public voice and whose voices are silenced" (p. 4).

This is entirely non-trivial in an increasingly multicultural society. As large universities (like the University of KwaZulu-Natal) sought to engage with "the community", it became increasingly clear that some voices were louder than others, some easier to access than others and some accorded more importance than others. Some were indeed silenced completely. Cultural boundaries between men and women in a large number of societies in this world are one easy example of this. Universities in societies where social transformation is taking place are often symbols of the old order, not the new — and this, too, further complicates the issue of university-community engagement.

At the University of KwaZulu-Natal, initially existing in the "old" South Africa where boundaries were drawn by an illegitimate government, engagement with community was exceptionally difficult. Demands and expectations of an expanded view of "community" could not be met within conventional funding models so different sources of funding also had to be found. Necessity, courage and imagination all played a role. For example, during the repressive years leading up to 1994 the university gave refuge to a whole range of NGOs that had their headquarters on one or other of our campuses. They represented "community" in these unusual circumstances and played a vital role in the formulation of the agenda on campus just by virtue of their presence. They also vastly improved the quality of the strategic conversations in the university. Their perspectives were different and they pointed the university to new areas of curriculum and research.

In the "new" South Africa, it was only by being visible in the community, accessible to students from all walks of life, and delivering some tangible improvement to daily circumstances that the university could be credible and secure, let alone deliver on its mission. The university made every effort to incorporate the views of trade unions, local councils, employer organizations, leaders of non-government and community-based organisations, development agencies and funders, women's organizations, and youth organizations, as well as community leaders. Some were approached in consultative forums; others were co-opted onto governing structures. The university — really to survive — had to be open to its communities in ways that many traditional universities have not. Mission was one thing; government policy was another. The latter emphasized "reconstruction and development" as well as "equity" — and the university's demonstrable engagement with community was tangible evidence of delivering on government policy.

If engagement is difficult in a geographically located university, then how much more difficult (and important) is it for a university such as The Open University? It operates across many, many national boundaries and its presence is more real in cyberspace than it is in physical presence on the ground. E-learning and the possibilities it presents make more and more universities part of this reality.

As we all become more aware of the importance of higher education in uplifting the peoples of the world, as we more and more seek social justice across our global society, so it becomes clear that it will not be possible to build enough physical facilities of conventional universities equal to this task. The model of open and distance learning will be far more able to cope with the reality of large numbers than traditional models of higher education — however much we may wish otherwise. It does however challenge our concept of "community" — and brings us much closer to Manuel Castells' "network society" (Castells, 2000). The Open University grapples with this reality. In contrast to universities where most of the students are very young, it has a student body of 200,000 which ranges in age from very young to very old, from employed to unemployed, from public sector to private sector; across 100 different countries, although 80% are British. In many important ways this huge body of students represents "community" in a way that few would contest. The university's very mission is about finding people who have not had the benefits of education in the conventional forums and who need second and third chances. Reaching these kinds of people remains its special challenge. Having reached them, they provide us with important footholds into their particular communities. The ubiquity of the Internet also gives us marvelous opportunities to broaden this engagement — although the challenge of the "digital divide" remains.

The Open University in a sense "constructs" community for three main (and strategic) purposes: first, to reach students across a range of networks (learning networks, health authorities, trade unions, refugee organizations), workplaces (employers and employer groups, as well as professional accrediting agencies), institutions (prisons, other providers) and other social communities; secondly, to deliver, contextualize (and sometimes create) curricula in different regional and national settings (with public and private-sector higher education providers with whom we have formal partnerships to deliver curricula); and, thirdly, to improve the information and strategic conversation and debate in the university (where we appoint representatives of important parts of these communities to our governing structures, as well as inviting them into consultative bodies). The university also actively engages with its virtual community is a variety of ways. This community logs over 250,000 transactions a day between its members. These transactions might be formal, mediated seminars or conversations; they might be students' support-group interactions or chat-room activity, or clubs' and societies' business. They might be providing evaluative feedback or even market research on planned activity. They also constitute an active research community doing distributive research in very new ways. One example of this is the operation of a climate-research activity where the capacity of over 100,000 computers around the world is harnessed to record and analyse climate change across the world. The possibilities are limited only by our imaginations.

If it is a complex matter to define "community" for the purposes of this paper, how much more so for universities expecting to engage with communities that are geographically spread and which may well be in conflict or tension with each other. The desirability of community engagement should not disguise the difficulties of achieving it.

STRATEGIC ALLIANCES THAT CHANGE ASPECTS OF CORE BUSINESS

The idea of a "strategic alliance" indicates a rather strong form of collaboration or partnership, something that one would expect to see formalized and enshrined in the mission and strategic plans of the alliance "members". Before we move to pondering the implementation of university mission, it is important to understand that not all individual members of a university community would accept the imperative of engagement with community. Those of us who do would see it as so important that it might well be the saving grace of a traditional university model otherwise terminally doomed. The nature of our networked society suggests that the university as we know it, in particular the university that integrates teaching and research under one (physical) roof, might well be at an end. Certainly management guru Peter Drucker thinks it is (Drucker, 2002). Change is on the agenda (whether we like it or not) and the introduction of engagement as a purposeful strategy is a necessary response to a complex and globalized world where we must aspire to being both local and global citizens, and prepare our students to be both local and global citizens as well. In this globalized, networked society, communities have vastly differing perspectives on the priorities of the real world and these perspectives need to be part of the living and dynamic university of today if a continued relevance to this real world is to be maintained. Certainly the record in this respect is mixed (see Brennan *et al* [2004], discussed briefly below). The point does, however, need to be made that no university can be so dominated by "community" concerns — from whatever source — that it loses its international and global role (Singh, 2003, p. 288). Community engagement is not a replacement for a critical and independent stance by the university, but an essential part of it.

The Association of Commonwealth Universities consultative document, "Engagement as a Core Value for Universities" (2001), also made the point that "21st century academic life is no longer pursued in seclusion (if it ever was) but must rather champion reason and imagination in engagement with the wider society and its concerns". (p. i). It goes on to assert that "engagement implies strenuous, thoughtful, argumentative interaction with the non-university world in at least four spheres: setting universities' aims, purposes and priorities; relating teaching and learning to the wider world; and back-and-forth dialogue between researchers and practitioners; and taking on wider responsibilities as neighbours and citizens." (p. i). These broad categories will be used in this paper for the sake of example. It is interesting to ponder the passing of a time where democratically elected governments represented "society and its concerns". It is clearly the varying extent of universities' autonomy and the growing complexity of society that make the national policy process no longer a sufficient basis for social and community engagement by the university.

The four aspects of university endeavour (identified by the ACU study, 2001) that can be influenced and even profoundly changed by our alliances outside the campus "walls" are taken in turn:

Setting universities' aims, purposes and priorities

The alliances described in this paper are "strategic alliances" and no alliance is likely to be "strategic" unless it is serving the university mission — either at a generalized level or a more specific one. In this context the UNESCO Declaration on Higher Education (1998) is useful. It states that higher education is "for citizenship and active participation in society, with a worldwide vision, for endogenous capacity-building, for the consolidation of human rights, sustainable development, democracy and peace, in a context of justice." (p. 21) While other statements (e.g. World Bank, 2002), and in particular those of national governments, have tended to place most emphasis on the economic case for higher education, what virtually all statements of this sort share is a highlighting of higher education's role in social change and transformation. In the developing world at least, this is a relatively recent emphasis.

The fact is that as higher education consumes a larger and larger proportion of national budgets, the debate about how this cost should be funded (and by what mix of beneficiaries) becomes more intense. The very idea of a remote group of people, teaching in a disinterested sort of way — and, perhaps more importantly, researching in a disinterested sort of way — seems less and less feasible. Yet "disinterestedness" lies at the very heart of why academic freedom is seen to be a significant matter, at the very heart of what universities can and have contributed, while not being even part of the public discourse. We are quite understandably more and more in societies where accountability is demanded, yet we are also more and more in a world where it seems that everything is determined by the marketplace, and almost everything is for sale. It is not always possible to serve these basically opposing forces. "Disinterestedness" may be the only distinctive feature left of what many of us regard as "universities".

Derek Bok, former President of Harvard University, has written about these concerns being linked to "a broader disquiet over the encroachments of the marketplace on the work of hospitals, cultural institutions and other areas of society that have traditionally been thought to serve other values. Almost everyone concedes that competitive markets are effective in mobilizing the energies of participants to satisfy common desires. And yet the apprehensions remain. However hard it is to explain these fears, they persist as a mute reminder that something of irreplaceable value may get lost in the relentless growth of commercialization." (Bok, 2003, p. 17).

And we do know that by no stretch of the imagination can the "market" substitute for "community" or "society" at large. We know also, as Ron Barnett has so powerfully written in his excellent book, *Beyond all Reason* (2003): "The university remains an extraordinary institution. (But) a higher education system that educates upwards of 40% of the population cannot be what it was when it educated, say, less than 15%. It can be much more. Its scale, its reach into society, the intermingling of its knowledges with those of the wider world and the wider forms of human being that it promotes are already enabling it to be much more. But it can be even more still." (p. 173).

In society as we know it today, it is clear that no university can separate itself (nor should it) from the larger problems of the world, much less its immediate community setting. The University of KwaZulu-Natal, after extensive consultation and debate with a huge range of different representatives of community made a very deliberate commitment in its mission: to not only commit to the conventional assertions about teaching, research and community outreach but to make specific commitment to "development". This may be unsurprising for a university located in sub-Saharan Africa — but is significant nevertheless and a radical departure from the past — and focused the mind of those developing strategy to deliver on this mission. It had major implications for all three legs of university activity: teaching, research and community development. Interestingly, it made our endeavours even more important to local business than it was before.

The Open University also broke from the past in a radical kind of way, a way that served the cause of social justice and set in motion a whole new method of delivering higher education. Given that its reach is global (and its government funding local), this mission is one which needs careful management — as well as several international partners (both in educational, business and donor community) — and an imaginative harnessing of technology. Its mode of delivery makes it possible for students who are geographically or financially constrained to obtain a British degree without having to leave their home country.

One of The Open University's major legacies lies in self-replication: in consultation with partners in other countries (some private sector), it extends its mission by assisting other organizations to set up open universities and, over time, to become independent. While this is an admirable extension of its mission, it may well not sit easily with those who espouse "the market" as the solution to higher education demand.

The conclusion must be that "mission" is not something to be taken for granted as it was in a bygone era of privilege and elitism — but rather something which may well need to be negotiated in the context of the social needs of the time. The social needs of our time, in turn, may extend well beyond our immediate physical boundaries as we all come to realize that we are part of a global society. At the same time, however, we need to understand, as we embark upon more and more engagement, that we are walking a tightrope where the balancing of disinterestedness, responsiveness and market forces may well overwhelm our best intentions.

In conclusion, let us be in no doubt that bringing outsiders' views into the sometimes secluded world of the university can have a profound change on the university. So, indeed it should, otherwise what would be the point? And let us also be in no doubt about its being difficult. With a range of world views being brought to bear on mission and strategic priorities, there will be disagreement. But, it is argued, it is precisely in the resolution of such disagreement that the university demonstrates its relevance to our modern, complex society.

Curricula changed by engagement and alliances

Not all cases of societal engagement require the creation of formal alliances and the following examples cover a spectrum of types of engagement that profoundly changed the university.

Five examples are cited of curricula transformed by development concerns at the University of KwaZulu-Natal:

- An architectural department surrounded by inadequate housing trained its students for many years for a first-world environment before recognizing the need to address the imperatives of alternative and low-cost housing, as well as built environment support in its curriculum. As a result the students and staff found themselves in great demand internationally because the problems of urbanization they were addressing are indeed global problems.

- An agricultural faculty that concerned itself exclusively with large-scale commercial farming turned its attention to the problems of small-scale and subsistence farming, and established a Farmers' Support Group to assist local farmers.

- A realization that a great many jobs are generated in the small business and voluntary sectors led to the tailoring of appropriate degree programmes.

- Service learning (or reflective community work) was added to the curriculum. This enabled students to become acquainted with development issues at first hand and also to obtain an insight into what they could do to improve matters.

- Development Studies as an area of teaching and research was strengthened and, indeed, in the course of time the Faculty of Social Sciences changed its name to the Faculty of Community and Development Disciplines — a strong signal to community and potential students alike.

At The Open University similar examples can be cited of where alliances have helped influence curricula:

- With so many students in employment, the university developed work-based learning (with unions, health trusts, business and other partners) and is finding new ways of recognizing and crediting learning done in the workplace. For example, there are programmes to turn nurse aides into fully qualified nurses and teaching assistants into fully qualified teachers.

- There are programmes where students acquire professional qualifications with alliance organizations such as Microsoft and Cisco at the same time as they earn their university qualifications.

- An alliance with the College of Law whereby the college supplies legal curricula in accordance with professional requirements and the university uses its experience and infrastructure to support the students in the shape and delivery of those curricula.

- Gradually, alliances with international partners enable their curriculum innovations to be absorbed into the curricula available to Open University students everywhere.

Alliances that impacted on the research agenda

What about research initiatives that flow from community alliances or need alliances to be successful? In a society defined as a knowledge society, as the ACU document (2001) makes so abundantly clear, "increasingly, academics will accept that they share their territory with other knowledge professionals. The search for formal understanding itself, long central to the academic life, is moving rapidly beyond the borders of disciplines and their locations inside universities. Knowledge is being keenly pursued in the context of its application and in a dialogue of practice with theory through a network of policy-advisors, companies, consultants, think tanks and brokers, as well as academics and indeed the wider society." (p. iii) Michael Gibbons (1994) has described what he calls "mode 2 knowledge production" where alliances between researchers are formed around particular problems or applications which, once solved, dissolve.

At one level, it is true to say that academics have always pursued research alliances (often at an individual level) and hardly need encouragement to do so. It is, however, important to look at the current climate and recognize three factors which might well not work in favour of academics pursuing community engagement and development in the research endeavour. The first has to do with the commercialization of research, whereby researchers are more often engaging in research which funders (business, government and other agencies outside the university) are prepared to pay for, rather than research that is important to society. It is regrettable that some of the most pressing of society's problems are not on the research agenda of universities. The second factor has to do with "disinterested" research (an issue referred to above). Disinterested research is increasingly difficult to fund and we live in a university world where the number and size of grants are seen as one of the main criteria of success. Yet "disinterestedness" lies at the heart of what universities can contribute, and have contributed over the years, and has led to some of the more spectacular breakthroughs in human knowledge. Some kind of balance needs to be maintained on the university research agenda to ensure that cognizance is taken of community needs without sacrificing essential independence and distinterestedness. The third factor has to do with interdisciplinarity and multidisciplinarity. Any focus on community problems and, indeed, many of the big problems of the world today rapidly makes clear that people working from the perspective and knowledge of one discipline will not reach solutions. The problems of the real world are seldom so kind as to divide themselves into disciplines. Most community development issues require a multidisciplinary approach.

Let us give some examples of where the preoccupation of the community and imperative of "development" in the mission of the university did and does drive the research agenda. The University of KwaZulu-Natal, for example, is located in a region of massive disparities, terrible sickness, poverty, unemployment, illiteracy, inadequate schooling and violence.

One excellent example of putting development at the heart of the university endeavour at Natal was the number of research projects devoted to one dimension or another of the HIV/Aids pandemic (a pandemic at whose epicentre the university found itself located). Over 150 research projects necessitated the setting up of a Networking Centre to coordinate the projects and disseminate information. Formal community agreements and partnership were essential to success, and since all the necessary expertise did not reside in one university, alliances with other universities inside and outside South Africa were formed and partnerships entered into with major funders from various parts of the world.

The university also had large projects in violence prevention, illiteracy, teacher education, low-cost housing and subsistence agriculture — to name but some. All of these projects were carried out in large and quite formal community alliances. Community issues often require what has come to be called "action research", and it is clear that large projects of this sort require particular skills in their management and implementation. The point, of course, is that community problems informed the research agenda of the university and shaped the policies that went with the funds available.

The Open University also has excellent examples of "community" impacting on research: its very mission defines an important part of its research agenda — and that is the use of technology, to reach and serve people who would not otherwise be able to access higher education and give them the best learning environments possible. The establishment of an Institute of Educational Technology and the Knowledge Media Institute as two large bodies of people focusing on these issues is evidence of this. This has extended into "ambient technology" and this too must become an important part of the knowledge base if the O.U. is to continue to be at the forefront of "distance" learning. There is also ongoing research on technology for various types of disability and it is no accident that The Open University has over 10,000 disabled students. The researchers in the university also use the possibilities presented by such a large virtual community and engage members of that community in research projects such as the climate-change model described above.

It may not be entirely fair to assert that many of societies' most seemingly intractable problems are not presently occupying high priority status on the research agenda of universities and yet it must be clear that better research should inform public policy debates at local, municipal, national and even international level. Often it is politics rather than hard evidence that dictate one course of action over another. Universities that give their academics the freedom and encouragement to make public the issues and make public the intellectual debate that should inform the politicians play a valuable role — if they care sufficiently and take their role of intellectual leadership seriously. But if we find ourselves concerned only with that research which attracts the largest grants, selling our intellectual skills to the highest bidder, then increasingly it will mean abrogating our responsibilities to the communities which sustain us, abrogating the most basic human responsibility — that of making the world a better place for all its citizens.

Responsibilities as neighbours and citizens

It is interesting to realize that it is during hard times that universities really demonstrate their core values because it is during hard times that society needs a place where some semblance of free speech and academic freedom prevails and the real issues of the day can be freely and robustly debated. In such circumstances, universities are faced with engagement with an existing social order while at the same time sowing the seeds for its transformation or transition into something else. And following regime change, there are major challenges for universities in both changing themselves and in contributing — both constructively and critically — to the wider changes around them. There are many places in the world which have experienced or are still experiencing transformative change in their immediate societies, change with which universities have, perforce, to contend. It is interesting to consider the contribution of universities to such change.

To do this, the findings of a large international research study led jointly by The Open University and the Association of Commonwealth Universities are drawn upon. The study was entitled "The Role of Universities in the Transformation of Societies" (Brennan *et al*, 2004), and it focused on roles played by universities in contexts of radical political and economic transformations in their host societies. The project sought to examine the extent to which universities generated, contributed to or inhibited change in such contexts. In choosing which 15 countries to study (Central and Eastern Europe, sub-Saharan Africa, Central Asia and Latin America) there was an assumption that by focusing on places where there was a lot of change going on, the part played by universities might be more visible.

Three roles for the university were highlighted:

An *economic* role: Overall, the project's case studies did not suggest that universities were not playing an economic role, rather that the role was not necessarily a matter of major debate, and that it was not considered to be "transformative". And while economic transformations were clearly taking place in a majority of the countries considered by the project, what was much less clear was the extent to which these were "knowledge-driven" developments and whether universities were playing a significant part in them. The report suggests a number of possible reasons for this relatively downplayed economic role. One was that many countries did not possess adequate steering mechanisms to change curriculum and pedagogy in directions required by economic and employment considerations. A second reason was that funding formulae for higher education in terms of staff numbers and other relatively fixed costs meant there was little pressure on institutions to take account of market responsiveness or other demand-side pressures. A third reason was an absence of staff to teach new subjects. One consequence of all this was the emergence of quite large private sectors of higher education to fill the economic gap created by the lack of responsiveness from the state institutions.

A *political* role: As far as a political role in social transformation was concerned, the project found the notion of "protected space" to be useful and near universal. In it, universities could provide at least some of their members with "islands of autonomy" from existing regimes and political cultures. On some of these islands, the seeds of future political opposition could grow but there were probably as many examples in the case studies where the islands had either provided succour to previous regimes or showed general indifference to local conditions. The islands, while isolated at home, were often connected to the rest of the world through cooperation programmes and research networks.

An interesting comparative study by Chowdhury (2004) of universities in India, Bangladesh, Poland and Slovenia described the role of universities in socialising "elites in waiting" and the creation of the human resources needed after regime changes, even though the changes themselves owed little or nothing to higher education.

The Transformation report (Brennan *et al*, 2004) concludes that universities are as much concerned with reproducing the old and protecting existing interests as they are about fermenting and supporting political transformation. Both processes can be found, sometimes even side by side in the same institution. One question the project sought to explore was whether the universities' political role was largely dependent or autonomous. It concludes: "On balance, we take the view that universities are used by different internal and external groups to attempt to achieve their various political ends. These reflect the particular group's strategic position in their society rather than an institutional strategy." (Brennan *et al*, 2004, p. 35)

Social and *cultural* aspects: The social and cultural aspects of the university's role in social transformation were also mixed and complex and as much concerned with social reproduction as they were with social transformation. South Africa provided the strongest example of concern with social-equity issues and the case study report recorded some impressive achievements as well as policy initiatives (Reddy, 2004). In Central and Eastern Europe, social-equity issues appeared to be lower on the agenda with universities possibly playing a less important part than they had under the old regimes. Culturally, universities had in some places provided a kind of repository for national sentiments that could come out of "storage" when time and circumstances permitted. But there could also be tensions between the "international" and "national" elements of the cultural role.

The project also looked at the *ways in which universities had themselves been transformed by external societal changes* and distinguished between:

- changes in curriculum, quality and standards;
- diversification;
- changes in access policies, student profiles and experiences; and
- academic responses to change.

Once again, a mixed picture emerged. There were pressures to change in all four areas, but responsiveness varied considerably. In Central and Eastern Europe in particular, emphasis on newly recovered "autonomy" tended to work against responsiveness and institutional change in the state sectors of higher education. One might also note that the responsiveness of many individual academics entailed escape by emigration rather than change and adaptation at home. In some cases, the project noted a tension between the demands of responsiveness to changing local contexts and the demands of increasing internationalization. A concern for legitimacy among new institutions could lead to a referencing against international standards through accreditation arrangements with foreign universities. National governments were generally introducing national, quality-assurance arrangements, again largely for purposes of legitimacy. The effects of these regulatory processes, however justified, tended to be to standardize provision and reduce the possibilities of responsiveness to more local needs and circumstances.

Conclusion: The Transformations project concluded that higher education's contribution to social change and development in societies undergoing radical transformations had been both modest and mixed. Schematically, from this project it seems possible to identify five models of higher education's engagement with their communities, whether local, regional, national or global. These are:

- "innovation" — universities providing new knowledge and people with new skills leading to transformation of enterprises and civil society;

- "maintenance" — universities reproducing the professionals needed by existing organizations and codifying the cultural knowledge to maintain identity and loyalty to existing structures and social hierarchies;
- "critique" — universities providing "protected space" for the thinking of the unthinkable and the possibility of challenge to existing structures and social practices;
- "shelter" — universities providing the conditions for their members that would allow an absence of social engagement, an isolation and protection from external change and development;
- "escape" — universities providing a route out of the host societies, especially for the young.

In fact, all five models can suggest "impact", whether positive or negative. And the Transformations project provided examples of all five models, often in combination even in the same university or even department. The project also demonstrated that universities generally have not been seen as the obvious sites of transformation nor have they seen themselves as such sites. However, it must also be acknowledged that, even if not crucial as originators of social transformation, universities may nevertheless be part of a vital set of mechanisms — developing human capital, supporting new institutions of civil society — that are essential to the success of the transformation process, even if that process is largely driven by other social forces.

There is, however, a further way in which universities could conceive of themselves as forces for social change and agents of global citizenship — and that is in their support of their fellow universities elsewhere in the world. In this way, engagement and impact are not within the host society of the university, but quite possibly with societies on the other side of the world. One can cite several examples:

- There are many universities that have link programmes with universities in other countries, and staff undertake teaching duties as well as make it possible for staff in either university to spend time in the partner institution. This is helpful to new curricula initiatives as well as to research programmes, including those involving community development. There are several initiatives at the moment (for example) where staff in "top" universities donate their time to teach in disciplines where local expertise is insufficient to the need. These are however usually individual rather than strategic, institutional arrangements.
- Of the many ways in which universities can (and should) fulfil their citizenship role, the Open Source and Content movements represent a particular challenge and opportunity. If universities are to be serving

the long-term benefits of society, if scholarship and knowledge are to be shared for the benefit of all, then it is difficult to argue against the placing of our material on the Web. This has been done by some universities — most notably M.I.T. — but what M.I.T. is sharing is its lecture notes, not material that is likely to endanger its business model. For The Open University to share its carefully constructed, student-centred material could well threaten its business model — and yet what an amazing difference it could make to colleagues in those parts of the world where libraries are poor and books hard to come by. The Open Content movement may well have other fundamental consequences. Quality assurance would assume a whole new meaning if it opened individual university offerings to comparison with the best of what is available on the Web. It might also change the economics of higher education. What is the point of individual academics in each institution endlessly reinventing undergraduate courses when excellent material is available on the Web?

• In a similar vein, one could cite the call being made by the Association of Commonwealth Universities, the Association of African Universities and the Higher Education South Africa Association to the world's universities to help revitalize the universities of Africa. One hopes that their call will be heard and their needs may well overlap with the possibilities of the Open Content movement.

ALLIANCES BETWEEN UNIVERSITIES

There is a lot of higher education about. In consequence, and linked to the general "rightward shift" in political economy in recent years, competition is an increasingly important feature of the contexts in which most universities operate. Even in this environment, collaboration is often a sensible "business" proposition. It is interesting to reflect on alliances that our two exemplar universities have forged.

Post-apartheid consortium

In KwaZulu-Natal, the five universities and polytechs in the region were driven to form a consortium by the recognition of three main issues:

• Recognition that apartheid had produced strange arrangements and the new South Africa had to find a way of moving beyond the "geopolitical imagination of its apartheid planners" (to use a phrase coined by the then Minister of Education, Kader Asmal);

• In a financially constrained system, recognition that (a) students were bearing more costs than necessary (for example, by paying application fees to all institutions in the hope of being selected by one); and (b) institutions were bearing more costs (for example, by each processing all these applications — as an obvious example); and

- The hope that a federal system (of some sort) could provide some mobility for our students and some benefits for the institutions.

The consortium was a success only in a very limited way. In a system which was hopelessly unequal, it was naïve to imagine that students (and their parents) and employers were not adequately informed as to the academic ranking of the participating institutions — or indeed that the unhappy history didn't bring with it baggage in the nature of trust relationships, to name but one aspect. The mix of student bodies, unions (and each participant had separate unions), senates, unequal competencies and capacities in administration and management, and leadership (with differing commitments to the consortium [and varying loyalties within their institutions]) — was altogether too complex a mix to go beyond the most obvious cost-saving measures. The issues were not helped by the administrative incapacity of the central body. Eventual government legislation enforced formal mergers — and the jury is still out as to whether these could be called successful. It would take a long time to even agree on the criteria for success — and those institutions with the most to gain would have different criteria to those with the most to lose. By the criteria of the business world, where mergers are common, universities are difficult and unusual bodies. Their governance structures are such that many people in the organization are in a position to block or jeopardize the implementation without sanction — and the managers manage more by influence than by exertion of authority in the formal sense. This is not a sensible cocktail — nor has it proved to be so.

O.U. alliances

The Open University is also a university with several "academic" alliances. Since its model of learning requires local support to its students wherever they are, it provides such support to international students (of which it has about 40,000) through local partners. These partnerships can be divided into four main sorts:

- Those enabling public-sector and even private-sector bodies to establish their own open universities and negotiate over time to achieve independence from the facilitating partner (O.U.), as well as title in their own countries. Examples of this sort are the Arab Open University which used O.U. material (suitably amended and contextualized) to start up. The partnership included training of staff and even use of systems — and ensured that a large number of students could be enrolled in a relatively short period. The institution started in 1999 and already has about 30,000 students — a large number of them women. Another example is the Singapore Institute of Management and similar arrangements were in place. It has established its reputation, weaned itself off O.U. material, been granted university title in its home country and will soon be independent. The O.U. also offers a Masters in Distance Education to assist staff acquire the knowledge of a specialist type of education.

- Those which are essentially business/private sector bodies in a foreign country where there is a market for business/management type courses, where the fees are relatively high (but still much lower than they would be if enrolled in another U.K. institution) — and, of course, "open" in the sense of entry qualifications.

- Those where the local partner is simply delivering tutorial support to students working to an O.U. curriculum. This may be a long-term arrangement or a short-term arrangement. In Ethiopia, the Civil Service College (in partnership with the O.U. and financed by the World Bank) offered the M.B.A. to a limited number of senior politicians (including the Prime Minister) and civil servants.

- Those which are essentially contractual arrangements to deliver a particular outcome. This would cover consultancies, often in the specificities of distance learning.

These have been successful partnerships and it is instructive to consider why. Opinions will differ on this, but the strongest possibility is that both types of partnership accept the "senior" status of the O.U. As the O.U. becomes more venturesome and seeks alliances with partners who see themselves as equal and even superior partners, the question of partnership becomes more difficult — and even impossible. Faculty are seldom inclined to accept others' considerations about curricula; national quality assurance mechanisms seem to baulk at even the idea that some countries might have an acceptable way of ensuring quality different to our own; and the pound is so strong that only relatively affluent partners can make the economics work. However as the O.U. becomes more conscious that it cannot deliver curriculum to a global audience from a mono-cultural base, it seeks opportunities for curriculum partnerships, perhaps with "virtual" staff members, albeit part-time, living in places outside Britain.

A regional alliance

Another example of a large and more complex alliance of institutions is the Greater Manchester Strategic Alliance involving five universities, 19 other tertiary education providers and seven existing social, economic or educational agencies or networks. Created only a year ago, the principal initial aim of this alliance was the widening of participation in higher education in a region marked by very sharp differences in economic prosperity and prospects between areas. The alliance was created precisely because of the very large volume of current educational provision. The complexities of choice facing individuals wanting access to higher education were considerable. And the challenge of inducing sufficient numbers of additional people to want access, in order that deeply rooted patterns of social inequality in the region could be overcome, could not be addressed adequately or cost-effectively by individual institutions working separately. Thus, the creation of the alliance.

What will be interesting about the Manchester alliance is the extent to which the initial impetus to cooperation — widening participation — will broaden to encompass a fuller range of community-linked functions. Already, considerable emphasis is being given to local and regional economic needs, along with concerns about social inclusion and cohesion. (Some of the northern parts of the sub-region witnessed race riots not so long ago.) The key here to making cooperation between institutions override competitive instincts is the commitment to extending higher education: in this way, competition for existing students becomes replaced by collaboration to increase student numbers overall. Ideally, all partners can be "winners"!

New technology and new ways to learn

The Open University and the University of Manchester are in discussion about an alliance that will pool the benefits of e-learning without both partners incurring the considerable costs and ongoing research that is essential to delivering education using the latest technology. As educators come to realize that the new technology introduces entirely different ways of student learning, they will also come to realize that the costs of delivering the best learning experiences are very high. Institutions have not been very forthcoming in sharing their knowledge in the teaching and learning domain so far. Faculty members are also unwilling to spend the time away from their disciplines necessary to become (and stay) educational technology specialists. Maybe, now with the costs so substantial, the climate for alliances of this sort will improve. It remains to be seen.

Milton Keynes alliance

An unusual alliance has been growing in the Milton Keynes district where there is an under-representation of the population in higher education. The alliance is dubbed "Universities of Milton Keynes" and represents an attempt at a new form of educational provision whereby all the universities in the area (four, including The Open University) and the local college combine to make their particular educational offerings available to students and, in an alliance with the City of Milton Keynes, run a central facility where students can have access to some central facilities and campus life. It is an unusual response to under-provision and recognition that it is no longer feasible to build more and more physical facilities.

Conclusion

The need seems to be for cooperation in doing new things. The question is whether this can be achieved while competing over the "old things" at the same time? One of the questions to be asked must concern the extent to which regulatory frameworks — whether national or international — support or hinder co-operation. It is difficult to encourage "market" forces while at the same time expecting cooperation.

LESSONS TO BE LEARNED

Permeable structures

It should not require extraordinary circumstances or incentives to get universities to engage with their communities. It is good practice to make our governing structures as permeable as possible; to pay careful attention to diversity so that other world views may be heard (which calls to mind Peter Senge's "learning organization" [Senge, 1990]); in short, to ensure our debates about important issues are as informed as possible. It should not be imagined that all views can be accommodated. Some can — and some cannot. The process, however, is vital — and provides a good example of democracy at work.

Finding resources

It is not the leadership and administrations alone that can make such engagement real for the universities' core functions. It is mostly in the faculty that tangible expression will be given to whatever alliances the institution will make. Faculty will not be instructed to engage and the nature of their engagement will not be controlled from above. They will engage if they are genuinely interested and it is in their interests to engage. It is up to university leaders to ensure promotion criteria support strategic alliances; it is up to leaders to find resources to support alliances (including, importantly, research projects) and resources may well be found from business interests, even if such resources are drawn from "corporate responsibility" funds; and, crucially, it is up to leaders to find and support good faculty leadership that understand and pursue institutional goals as well as faculty goals.

Sustaining partnerships

The capacity to sustain partnerships and alliances may well be the distinguishing feature of universities that will thrive in this new world of "engagement". This is not as easy as one would imagine. The locus of decisions about partnerships, curricula, financing and other matters that impact on any one partnership are often in several different parts of the university — and sophisticated structures have to be found to bring them all into line with strategic intent.

Engaging with society

It is important that individual academics publicly engage with different parts of society. The university, as an institution, will always find it very difficult to engage with the many and complex parts of modern society. But its individual academics can be in many forums and part of many different "communities", and it is there that the "voice" of the university can be heard and the role of the public intellectual understood. Without that kind of engagement, the institution, however assiduous its leaders, cannot be truly seen to be in the community. It means that academics must move out of their "tribes and territories" (to quote Tony Becher [1989]) and take the university into the community — and bring the community into the university. The worth of this kind of engagement must be formally recognized by the institution as a whole.

Blurred boundaries

Boundaries are becoming blurred and include the spatial (where learning takes place), time (when learning takes place), knowledge (where it is produced), environments (local, national, global), control (learners, providers, funders), and roles (teacher, learner, assessor, enabler, manager). And to these boundaries must be added the boundaries of our universities themselves. Fewer of our students will attend a single institution. Many will expect increasing recognition to be given for learning that has been accomplished elsewhere, including — but not exclusively — in the workplace. Alliances facilitate these arrangements.

Multiple identities

Identities will become increasingly multiple and will change throughout the life course. Some identities will be easier to integrate than others. Identities will be parallel (student, worker, parent) rather than sequential, and some identities will be increasingly contested (entailing both mobility and mobility blockages) and insecure ("Do I really belong here?" — "Am I good enough?"). Academic identities will not be immune from these changes.

Social responsibilities

More and more (and especially after the spate of scandals in recent years) business is being pressured to demonstrate its commitment to its social responsibilities. Working together with universities in communities (especially communities where development is clearly needed) is a mutually satisfactory way in which to make a tangible difference.

Openness

Taken together, these trends will require a much greater "openness" from our institutions of higher education, including an openness to change themselves into quite different kinds of institutions, institutions which are able to be more collaborative in nature, more diverse in composition, more responsive to addressing the major issues of our time. We must surely share the vision that derives from the idea that the world will be better off, at best healed, by educational intervention that is conducted in alliances that, quite literally, share our common wealth. The task is worthwhile and possible if it can overcome the acquisitiveness that characterizes so many of the initiatives that currently ride the spirit of globalization.

A new collegiality

We noted earlier that "alliances" sit at the stronger and more formalised end of a spectrum of forms of collaboration and partnership between universities and the increasingly wide varieties of communities with which they must engage. But relationships of this sort should not blind us to the importance of other — and in some senses weaker — forms of collaboration, both for institutions, for groups within them and for individual academics. In some ways, these direct us back to older ideas of collegiality, but also to a new collegiality that extends beyond the boundaries of academe to embrace wider communities — locally, nationally and internationally. Though weaker in form, such relationships may nonetheless have considerable impacts. But whether one uses "alliance" or some other word, whether one talks about institutions or individuals, the message is the same one — working together, we can achieve so much more.

REFERENCES

Association of Commonwealth Universities (2001). "Engagement as a Core Value for the University — a consultative document".

Barnett, Ronald (2003). *Beyond All Reason*. SHRE and Open University Press.

Becher, T. (1989). *Academic Tribes and Territories: Intellectual Enquiry and the Cultures of Disciplines*. Open University Press, Buckingham.

Bjarnason, Svava & Coldstream, Patrick (2003). *The Idea of Engagement — Universities in Society*. Association of Commonwealth Universities.

Bok, Derek (1982). *Beyond the Ivory Tower: Social Responsibilities of the Modern University*. Harvard University Press.

Bok, Derek (2003). *Universities in the Marketplace*. Princeton University Press.

Brennan, J, King, R. & Lebeau, Y. (2004). *The Role of Universities in the Transformation of Societies*. Association of Commonwealth Universities and Centre for Higher Education Research and Information.

Castells, Manuel (2000). *The Information Age: Economy, Society & Culture*: Volume 1: The Rise of the Network Society. Second edition. Blackwell, Oxford.

Chowdhury, Roy S. (2004). "Mapping Minds, Changing Maps: Universities, Intelligentsia, Nation States (Slovenia, Poland, India and Bangladesh)". CHERI/Open University, www.open.ac.uk/cheri/TRhome.htm

Drucker, Peter (2002). "The Near Future" (Part 1). *The Economist*, 2 November 2002, London.

Friedman, T. (2000). *The Lexus and the Olive Tree*. Anchor Books, New York.

Gibbons, M. (2001). "Globalisation and Higher Education: the tension between co-operation and competition". *Higher Education Digest*, no 41. The Open University, London.

Gibbons, M., Limoges, C. *et al.* (1994). *The New Production of Knowledge: The Dynamics of Science and research in Contemporary Societies*. Sage, Thousand Oaks, California.

Newman, Janet (2005). http://www.open.ac.uk/inaugural-lectures/pics/d35754.doc

Reddy T, (2004). *Higher Education and Social Transformation, a case study of South Africa*. http://www.open.ac.uk/cheri/Trhome.htm.

Senge, P. (1990). *The Fifth Discipline: The art & practice of the learning organization*. Doubleday/Currency, New York.

Singh, Mala, (2003). "Universities and Society — Whose Terms of Engagement?" in Bjarnason, Svava & Coldstream, Patrick (2003), *The Idea of Engagement*. Pp. 272-305.

Tomusk, Voldemar (2004). *The Open World and Closed Societies*. Palgrave Macmillan, New York.

Higher Education in the Twenty-First Century: Vision and Action (1998). UNESCO Publication, Paris.

Task Force on Higher Education and Society (2000). *Peril and Promise: Higher Education in Developing Countries*. The World Bank, Washington D.C.

"Constructing Knowledge Societies: New Challenges for Tertiary Education", (2002). The World Bank, Washington, D.C.

CHAPTER 5

Higher-Education Systems Dynamics and Useful Knowledge Creation

Frans van Vught

INTRODUCTION

Economic history is about the economic successes and failures of companies, regions, countries and continents. Generally speaking, economic historians argue that economic growth is the result of the accumulation and application of knowledge. Economic growth is created because individuals develop new ideas and apply these in processes of production and distribution. And because the capacity of each individual to acquire knowledge is limited, the processes of knowledge accumulation and application are in essence social processes: only by means of specialization of labour and cooperation will we be able to continue our processes of creating and applying new knowledge.

This argument is certainly not new. It was already developed by Adam Smith in 1776 and it has played a central role in economic theory ever since. Economic growth implies the continuous development of increasingly complex patterns of division of labour, in which the market usually plays a crucial coordinating role.

Generally speaking, the market is a system for the allocation of scarce resources. In the economic sense, a free market allocates resources through the price mechanism, subject to the discipline of supply and demand.

The market also is a mechanism of social coordination. Out of the decisions of many actors it creates a "spontaneous social order" (Hayek, 1967), not so much by grand design and rational planning, but rather by allowing autonomous actors to develop mutual relationships. The market is a mechanism for "coordination without a coordinator" (Wildavsky, 1979, p. 90).

The market as a coordinating mechanism, in its turn, is embedded in a context of rules, norms and practices, leading to specific processes and outcomes of coordination. Trying to influence these rules, norms and regulations in order to stimulate the coordinative capacity of the market appears to be the objective of many current policies in our modern knowledge economies.

According to the general policy arguments in these modern knowledge economies, the key to economic success is the ability to develop new knowledge and to apply it in economic processes. In addition, this ability is assumed to be to a large extent determined by institutional economic contents. One of the major challenges for policy-making in our knowledge economies is to find and influence the institutional factors that have an impact on the processes of the accumulation and application of knowledge.

In this paper I intend to explore the dynamics of higher-education systems. I will especially focus on the behaviour of higher-education institutions in policy-contexts in which market coordination plays a major role. My objective is to analyse the dynamics of higher-education systems and to explore some of the conditions that might stimulate the processes of the accumulation and application of knowledge in modern societies.

USEFUL KNOWLEDGE

In order to be able to conceptualize the role of knowledge in economic development, we need a theoretical framework. For this, let me first once more go back to Adam Smith. According to Smith, the "improvement of machines" (which is crucial for economic development) is the result of the efforts of two groups: the "common workmen" and the "philosophers or men of speculation". The common workmen are continuously looking for ways to improve their operations: "A great part of the machines made use of in these manufactures... were originally the inventions of common workmen who, being each of them being employed in very simple operation, naturally turned their thoughts towards finding out easier and readier methods of performing" (Smith, 1776/1976, p.115). The philosophers form a second source of innovation. "Improvements have been made by the ingenuity of those who are called philosophers or men of speculation, whose trade is not to do anything, but to observe everything; and who, upon that account, are often capable of combining together the powers of the most distant and dissimilar objects" (Smith, 1976/1976, p.115-6).

Adam Smith here addresses one of the most crucial institutional factors that, according to economic historians, appears to have influenced the economic development of the Western world. The historical argument is that, until the Industrial Revolution took place, technological progress was the result of serendipitous discoveries. "Although new techniques appeared before the Industrial Revolution, they had narrow epistemic bases and thus rarely if ever led to continued and sustained improvements. At times these inventions had enormous practical significance, but progress usually fizzled out after promising beginnings. Such techniques are also less flexible and adaptable to changing circumstances..." (Mokyr, 2002, p19). After 1800 a transition took place which allowed for the growth of useful knowledge as a moving force in economic development. This transition implied the inter-action between the knowledge of the "common workers" and that of the "men of speculation".

In a recent book Joel Mokyr (2002) develops the argument that the genesis of the Industrial Revolution can be interpreted as the result of the specific development of the knowledge economy of Western Europe in the 18th century. Building on a wide variety of studies on the Industrial Revolu-tion, he stipulates the well-known theory that this Revolution is the effect of the application of the scientific knowledge gained during the 17th and the 18th centuries to the processes of industrial production. However, Mokyr also develops a theoretical framework that tries to explain the interaction between two layers of knowledge: propositional knowledge and prescriptive knowl-edge, two types of knowledge that are clearly related to the two groups of Adam Smith. It is this theory that might help us to analyse the role of knowl-edge in economic development.

According to Mokyr "useful knowledge" consists of knowledge "what" (propositional knowledge, or sets of beliefs) and of knowledge "how" (pre-scriptive knowledge, or techniques). Propositional knowledge is the knowl-edge of scientists and scholars, the men of speculation. Prescriptive knowledge is the practical knowledge of artisans and craftsmen, of the common work-men. It is the interaction between these two types of knowledge which, according to Mokyr, explains the dynamics of a knowledge economy. In this process of interaction propositional knowledge is "mapped" into prescriptive knowledge, while prescriptive knowledge can produce a feedback into propo-sitional knowledge. The characteristics of both types of knowledge have an effect on the conditions of the process of interaction, and thus on the results in terms of the economic dynamics.

Mokyr argues that the existence of some piece of propositional knowledge can serve as an epistemic base for new techniques. However this existence does not guarantee that any mapping into prescriptive knowledge will occur. "... the existence of a knowledge base creates opportunities, but does not guar-antee that they will be taken advantage of" (Mokyr, 2002, p.17). If the epistemic base (the propositional knowledge) of techniques (prescriptive knowledge) is wide, inventions occur rapidly and efficiently. If the epistemic base is narrow, solutions to problems are costly or even impossible. The propositional knowledge sets thus are potential preconditions for the development of useful knowledge. But also the feedback from prescriptive knowledge sets to propositional knowledge is of importance. Such feedback processes can direct the epistemic bases, and increase their width and density. The combination of the two processes is crucial. "If there is sufficient complementarity between an upstream and a downstream process in the system, persistent, self-reinforcing economic change can occur" (Mokyr, 2002, p.21).

The crucial question of course is when this "sufficient complementarity" occurs and whether it can be stimulated. I would like to argue that the appearance and the nature of the processes of interaction and complementarity between the two types of knowledge are an effect of the institutional contexts in which they are situated. In our modern knowledge economics the relationships between universities and society at large form a crucial aspect of these relationships. In the rest of this paper I will focus on these relationships. I will analyse the dynamics of the present-day higher-education systems of the Western world, looking both at their internal driving forces and their external policy-environments.

CONSUMER SOVEREIGNTY IN HIGHER EDUCATION?

It is a familiar argument by now: the Western world has entered the phase of the "knowledge society"; our future prosperity and welfare will to a large extent depend on our ability to create and apply knowledge; our economic growth is dependent upon the ways we are able to work with useful knowledge. Nation states and whole continents underline their ambitions to become global competitors in terms of the knowledge economy. The European Union has, for instance, indicated that it intends to become the world's most dynamic and competitive knowledge economy by the year 2010.

The "knowledge economy" is at the heart of many governmental policies these days. Governments design policies that intend to stimulate the creation and application of knowledge in economic activities; they try to stimulate "academic entrepreneurialism", the use of IPR, the setting-up of venture capital funds and the intensity of cooperation between universities and business and industry.

Given these ambitions, political leaders increasingly address higher-education institutions. They craft higher-education policies that intend to influence the behaviour of these institutions and of the faculty working within them. Generally speaking these policies regard the trade-off between autonomy and accountability; between less state control and more self-management on the one hand (Van Vught, 1992) and more efficiency and especially responsiveness to societal needs on the other (Meek, 2003).

The policy-argument that governments use is rather straightforward and goes as follows. Higher-education institutions need to become more responsive to the needs of the knowledge society. They need to increase their capacity and willingness to become engaged in the production of useful knowledge. In order to stimulate these institutions to do so, the mechanism of market coordination can be used. Reinforcing the demand side of the market (by increasing consumer sovereignty) will increase both the sensitiveness to consumers' wishes and the level of competition between universities. The result will be higher-quality outputs and an increased responsiveness to societal needs.

It seems to me that the validity of this policy-argument can be questioned. First, the outputs of higher-education institutions are usually heavily subsidized, both by public funding and by private gifts. Supply and demand do not set a market-clearing price for the outputs of higher-education institutions (Geiger, 2004, p.17). The subsidization processes also create market distortions, especially because of the uneven distribution of the public and private resources that are poured into higher education (Newman, et al., 2004, p.90). In higher-education systems the price mechanism works imperfectly.

Secondly, the introduction of more consumer sovereignty in higher-education systems does not necessarily trigger the behaviour of higher education institutions that governments are trying to accomplish. Given the specific nature of their "products and services", higher-education institutions often are able to use their autonomy to resist the pressures of the increase of consumer power.

There is simple explanation for this. The products and services that higher-education institutions offer are "experience goods" (Dill, 2003): the clients of universities are only able to judge the relevance and the quality of the outputs of higher education, when they are able to experience them. Students can only really judge the quality of a course when they take it; and research clients can only really judge the quality of a research project when they are offered the results. When confronted with the question to take a decision in favour of a certain product or service of an institution for higher education, clients (including potential students) are hampered with the well-known market failure of imperfect information. Higher education institutions, on their part, are enticed by these conditions to represent themselves in the best possible ways. They underline their self-acclaimed qualities hoping that by emphasizing these, they will be able to convince the clients of their attractiveness.

As a result of this the consumer market works imperfectly in higher-education (Massy, 2003, p.42). In the words of Joseph Stiglitz: "Recent advances in economic theory have shown that whenever information is imperfect and markets incomplete,… then the invisible hand works imperfectly" (quoted in Friedman, 2002, p. 50). Increasing consumer sovereignty therefore does not automatically lead to an increase of responsiveness to societal needs by higher-education institutions. Rather the behaviour of these institutions is triggered by the conditions of another market, that of competition for institutional reputation.

MARKETS AND REPUTATION IN HIGHER EDUCATION

In his classic *The Higher Education System* Clark explores three major types of markets that are relevant in higher education systems: consumer markets, "where people normally exchange money for desired goods or services" (Clark, 1983, p. 162), labour markets, "in which people offer their capabilities and energy for money" (p.164) and institutional markets, "where enterprises interact with one another, instead of with consumers or employees" (p.165). It is the first market (consumer markets) that appears to be the object of many governmental policies that try to increase the coordinative capabilities of market forces in higher education. By increasing the capacity of the consumers of higher education outputs (students, clients) to choose among the various products of higher education institutions, these policies intend to strengthen the consumer market. However, exactly because of another higher-education market mentioned by Clark, these policies are usually only marginally effective. Let me explain this.

The actions of universities and other higher education institutions appear to be particularly driven by the wish to maximize their (academic) prestige and to uphold their reputations (Garvin, 1980; Brewer *et al.* 2002). Universities seek to hire the best possible faculty (on the higher-education labour market) and they try to recruit the most qualified students (on the higher-education consumer market). They do so because they are "intensely concerned with reputation and prestige" (Geiger, 2004, p.15).

Given this drive, higher-education institutions are first and foremost each other's competitors (on the institutional market). They compete amongst themselves for the best students, the best faculty, the largest research contracts, the highest endowments, etc. They compete for all the resources that may have an impact on their institutional reputation.

Geiger (2004) argues that this competition for reputation is played out in two principal arenas, one comprising faculty scholarship, and the other reflecting the recruitment of (especially undergraduate) students. In the first arena, universities try to recruit and employ the best scientists, i.e. those scholars with the highest recognition and rewards, the highest citation impact scores and the largest numbers of publications. In order to be able to do so, they continuously feel the need to increase their staff expenditures, especially in research (since it is this context that scholars are attracted to), creating a continuous need for extra resources. The second arena regards the recruitment of students. Given their wish to increase their reputation, universities try to attract the most talented students. They use selection procedures to find them, but they also offer grants and other facilities in order to be able to recruit them, again leading to a permanent need for extra resources.

The concept of "reputation in higher education" needs some further exploration. The reputation of a higher-education institution can be defined as the image (of quality, influence, trustworthiness) it has in the eyes of others. Reputation is the subjective reflection of the various actions an institution undertakes to create an external image of itself. The reputation of an institution and its quality may be related, but they need not to be identical. Higher-education institutions try to influence their external images in many ways, and not only by maximizing their quality.

The dynamics of higher education are first and foremost a result of the competition for reputation. Higher education systems are characterized by a "reputation race". In this race higher-education institutions are constantly trying to create the best possible images of themselves as highly regarded universities. And this race is expensive. Higher-education institutions will spend all the resources they can find to try to capture an attractive position in the race. In this sense Bowen's famous law of higher education still holds: "...in quest of excellence, prestige and influence... each institution raises all the money it can... [and] spends all it raises" (Bowen, 1980, p.20).

THE UNINTENDED CONSEQUENCES OF PUBLIC POLICY

As indicated before, in many countries across the world, a shift is taking place in public policy regarding higher education. Even in countries where state regulation used to be the dominant factor with respect to the dynamics of higher-education systems, now new polices are emerging designed to create markets in higher education and to encourage inter-institutional competition.

Newman et al. (2004) see two main causes for this international development in public policy. One is the previously mentioned wish of political leaders to use the assumed positive forces of increased competition and consumer sovereignty to make higher-education institutions more responsive to the needs of society, especially with respect to the knowledge economy. I argued before that this argument fails to appreciate the strength of another market in higher education, that of institutional reputation.

The other cause for the international shift of public policy towards markets and an increase of competition, is the behaviour of universities themselves. When confronted with the temptations of more autonomy and self-management, university leaders are most willing also to accept the increased competition that usually comes with them. As a matter of fact, the increase of competition is often used as an argument for even more autonomy: "We need greater autonomy in order to compete" (Newman, et al., 2004, p. 34).

However, the introduction through public policy of increased competition may lead to a number of unintended consequences in the dynamics of higher-education systems that do not necessarily contribute to a better responsiveness to societal needs.

First, the total cost of higher education appears to be growing immensely. The reputation race implies that universities are in constant need of more resources. They need these resources to recruit better staff, to offer more study-grants, to upgrade their facilities, to improve their PR, etc. "Universities press their pricing up to the limits that markets, regulators, and public opinion will allow. They justify their actions in terms of the rising cost of excellence and other factors beyond their control, but that is only part of the story. The impetus for price hikes stems from the university's own choices…" (Massy, 2003, p. 39). It stems from its drive to engage in the academic reputation race.

The effect is an impressive increase of the spending levels of higher-education institutions. Geiger (2004), for instance, shows that the per-student spending between 1980 and 2000 in the U.S. rose by 62% at public universities and more than double that at private institutions (Geiger, 2004, pp. 32, 262). In the U.S. higher education has become far more expensive during recent decades. And although participation rates have grown and students have certainly benefited from these increases of spending levels, it may also be pointed out that, in particular, the private costs of higher education have gone up dramatically. In the U.S. "the costs of higher education borne by students nearly doubled in real terms from 1978 to 1996… The costs of going to college… grew nearly twice as fast as the economy" (Geiger, 2004, p. 33). When public policies in other countries tend to follow the U.S. example of increasing the competition in a system where reputation is the major driving force, similar cost explosions should be expected.

It should also be pointed out that the shift of the costs of higher education from public to private sources implies that the social returns of higher education are increasingly being overshadowed by the private benefits. In this sense, the introduction of consumer sovereignty and competition implies a "privatization" of higher education. Students and graduates increasingly demand "value for money" for their investments, and higher education institutions may be tempted to "reduce the value of learning to simply the opportunity to earn more upon graduation" (Newman et al., 2004, p. 44).

A second consequence of the introduction of increased competition appears to be an increase of the wealth-inequalities among institutions. In traditional continental European public policies with respect to higher education, institutions were assumed to be equal and (largely) similar. The new policies however emphasize the importance of differences between institutions. Universities are stimulated to compete and to develop specific roles and profiles, to relate to specific stakeholders and to respond to regional needs. This increase of competition leads to greater inequalities among institutions, because there is no "level playing field". The reputation race works out differently given different levels of resources; the higher these levels are, the more an institution will be able to climb the ladder of reputation. Higher-education institutions can only hire the faculty whose salaries they can afford. But they can also only charge the tuition fees that are justified by the level of their reputation. The reputation race is fuelled by an insatiable need for funding. Richer institutions are more easily able to increase their reputation than poorer institutions. And this process is self-reinforcing: as the race goes on, the wealth-inequalities and the differences in reputation tend to increase. The result is the establishment and strengthening of institutional hierarchies. Increased competition thus creates hierarchical differentiation in higher-education systems.

Thirdly, the new public policies (and the creation of institutional hierarchies) are accompanied by a greater social stratification of students. Highly reputable institutions try to enrol high-ability students. In order to accomplish this, they apply high-tuition/high-aid strategies, trying to attract and select those students who are most talented and whose enrolments reflect on their prestige. The result is a social stratification based on merit. Higher-education systems become more stratified by academic ability. Both students and institutions act in such a way that a meritocratic stratification is produced.

Even though student-aid policies are designed to create opportunities for the least advantaged, increased competition leads institutions to focus either on those students who have the financial resources themselves, or on those who have the highest abilities (and who can be offered grants). According to Newman et al. (2004), in the U.S. the less-advantaged students have become the victims of this development. "The price war that has broken out among institutions and even among states, grounded in the financial aid offered to attractive students, favours the already advantaged. They are also the ones knowledgeable enough about the system to seek out and attract competitive offers" (Newman, et al., 2004, p. 87).

Cost explosions, institutional hierarchies and the social stratification of the student body are not necessarily the consequences that political actors have in mind when they design the public policies that should stimulate higher-education institutions to become more responsive to societal needs. They are, however, possible effects of the introduction of an increase of competition in higher education systems. Because of the dynamics of the reputation race, these effects may very well occur. The more autonomy higher-education institutions acquire, the more they will intend to engage in this competition for reputation. Public policy makers in higher education should be aware of these dynamics and look for more effective ways to create the contexts that can stimulate the accumulation and application of knowledge in our modern societies.

THE INSTITUTIONALIZATION
OF USEFUL KNOWLEDGE CREATION

What then could such a more effective way be? Let us go back to Mokyr's theory of useful knowledge. Mokyr argues that useful knowledge is the combination of propositional and prescriptive knowledge. The mutual interaction between these two types of knowledge (through processes of mapping and feedback) can lead to self- reinforcing economic development (see paragraph 2, above). The challenge, of course, is designing an institutional context that will stimulate a strong interaction between the two processes of knowledge creation.

Our analysis of the dynamics of higher-education systems shows that the introduction of more consumer sovereignty and competition on the consumer market does not necessarily lead to more responsiveness from higher education institutions to the needs of the knowledge society. The behaviour of higher-education institutions is driven by a competition for institutional reputation rather than by a competition for consumer needs. In addition, introducing more autonomy for higher-education institutions in such a "reputation race" creates several unintended consequences (costs explosions, institutional hierarchies and social stratification of the student body).

An effective institutionalization of the interaction between the two processes of knowledge creation should take this into account. It should even take the existence of the reputation race as given and offer a context in which the reputation-driven behaviour of higher-education institutions can stimulate a fruitful interaction. Rather than on the objective to stimulate competition for consumer needs, increasing institutional autonomy should be focused on a successful and effective interaction between the two types of knowledge creation. Higher-education institutions should be challenged to address this interaction and they should see the positive effects of it as contributing to their reputation. This is what public policies for the knowledge economy should do. This is the way the coordinative capacity of the market should be used.

This is, of course, more easily said than done. The design of an effective institutionalization of useful knowledge creation is a challenge that many countries are facing and that is only beginning to be addressed. Let me, by way of conclusion, offer a few elements that might perhaps contribute to further facing this challenge.

Through human history, curiosity and the thirst for knowledge for its own sake have been the major driving forces behind the growth of propositional knowledge. And although these forces are still important and powerful today, their importance is declining relative to the importance of the motives for the accumulation of prescriptive knowledge. Even "pure" science today is no longer completely detached. "Somewhere in the back of the minds of most pure scientists are funding considerations. Funding agencies, somewhere in the back of their minds, think of legislators. And legislators, one hopes, in a remote corner of the back of their minds, have society's needs at heart" (Mokyr, 2002, p. 288). In our modern knowledge societies curiosity-driven research certainly has not disappeared, but it is increasingly being combined with the more pragmatic mechanisms of prescriptive knowledge creation.

A potentially fruitful way to stimulate the creation of useful knowledge is, I argue, to reinforce this combination of curiosity-driven and solution-driven research. This implies that the growth of propositional knowledge should be stimulated both by allowing for maximum freedom for curiosity-driven efforts and by processes of agenda-setting (trying to steer research efforts into specific fields of application). Alternatively, the growth of prescriptive knowledge should be reinforced not only by the search for pragmatic solutions for high-priority problems, but also by stimulating researchers to scour the bodies of propositional knowledge for guidance on how to create new mappings for new techniques.

In order to realize a stronger interaction between the two processes of knowledge creation, new partnerships between the public and the private sector should be developed. Substantial combinations of public and private funds should be made available for the universities that (either by themselves or in consortia) are willing and able to engage in these interactive research processes. The level of these combined budgets should be such that they can have an impact on the positioning of the institutions in the academic reputation race. Higher-education institutions should feel challenged by these budgets and they should accept it as self-evident that their efforts in this context will bring them a higher potential to increase their reputation.

The budgets for useful knowledge creation should of course be allocated in competition. Higher-education institutions should feel the necessity to compete for these funds. They should be willing to hire the best scientists and scholars to contribute to the programs that are funded by them. And they should feel challenged to adapt their curricula to reflect the characteristics of useful knowledge production.

Given this content, public policy making should not so much be focused on increasing competition between higher-education institutions on the consumer market. Rather it should consist of a set of "social contracts" between public authorities and higher-education institutions in which the mutual responsibilities are laid down. In these contracts governments should provide a large autonomy to higher-education institutions, but at the same time keep them accountable for fulfilling their specific missions and roles. Higher-education institutions should accept the social and economic responsibilities of the modern knowledge societies. They should design their missions with these responsibilities in mind. Depending on their specific positions and roles in society, these missions will imply different contributions to society in the crucial fields of teaching, research and social service.

The institutionalization of useful knowledge creation thus asks for new partnerships between political actors, business and industry, and higher-education institutions. In these partnerships each group of stakeholders has its own role to play. The political actors should carefully design the trade-offs between more (conditional) autonomy for universities and their willingness to fulfil their missions and to compete for the budgets of useful knowledge creation. Business and industry should accept their role in the processes of agenda-setting, guiding the accumulation and application of knowledge. Higher-education institutions need to understand their crucial social responsibilities and to face the challenge that the creation of their reputation can be influenced by external considerations and budgets. But more important in these new partnerships are the cooperative efforts of the three groups of stakeholders. Only by cooperating will they be able to show the many positive effects of the creation and application of knowledge as a social process.

REFERENCES

Bowen, H. (1980), *The Cost of Higher Education*, Jossey Bass, San Francisco.

Brewer, D.J., Gates, S.M. and Goldman, C.A. (2002), *In Pursuit of Prestige: Strategy and Competition in U.S. Higher Education*, Transaction Press, New Brunswick, NJ.

Clark, B.R. (1983), *The Higher Education System, Academic Organization in Cross-National Perspective*, University of California Press, Berkeley.

Dill, D.D. (2003), "Allowing the Market to Rule: the case of the United States", *Higher Education Quarterly*, vol. 57, no. 2, pp. 136-157.

Friedman, B.M. (2002), "Globalization: Stiglitz's Case", (Review of Joseph E. Stiglitz, *Globalization and its Discontents*), *New York Review*, August 15, 2002.

Garvin, D.A. (1980), *The Economics of University Behavior*, Academic Press, New York.

Geiger, R.L. (2004), *Knowledge and Money, Research Universities and the Paradox of the Marketplace*, Stanford University Press, Stanford.

Hayek, F.A. (1967), *Studies in Philosophy, Politics and Economics*, Routledge & Kegan Paul, London.

Massy, W.F. (2003), *Honoring the Trust, Quality and Cost Containment in Higher Education*, Anker, Boston.

Meek, V.L. (2003), "Governance and Management of Australian Higher Education: Enemies Within and Without", A. Amaral, V.L. Meek and I.M. Larsen (eds.), *The Higher Education Management Revolution?*, Kluwer, Dordrecht.

Mokyr, J. (2002), *The Gifts of Athena, Historical Origins of the Knowledge Economy*, Princeton University Press, Princeton.

Newman, F., Couturer, L. and Scurry, J. (2004), *The Future of Higher Education, Rhetoric, Reality and the Risks of the Marketplace*, Jossey Bass, San Francisco.

Smith, A. (1776/1976), *The Wealth of Nations*, Penguin, Harmondsworth.

Vught, F. van (1992), *Governmental Strategies and Innovation in Higher Education*, Jessica Kingsley, London.

Wildavsky, A. (1979), *Speaking Truth to Power, the Art and Craft of Policy Analysis*, Little, Brown & Co., Boston.

PART II

•••••••••••••

Knowledge Transfer

CHAPTER

European Research Policy: Towards Knowledge and Innovation or Trivial Pursuit

Bertil Andersson

EUROPE NEEDS SCIENCE

Today 25 European countries from both sides of the former Iron Curtain belong to the European Union with an increased political, economic and cultural integration, where research and innovation are seen as strategic tools to promote European competitiveness in a more globalized world. This is reflected in the ambitious political declarations of the European Council of the E.U. Heads of Government in Lisbon (2000) and Barcelona (2002), which state that, by the year 2010, Europe should have become the most competitive knowledge-based economy in the world and have reached spending of 3% of its GDP as a goal for investment into research. These declarations also reflect the political awareness that European research has lost strength to the United States and that is also being challenged by the fast-growing economies of Asia. It will remain to be seen to what extent Europe can live up to these high goals which will very much depend on the level of economic growth and the political ability to re-orient current priorities, especially as two-thirds of the 3% target should come from the private sector. Another uncertainty is how the recommended increase in public research funding will be divided between the national and European levels.

THE NATIONAL APPROACH TO EUROPEAN RESEARCH

Historically, research has been a national responsibility and regarded as a means to increase a country's competitiveness. For example, Swedish tax

79

money should pay for a Swedish researcher's innovation carried out at one of the national universities which should then be exploited to create new job opportunities and economic growth in Sweden. This "virtuous circle" is a deeply rooted tradition that can be traced back to 1896 when Alfred Nobel died, and the openings of his famous will that provided the foundation for the Nobel Prizes. The implementation of the will was not an easy task, with many potential obstacles, including one imposed by the Swedish King Oscar II. Nobel, who had a true international perspective from his industrial activities in many countries, wrote: "It is my wish that in awarding the prizes no consideration whatsoever should be given to the nationality of the candidate, but that the most worthy shall receive the prize, whether he be a Scandinavian or not." The king despised this statement and considered that Nobel had acted in an unpatriotic manner by not reserving the prize for a countryman, and even boycotted the first Nobel Prize award ceremony.

The national predominance on science policy and research funding has prevailed from the early days of Nobel throughout the last century. Around 95% of public research funding in Europe is national, with the remaining 5% coming from the E.U. Framework Programmes (FP) (see below). There are many indicators that this overwhelmingly national approach is no longer optimal to develop European research, innovation and technological development across the European Union.

Certainly, Europe contributes to global research with high-level science and, in quantitative terms, produces approximately the same number of scientific publications as the U.S. However, in qualitative terms, the U.S.-based publications are clearly ahead when one uses parameters such as the average number of citations per paper, in particular when counting the papers with the highest impact factor (the top 1% cited papers). This high impact research in the U.S.A. is particularly evident in rapidly emerging fields such as ICT, nano-science and technology and biotechnology, while Europe performs relatively better in the more mature ("traditional") scientific areas, such as inorganic chemistry and the humanities.

It is also very important to note that the top 20 institutions in the world contain about 30% of the most quoted scientists and yet only 2 of these top institutions are European (Academic Ranking of World Universities, 2003). The dominance of U.S. institutions, when it comes to high level research, is also apparent from the distribution of Nobel prizes in physics, chemistry and medicine. However, the use of Nobel prizes for tracing excellence also shows that the dominance of U.S.-based scientists (today up to 80%) is a fairly recent phenomenon. For example, as late as 1980 the number of prizes in chemistry awarded to European scientists was equal to American prizes. However, it does illustrate a rapidly increasing trend which is bearing the fruit of an earlier and consistently high investment in research over several decades.

The benchmarking with research in the U.S.A. receives much attention in the current debate, somewhat overshadowing the fact that Europe today is also beginning to be challenged by fast-developing Asian countries. There is also the so-called European paradox. The large amounts of resources that Europe is investing in science do not, to any significant extent, materialize into innovations of commercial potential. The reasons are complex and also relate to cultural attitudes not only in the research world but also in the risk finance industry in Europe. It is an often used argument that investment into basic research is not a limiting factor for European growth. This is the major reason why the common E.U. budget has almost entirely focused on applied research. As will be discussed below, this analysis is being challenged at the same time as the traditional classification of basic and applied research is no longer so obvious as it once was.

THE PLAYERS IN THE ERA

Which are the major organisations that today have an influence on European research funding and science policy? As indicated above, the major part of research in Europe is funded via national research funding organisations. The pan-European impact of these resources has, however, been limited by the strong national emphasis, variations in funding procedures and big differences in economic resources between countries. However, currently, there is a combination of political and economic, as well as scientific pressure, for the national funding organizations to increase their collaborative efforts at the European level and work towards a better coordination of their funding institutions and procedures and so maximize the potential of this investment.

CERN, EMBO, ESO and ESA are all examples of European intergovernmental cooperation with a specific disciplinary focus. Their impact on European (and world) science and science policy within their areas of expertise has been profound, and their position vis-à-vis their scientific communities is very strong.

Since the mid-1980s the single largest actor on the European science scene has been the E.U. Framework Programmes (FP) which represent a considerable financial strength and political influence. Indeed, because national resources also have to cover infrastructure of all types, as well as salaries and running costs, the influence of the FP is far higher than the 5% proportion of European research investment would suggest. The mission of the FPs is, primarily, to promote European competitiveness and to support the policy goals of the Union. Hence, as indicated above, the major emphasis has been placed on top-down initiated and applied research.

Thus, tackling the European paradox has been a mission for E.U. research while so-called basic research has remained a national responsibility. This division of responsibilities is now being challenged. There are arguments to suggest that it would actually have been a better approach to exchange the responsibilities. Basic research does not normally see any borders and is by nature truly international. Applied research, on the other hand, is strongly connected to the national (or even regional) economy.

At the same time, one must recognize that the concepts of basic and applied research are becoming more and more obsolete. In many emerging areas of science and technology, it is difficult to define what is basic or what is applied. Is research in functional genomics basic or applied? In nano-sciences, the production of various forms of nano-tubes, which have many potential applications, is based upon the entirely unexpected result of "blue sky" research, namely the discovery of the fullerenes as a third crystallographic form of carbon. A study for the U.K. Treasury showed that the so-called "linear model" of basic research leading directly to applied research and then on to innovation and economic development rarely holds true and the process is actually a complex diffusion process with many stages and feedback loops. This is also the conclusion of the European Commission's High Level Expert Group in its recent report, which points out that the division, or rather frontier research, and innovation are becoming increasingly hard to define and that the relationship is becoming increasingly strong. When analysing the scientific publications from frontier research quoted in registered patents, one can see a clear and growing trend which is most obvious within the field of biotechnology. Furthermore, a considerable portion of "frontier" research is today taking place in industrial laboratories.

THE EUROPEAN RESEARCH COUNCIL

There are currently new winds of change in European research policy, in particular, the proposal for the establishment of a European Research Council (ERC) (2003). The idea of such a pan-European research council has been debated on and off during the last 30 years, but has always been dismissed as a political impossibility because of the missions of existing national and European research funding structures and their concern to defend their "fiefdoms" as discussed above. Some five years ago, many organizations representing European research, including the European Science Foundation (ESF), which includes most of Europe's research funding agencies in its membership, gave a new and strong push for the establishment of an ERC. Two financial options could be foreseen: the national research councils top slicing themselves to create a common European fund, or that the resources should be provided centrally by the European Commission. The former alternative was hampered by a general unwillingness to export national research money combined with restrictive legislation in many countries. The concern with the second option was to ensure a bottom-up approach for frontier sciences under the commission. In 2002, the Danish Presidency of the European Union brought the ERC concept to the political level. In a relatively short time, a consensus was reached and the ERC is now one of the major pillars of the FP7 proposal from the commission. However, the task has been limited to a competition for the best individual research teams in Europe. In the recent budget proposal for the FP7, €1.5 billion have been allocated for the ERC. There are many potential benefits of such a "European Championship" in research. It will give additional significant economic support to Europe's best scientists — it will move the frontiers of European science forward. It will also undoubtedly have dynamic effects on the European research system. Potential "national heroes" will get a European benchmark, the priorities of national research councils will be tested and, most likely, it will lead to a clear ranking of the European universities and research institutions. The ERC will also, by promoting frontier research in emerging areas, stimulate innovation and European competitiveness. There are risks with the ERC project. One could be the discrediting of the system through a very heavy over-subscription application rate. The second is that the ERC may only have limited independence under the umbrella of the commission. This issue will be dealt with by a high-level senate of highly reputed scientists who can defend scientific independence and who will set the frame for operation of the ERC.

COORDINATION OF NATIONAL EFFORTS

European research has constantly suffered from fragmentation and unnecessary duplication of efforts and resources. Within Europe, we seem very adept at the creation of new and frequently overlapping and duplicating structures. What is clear is that there is an urgent need for a science-driven scale and scope in research. Even though research progress will continue to be driven by individually excellent principal investigators (the best being supported by ERC) it is also becoming increasingly clear that many future research problems are so complex that they cannot be solved in one institute or even in one single country. Progress to solve research questions and pave the way for new innovations will require a critical mass of competences and resources. Such critical masses will require the combination of multi- and interdisciplinary skills. Such interdisciplinary constellations are, for example, required to contribute to major global challenges such as the human genome project, as well as problems related to global environmental change, especially driven by climate change. A recent trend in Europe is that the national research councils are starting to create such critical mass through an increased coordination of their efforts in certain research areas. However, once one passes beyond bilateral, or, at most, trilateral cooperation, the complexities and difficulties of arranging such cooperation increase exponentially. Now the research founders are working through their joint organization, the European Science Foundation. For example, the so-called EUROCORES programmes (2005), which are a new kind of networking of national research councils and funding, are an important step in developing European "frontier" research. The EUROCORES programmes bring together substantial research money in contrast to previous collaborative schemes which have only provided networking costs. Nevertheless, the process still remains complex and rather lengthy.

We have all recognized the need to maximize the human potential of Europe, especially at the critical stage of transition to a fully independent researcher. The European Young Investigators Award Programme (EURYI) (2005) brings together national research founders, through ESF and the Euro-HORCS, in order to promote 25 young researchers to establish themselves as independent scientists. This is another example where national money is being converted into pan-European resources.

There has been a common view among researchers that the European science policy has been a kind of trivial pursuit with a political rather than a scientific mission. Now, many of the current developments exemplified in this brief account may herald a change in this attitude. It is not a trivial pursuit. There is a growing awareness that Europe needs science, but also that science needs Europe.

REFERENCES

Academic Ranking of World Universities. (2003). Shanghai Jiao Tong University, Institute of Higher Education. http://ed.sjtu.edu.cn/rank/2003/2003main.htm

ESF EUROCORES. (2005) *European Collaborative Research Programmes*. http://www.esf.org/esf_activity_home.php?language=0&domain=0&activity=7

ESF EURYI. (2005). *European Young Investigator Awards Programme*. http://www.esf.org/esf_genericpage.php?section=8&domain=0&genericpage=1879

E.U. European Council, Lisbon. (2000). *Presidency Conclusions, 23-24 March*. http://ue.eu.int/ueDocs/cms_Data/docs/pressData/en/ec/00100-r1.en0.htm

E.U. European Council, Barcelona. (2002). *Presidency Conclusions, 15-16 March*. http://ue.eu.int/ueDocs/cms_Data/docs/pressData/en/ec/71025.pdf

The European Research Council: a cornerstone on the ERA (2003). "Report from an Expert group", ERCEG — the "Mayor" report, Ministry of Science, Technology and Innovation, Denmark. http://www.ercexpertgroup.org

Frontier Research: The European Challenge. (2005a). "High-Level Expert Group Report", European Commission (EUR21619), Feb. 2005.
http://www.insme.info/documenti/
hleg_fullreport_frontier_research_april2005.pdf

Frontier Research: the European Challenge. (2005b). "Report of the High Level Expert
   Group". Chair, William Harris, European Commission.
   http://europa.eu.int/comm/research/future/pdf/
   hleg_fullreport_frontier_research_april2005.pdf
Jank, W., Golden, B. L. & Zantek, P. F. (2005). "Old World vs New World: Evolution
   of Nobel Prize Shares". *INFOR, Canadian Journal of Information and Operational
   Research*, Feb. 2005.
New Structures for the support of high quality research in Europe. (2003). "A report from
   a High Level Working Group constituted by the European Science Foundation to
   review the option of creating a European Research Council". Chair, Richard
   Sykes. http://www.esf.org/newsrelease/63/ERC.pdf
*Proposal concerning the seventh framework programme of the European Community for
   research, technological development and demonstration activities,* 2007 to 2013.
   (2005). European Commission, COM (2005) 119 final.
   http://europa.eu.int/eur-lex/lex/LexUriServ/site/en/com/2005/
   com2005_0119en01.pdf
Scott, A., Steyn, G., Geuna, A., Brusoni, S. & Steinmueller, E. (2001). *The Economic
   Returns to Basic Research and the Benefits of University-Industry Relationships: A literature review and update of findings. Report for the Office of Science and Technology,*
   SPRU. www.sussex.ac.uk/spru/documents/review_for_ost_final.pdf

CHAPTER 7

Knowledge Diffusion: The Prospects for More Productive University-Industry Partnerships

Anita K. Jones

Over recent years, technology has dramatically changed how industrial corporations partner with one another. Yet, there has been little change in the relations between universities and industry. In this paper we explore how technology and market forces have facilitated a fairly dramatic change in industry-industry partnerships over the past 15 to 20 years, and we ask whether those influences can engender more productive university-industry relationships. In the U.S. and Europe there are increasing concerns about innovation and the ability of those nations to compete in the global marketplace. University-industry partnerships should be a high-leverage contributor to innovation, and, therefore, to national economic strength. So, productive university-industry partnerships have very high value. And there are too few of them.

Partnering relationships between corporations have changed in quite remarkable ways. For example, some companies now outsource their customer care and maintenance support service, and rely on just-in-time supply by subcontractors. Some outsourcing involves companies off-shore. Corporations focus to a greater extent on exercising their competencies and they rely on partner organizations for support. A hallmark of such corporate relations is a much higher level of trust. This is evident because these new-relationship companies deliberately position themselves so that their ability to perform in the marketplace is utterly dependent upon the timely performance of partner corporations for whom there may be no back-up. Trust has always been a necessary element of university-industry partnerships, but it has not always been sufficiently present.

Technology is a first order enabler of new ways to address markets; perform customer care; deploy non-stop, 24/7 services; deliver one-of-a-kind, customer-tailored product configurations; deliver products just in time and collaborate in deep ways. To a great extent the new kinds of industry-to-industry relationships are enabled by the adroit use of information technology and communications. Yet, it is market forces that frame the relationships.

The Colloquium in Glion seems an appropriate venue in which to ask: do these new forms of corporate partnership give new scope or opportunity for university-industry partnerships? Do the new openness and trust in partnerships that are now a hallmark of today's industry carry over to new and better kinds of relationships between universities and industry? Are there opportunities for more effective partnerships between these disparate organizations than in the past?

NEW MODES OF INTERACTION

In this section we address the technology and the new modes of interaction that contribute to new types of corporate relationships. One enabler of partnerships is the ability to share data about products and services between partner corporations. For example, engineers across multiple organizations can share common engineering drawings that can be updated in real time by any partner as permitted by disciplined access control, and even collaboratively updated. Remote, (near) real time monitoring and control of instruments permits "corporately separate" individuals to remotely participate, monitor, or even control, some element of the laboratory or manufacturing activity of another partner. Computational simulations of natural and human-induced phenomena permit geographically separated individuals to collaborate in the study of on-going activity in industrial space or in a laboratory. Engineering data from one site can be fed into simulations in another in near real time.

Collaboration through remote data sharing has the added property that what is shared is just that which is represented in the data. Engineering specifications and drawings may not make visible proprietary aspects of the manufacturing or fabrication process by which the product is built. Sharing of data can be judiciously restricted and one company can conduct parallel activities with multiple corporate organizations without divulging the data of one partner to another. This aids a company in protecting what it considers proprietary by avoiding "too many" physical visits by personnel from supplier partners. Likewise, remote collaboration via shared data and shared visualization permits a participant to stay at their home site and interact with remote colleagues on a low-overhead, even no-notice, basis. The accuracy of shared engineering data makes it possible for one company to fabricate a component that is within tight specifications. It is shipped to a partner who can efficiently integrate that component into a larger physical system due to tight control of both system and component manufacture. So the new modes of interaction are not limited to information-based collaboration; information technology facilitates more efficient physical interaction as well.

Worldwide communications for tele-collaboration are cost-effective. The research universities, as well as industry, already have high-speed network and computing infrastructure in place and in routine use. A new relationship need not bear the cost of any unique communication infrastructure to underpin it.

Information technology has led to another change — one organization can capture domain expertise, processes and techniques in software (digital tools) which can then be used by others, even users who do not understand the inner working of the software. This new vehicle for knowledge diffusion allows organizations to exchange expertise and knowledge in a potent form. Industry may view digital tools that they develop as proprietary and restrict sharing to partners. University researchers typically post and promulgate such digital tools and data resources openly. When source code and not just binary code is available, such tools are described as "open source". This open promulgation of research results in a digital form that allows others to perform similar experiments or to replicate (or not) the results of the original researcher. Digital tools are yet another way that information technology facilitates collaboration and productivity in partner organizations — whether tool sharing is restricted, or whether open source code is posted publicly.

All the technology-based enablers for industry-industry partnerships should be equally as effective for university-industry partnerships. Remote sharing of data and collaboration are particularly helpful because industry is typically reluctant to send their best talent to work on longer-term research collaborations. Technology permits intermittent and remote interaction.

CORPORATE R & D LABORATORIES

In the U.S. when "globalization" became a reality of business in the early 1990s, substantial cut-backs of some large, premier research and development (R & D) laboratories began. Not even the most prestigious were spared. General Motors, Texaco, IBM, Bell Laboratories and Xerox were only a few corporations that substantially downsized their laboratories. Industry felt that it could not support the cost of those laboratories in the more competitive global markets that they necessarily had to address. As a result, less research and

advanced development are conducted by these corporations, and they typically emphasize development over research. In the U.S., these laboratories
have not been rebuilt to their former states.

In the past few years, at least a few high-tech companies have sited divisions of their corporate R & D laboratories in the locale of university research
activity. Intel has opened a laboratory near Carnegie-Mellon University, University of California-Berkeley, Cambridge University in the U.K., and the
University of Washington in Seattle. It is even more of a change that some
corporations are locating satellite R & D laboratories not just in the country
of their headquarters, but around the globe. Microsoft Research Laboratory
sites divisions in what appears to be a more market-conscious way, placing
R & D laboratories in Beijing, China, Silicon Valley, Cambridge in the U.K.,
and Bangalore, India. Mitsubishi Electric Research Laboratories include a
Telecommunication Lab in Rennes, France, a Visual Information Lab at the
University of Surrey in the U.K. and the long-standing Research Lab in Cambridge, Massachusetts. All have university relationships with at least those
universities in the local geographic vicinity. Today, corporate research laboratories are located internationally, not just in the home country of a corporation. Technological innovation knows no borders.

That may indicate that corporations can be expected to be more amenable
to building university partnerships with any strong university, not just those
in the country where their headquarters are located. The ease with which trust
relations can be built up with an individual university will play a role in the
development of partnerships. Intellectual property arrangements can be an
impediment to building a trust relationship. This will be discussed later.

Sematech, born of faltering U.S. microelectronics market share, created a
successful research and development activity with many partner corporations
in the semi-conductor business, as well as their supplier companies. After
declaring the success of Sematech, the Semiconductor Industries Association
told the U.S. government that it no longer needed the Sematech funds (being
routed through D.A.R.P.A. until the mid-1990s). The semi-conductor industry and Department of Defense then formed a follow-on partnership for basic
research. The industry funded $2 for every government matching dollar. The
purpose of the government participation was not so much as a source of funds,
but as a participant who could insist on the performance of basic research over
near term development (Barrett, 1996). Initial projects were determined by a
D o D sponsored workshop in the mid-1990s attended mainly by the university researchers.

High-tech industry critically relies on innovation which — over the long
run — is grounded in basic research. With the current structure of industrial
R & D laboratories, it is difficult to document whether there is less of a reser-
voir of basic research available to high-tech companies, whether there are less

or more substantive basic research relationships between university and industry, and whether the pipeline of students trained in the context of truly long-term basic research is of increasing or decreasing quality, particularly in rapidly advancing disciplines. It is also difficult to determine whether high-tech industries have access to an adequate pipeline of basic research. The bottom line is that there is need born of competition for industry to acquire appropriable research and the derivative innovation from somewhere, if not from in-house laboratories. And the most stable and robust source of basic research, at least in the U.S., is the research universities. A few selected government laboratories, such as the Naval Research Laboratory, are reliable sources of research results. But, for the most part, the government laboratories are focused on mission and related technology application. There is no rising alternative to the research universities as a source for both research ideas and the new graduates with expertise that advances innovation.

RESEARCH INFRASTRUCTURE

Financing affects the willingness for organizations to collaborate. In particular, the cost of the necessary laboratory infrastructure for the specific research to be conducted must be found if the laboratory is to function. Both in universities and in industry, the cost of laboratory equipment has increased in most areas of engineering, science and medicine. Researchers in physical science and engineering explore increasingly smaller and larger scale phenomena — nano-science to galaxies. Experiments are more complex as they move from 2-D to 3-D analysis (e.g. 2-D DNA string discovery to 3-D protein folding). The equipment to support such exploration is often more sophisticated and more expensive. The resulting financial reality has given rise to an increasing number of virtual research centres, particularly in the research universities in which researchers from multiple universities share equipment. The National Science Foundation supports numerous such centres across fields as disparate as earthquake engineering, nano-scale engineering, and astronomy. A virtual centre should as easily accommodate a corporate partner as a university partner. So, the trend to geographically distributed research collaborations and shared research infrastructure should positively impact the consideration of university-industry partnerships.

RESEARCH COLLABORATION

Some research questions have been out of reach of university researchers. This is especially true when the research involves engineered systems such as long-term performance of diesel engines in actual use, the behaviour of a molten material within a controlled manufacturing process, or retail marketing inventory management. Industry has direct access to the relevant data.

Today, information technology makes possible laboratory access to on-going social and business activities. Industry data could be made available to university researchers — the technology supports such sharing of information. However, again the issue of trust arises. A corporation will only share such data — which is likely considered sensitive, if not proprietary — if the two organizations trust each other. Numerous such trust relationships exist between a company and a trusted supplier. There may be more openness to establishing such relationships, if industry believes that it is receiving value from the relationship with a university.

Another gradual change is that "we are teaching more and more about less and less" (Mead, 2003). Individuals are educated to be expert in narrower and narrower fields as the amount of knowledge in each field increases. As a result, research collaboration is becoming increasingly interdisciplinary in order to have all the necessary expertise available. Over the past several decades — in the U.S. at least — there has been an increase of university research collabo-rations that involve researchers from multiple disciplines. Concomitantly, there has been a rise in the number of university-university collaborative cen-tres that tackle problems deemed to be too large for one university. The imper-ative to collaborate across disciplines incrementally grows over time. When a company focuses its efforts on just its "core competencies", its need for experts in related fields increases. This too augurs well for university-industry partner-ships.

Anecdotally, larger university research efforts increasingly appear to moti-vate their research by stating a need to solve social problems, e.g. predicting earthquakes and ameliorating damage from them; weather prediction; aiding ageing populations to live at home longer; and protecting the soldier. Whether this is driven by government funding focused on short-term objec-tives, or by the researchers' own curiosity, such rationales seem more abun-dant. Industry always has such rationales because their overall objective is to produce a better product or service. So, one might conclude the university researchers are now more comfortable with stating application objectives for their research, where sensible. Such motivations need not limit the long-term nature of research, if the motivations are suitable structured.

I conclude that many of the forces or trends affecting university research can be viewed as supportive of future university-industry collaboration. There is, I believe, a genuine increase in the opportunity for richer and more produc-tive partnerships.

Of course, the most profound partnership of all is that industry hires the students that come out of the research universities. Those students carry new knowledge into the corporation, and over time influence how the corporation adapts. That partnership does not seem to be changing, except that both industry and universities are more "internationally minded".

THE BASIS FOR PARTNERSHIPS

Now I want to turn to the fundamental relations between the organizations and the individuals involved in a university-industry partnership. First, such a partnership can work very well; there is a long history — at least in the U.S. — of university-industry partnerships. There are diverse staffing and funding arrangements. Industry may provide employees to directly participate with university researchers. Faculty may consult with a company, sometimes taking extended absences from the university to work at a corporate location. But a common arrangement is a partnership that only involves industry funding research in an existing university laboratory with no joint staffing. These partnerships are weak if the industry funding only pays incremental costs to an ongoing activity that is funded from other sources.

Genuinely close university-industry partnerships are typically more difficult to establish and maintain than industry-industry partnerships because the cultures of the two kinds of organizations are different and their reward systems and objectives diverge. A few specific reasons for difficulty in university-industry relationships include:

- industry is typically focused on the short-term development of a next product; universities are focused on discovering new knowledge for its own sake;
- university researchers seek the reward of recognition by their peers in the larger research community based on rapid and open publication of their research findings; industry researchers are rewarded by the corporation when they advance corporate products and services;
- industry is often unwilling to pay more than incremental research costs, while the university researchers attempt to amortize laboratory recapitalization across all research activity;
- industry needs to protect its ability to appropriate, perhaps uniquely, the ideas that derive from research; university researchers want to publish ideas broadly; wrangling over intellectual property is routine; and
- university researchers want to protect their ability to team with multiple corporations; industry needs to protect its proprietary information.

One influence on the formation of such partnerships in the U.S. is the appearance of a "new player". This is the University Patent Foundation or Technology Transfer Foundation. These organizations came into being after the passage of the Bayh-Dole Act that granted universities ownership of the intellectual property that their researchers developed. Essentially, all U.S. research universities have such an organization. These foundations typically hold the intellectual property of the university and are in business (1) to proactively ensure that a university's intellectual property is exploited for the good of the nation, and (2) to derive income from it. Consequently, the formation of a university-industry partnership involves not just the interests of the researchers and the university "sponsored programs office", but a foundation whose objective is to create wealth based on intellectual property. Anecdotally, industry complains that negotiation over intellectual property rights has become more complicated and constitutes the greatest impediment to university-industry partnerships.

The return of these foundations is mixed. In select cases universities have earned tens, or hundreds of millions, of dollars on a single "home run" patent. But such return is rare. Some foundations barely pay, or do not pay, their own expenses. The Association of University Technology Managers conducts a survey of results of technology management at research universities. Their A.U.T.M. Licensing Survey: Fiscal Year 2003 report can be found at www.autm.org. It reports on invention disclosures, patent applications, patents issues, licences/options executed, and new companies created. They report that 374 new companies were created in 2002 in the U.S. that depended upon university licensed intellectual property. These foundations do aid in the creation of new companies by faculty, and they fund both patenting and license marketing, activities that faculty may not pursue.

The 2003 report indicates that overall the A.U.T.M. universities that responded to their survey expended $31 billion of the $36 billion expended on research in the U.S. in 2002. The foundations earned $1.3 billion or roughly 4% compared to one year of research funding expended by the universities. Of course, part of this income must pay the cost of the technology transfer enterprise. So, return after expenses will be lower. This percentage return on investment is not particularly high. However, the patent foundation organizations are for the most part relatively new and still have not had time to mature. One thing is certain — the advent of the Bayh-Dole Act complicated the formation of university-industry partnerships in the United States.

THE AUDACIOUS IRISH

In this section we explore the climate for creating partnerships and whether a small population — in this case a small nation — can more productively and effectively nurture university-industry partnerships that out-perform their competition. Ireland provides an intriguing case of study of a country seeking to make a material change in university-industry partnerships.

Twenty years ago Ireland was a struggling agrarian nation with an economic growth rate just above 2%. By the late 1990s (1994 to 2000) Ireland
had transformed itself into the Celtic Tiger, a nation with economic expansion of 9.3% that led the world, eclipsing even the Asian Tigers as measured
by growth rate. Their strategy for aggressive economic growth relied upon low
corporate tax rates, cooperative unions, and an educated, English-speaking
workforce. Ireland established itself as an attractive place for corporations to
site new manufacturing and fabrication plants. In 2004 Intel's largest semiconductor plant outside America was upgraded and commenced manufacture
of an advanced line of components. Nine of the world's ten largest pharmaceutical manufacturers have plants in Ireland, as do Dell and Apple. Ireland
receives one third of all foreign direct investment into Europe in the areas of
health care and pharmaceuticals in recent years. Ireland's attraction in the
1990s was not technology-based, but financial, with an attractive business
operations climate.

Ireland is a nation of 4 million souls, less than the population of Los Ange-
les, California or Toronto, Canada, and half that of New York City. Ireland
offers an excellent example of how a small nation, a small population, can
craft and execute a strategy that changes the relation between industry and a
nation.

Such aggressive growth above 9% is difficult to sustain; no country has
done so for more than a few years. In the late 1990s India and Eastern Europe
could offer lower costs and gave Ireland competition that bled off investment.

So, what is Ireland's follow-on strategy to attempt to maintain vigorous
economic expansion? It is to further develop their good education system to
produce knowledge workers at an advanced level, and to establish the Irish
universities at the forefront of research in information technology and biotechnology. Ireland's "round two" strategy calls for attracting more than manufacturing plants; they want to attract research and development centres of
high technology companies to locate in Ireland with direct collaboration with
the Irish universities. So, the government has set as an objective to grow
world-class research activities inside their universities (third level organizations).

Ireland did not start with the best research universities in the world or with
many large, indigenous Irish companies. The Irish K-16 education is rated
highly. The government increased the number of students attending college
substantially between the mid-1990s and 2000. Their strategy is indeed audacious. Were the U.K., the U.S. or a few other nations to field such a strategy,
one could argue that they would start with world-class research universities.

A keystone of the "round two" Irish strategy is Science Foundation Ireland
(S.F.I.). Modelled after the National Science Foundation in the United
States, this government agency funds basic research in information technol-

ogy and biotechnology in Irish universities. The author served on the Board of Trustees of S.F.I. for the first three years of its existence as we were defining its principles of operation.

Grants are awarded based on international peer review. On a per capita basis, Ireland is investing more in research than the United States. S.F.I. has invested not just in principal investigators and in university research centres, but in creative university-industry partnerships. Recall, the objective is to attract industry R & D laboratories to Ireland, and to have them co-locate with universities, where appropriate. Executing a strategy that China, Taiwan and other countries have successfully used, Science Foundation Ireland has been particularly successful in bringing researchers with ancestral ties to Ireland back to Ireland permanently or as visitors.

There are indications that the overall Irish strategy is having a positive effect. Hewlett Packard, Servier, Siemens, and Proctor and Gamble all have entered into partnership in major research centres with Irish universities since 2002. Intel has a new research activity in nano-science with Trinity College Dublin, and Bell Laboratories is establishing a centre for research in telecommunications and supply chain technologies in Ireland.

These knowledge-based partnerships are based on small numbers of people, knowledge and expertise in pursuing new research ideas. The audacious and apparently successful Irish demonstrate that small groups — it need not be a national activity — can exert large economic leverage when the course that they chart is focused, financed and complementary to the interests of ever-evolving industry. These university-industry partnerships have the advantage that the education of the next generations of Irish researchers is intimately entwined with their operation. The Irish expect the process to be relatively self-sustaining.

CONCLUSION

The question addressed in this paper is whether the climate for university-industry partnerships has changed, and whether it offers new opportunities. In summary, I think that the answers are "yes" and "yes". The above discussion argues that information technology coupled with market changes has opened industry to the possibility of new relationships. Of particular importance is the increase of the level of trust that is endemic in these relationships compared to relationships of two decades ago. A number of companies have made their ability to perform deeply dependent on the performance of their suppliers. Further, we pointed out that global competitiveness has led companies to focus on their core competencies, and to a reduction of corporate R & D capability. Yet high-technology companies need not just modest product increments, but new ideas that can underpin whole new product lines.

Technology innovation is the life-blood of high-tech corporations, especially as they are driven to compete globally, not just regionally. Industry has embraced new relationships with other partners. Is there an opportunity for more and closer university-industry partnerships? Can a company invest such trust in a relationship with a university in order to gain a pipeline of new ideas at a stable and rapid rate as input to product innovation? It is the university whose core competency is research. My hypothesis is that if corporations are entering into much more intimate and dependent relationships with other corporations, then it is worthwhile to take a fresh look at the potential for future university-industry partnerships.

In the minds of some, the U.S. and Europe are losing their innovative advantage. The European Union has re-affirmed the Lisbon Agreement which states an objective of becoming the most innovative and productive economy in the world by 2010. One symptom of U.S. slow-down is that in 2003, America ceased to be the world's leading recipient of foreign direct investment, eclipsed by China. This is one measure of how markets judge the promise of competing nations. The U.S. has no clear statement of economic objectives and action that is comparable to the Lisbon Agreement.

If nurturing a knowledge-based economy that emphasizes university-industry knowledge partnerships is a sound strategy for a nation like Ireland, it may be a sound strategy for other nations. Both Europe and the U.S. have a culture of investing government funds in research and development, and in their universities. This positions them to be able partners of industry.

Can even a small national effort make a difference? The Irish accomplishments argue that it can. In his book, *As the Future Catches You*, Juan Enriquez, of Harvard University, says: "The future belongs to small populations who build empires of the mind." (Enriquez, 2001).

University-industry partnerships are a natural mechanism to use to relate basic research to industrial innovation, and speed knowledge dissemination. One major sticking point that we have not yet addressed is how appropriable research results are to a company's product lines and sales capability. It is industry's concern that they will not be able to appropriate the results that come from research, or not be able to do so in an acceptable time period. With government and the universities involved as co-investors, the opportunity for appropriable return should increase.

If the U.S. or Europe became seriously concerned about the productivity of their economies, then governments could reconsider both incentives aimed at encouraging innovation. For example, R & D credits — essentially government subsidies for industry to invest in R & D — could be an increased funding source for partnership with universities. The opportunity for more productive and more creative university-industry partnerships has never been greater, and in Europe and the U.S. the need for translation of new ideas into new products is greater than ever before.

REFERENCES

Barrett, Craig, (1996). Private communication with chief executive officer, Intel Corporation.
Enriquez, J. (2001). *As the Future Catches You*. Crown Business, New York.
Mead, Carver A. (2003). *Address to the National Academy of Engineering annual meeting* on the occasion of his receiving the Founder's Medal, October 2003.

CHAPTER

The Collaboration Imperative

Wayne C. Johnson [1]

INTRODUCTION

At the Glion IV Colloquium on "Reinventing the Research University", the author contributed a chapter on "Globalization of Research and Development in a Federated World", focusing on opportunities for strategic partnership using the concepts of the "knowledge supply chain" and the "partnership continuum" (Johnson, 2004). This chapter builds on that work, seeking to advance the thinking about university-industry collaborations and building strategic relationships, while recognizing some of the challenges in collaborating.

The chapter discusses the impact of the information technology evolution and its impact on research strategy and innovation from the conventional stand-alone wave, to the systems innovation wave, the network innovation wave and finally the innovation and knowledge exchange or systems of systems innovation wave. This results in the collaboration imperative and the need to manage the knowledge supply chain.

THE RISE OF SCIENTIFIC ACTIVITY AND VIRTUOUS ECONOMIC DEVELOPMENT AND SOCIETAL BENEFITS

During World War II, the Office of Scientific Research and Development oversaw much of the effort that resulted in radar, missiles, radio-controlled fuses, the atom bomb and penicillin. Vannevar Bush, the director of the OSRD, recognized that these scientific advances and new technologies had

1 The author would like to acknowledge, with gratitude, the assistance of Mr. Lou Witkin, of HP's University Relations Worldwide, and Mr. Ron Crough, of Vosara, Inc., in the preparation of this chapter.

enabled the U.S. and its allies to win the war, but that the margin of success was dangerously small (Zachary, 1997). Since that time there has been a series of events or "wake-up calls" that have emphasized the importance of government, universities and industry working together to create new knowledge and educate a new generation of engineers and scientists:

- World War II demonstrated that we needed sustainable and reliable processes to create scientific advances in order to insure national security, medical advances and economic prosperity. In his seminal report, "Science The Endless Frontier", Bush proposed the creation of a partnership between government, universities and industry to create new scientific knowledge (Bush, 1945).
- Because of Sputnik, Eisenhower supported the creation of the National Aeronautics and Space Administration in July 1958. He also signed the National Defense Education Act that encouraged the study of science.
- When the Soviet Union won the race to put a man into space, President Kennedy challenged the U.S. to "commit itself to achieving the goal, before this decade is out, of landing a man on the moon and returning him safely to earth". Kennedy also recognized the importance of education to this effort by starting "a new Manpower Development and Training program".
- The attacks on the World Trade Center on September 11, 2001, created a new national agenda on security, resulting in a partnership among government, universities and industry to advance science and technology in this critical area.
- The advent of the internet has enabled work to be broken down and dispersed throughout the world to where the various pieces can be done most effectively.

The Vannevar Bush model of the involvement of government, universities and industry to insure national security and economic security needs to be updated. New approaches need to be developed for these partners to achieve national security and economic competitiveness in a globalized world. Other countries have faith that America will solve this, but we need to heed the wake-up call. Fortunately, America has significant capabilities. Although America is a nation motivated by individualists, when the task is large, we come together. In doing so, we do what it takes to succeed and we always seem to be able to develop imaginative, creative new ways of accomplishing things.

INNOVATION WAVES IN THE 'IT' SPACE

The information technology ("IT") industry has followed a unique evolutionary history throughout the past five decades. The renaissance which began through the efforts of Vannevar Bush was propelled forward by the national science and technology focus, together with the attendant government funding and investment. In combination with the research activities of many universities and the work of the large industrial central research laboratories (AT&T, IBM, etc.), these elements came together to create the innovation engines and new technologies which gave rise to rapid progress across a variety of fundamental IT areas. The next sections will examine four different waves of innovation activity, together with the underlying research *modalities* or operating modes that seemed prevalent during these times. The first will look at some of the outputs of those waves of innovation, and then working backwards examine a few of the themes, motivations, assumptions and philosophies that underlie the university-industry interactions and partnerships of that time.

THE 'STAND-ALONE PRODUCTS' INNOVATION WAVE

One of the important contributions produced by this first wave of innovation activity was a multitude of individual and proprietary "stand-alone" products. At the time, these products enabled individuals and organizations to be able to do things, both computationally and commercially, that had previously been out of reach.

The prominent research and development *modality* that supported the development of this myriad of products could be characterized as one of *independent exploration* of distributed opportunities across many fronts, with undercurrents of a "go-it-alone" approach to product innovation and development. This mode of operation supported the goal of many companies to put wonderful new products into the hands of end-users as quickly as possible. It also supported the research interests of finding promising new areas to explore, and mapping out relatively unexplored fields to play in. Research and technological innovation delivered the hot new features, integration was deferred to the end-user environment, and any focus on solutions (in today's terminology) was virtually absent from the efforts to get the newest feature-enabled products to market quickly. Some have characterized the contribution focus as technologically-driven "features and functions", "mips and megabytes" or "speeds and feeds".

Looking a little deeper at the underlying research modality, we find a number of interesting subtleties. In the research space, the sponsoring and initiating of many decoupled activities and independent investigations seemed natural, given the ready abundance of problems to be solved and the wide-open spaces of undeveloped opportunities to be worked on. Philosophically, universities were optimizing their desire for open inquiry and basic research, and this was well suited to having an abundance of undeveloped areas to work in. Within universities, work was usually conducted on a departmental basis, and there wasn't a great deal of multi-disciplinary research to be had. Furthermore, the way in which research topics and problem areas were identified and configured among independent research teams also demonstrated a sort of "innocent independence" that was well suited to motivating simultaneous and uncoordinated research work.

In a parallel space, companies were looking for ideas that could contribute to their immediate problems in developing the point products that they were undertaking. They were challenged to attract researchers to focus on specific problems related to their product development interests, hoping to move university researchers beyond basic research interests and focus more of their efforts on solving some of the practical problems of the day. Companies were comfortable engaging their university counterparts only infrequently, and after some discussions and interchanges they would come back at a later time to see what had developed, without great expectations of finding significant practical applications.

In retrospect, both the university predisposition towards basic research and the infrequent industrial interactions and expectations of few practical contributions resulted in an unstated agreement around a serial technology transfer model, where relatively little "after-the-fact" accomplishments were exchanged between researchers and product developers.

THE 'SYSTEMS' INNOVATION WAVE

As technology advanced, research interests became more developed, and products grew more complex and sophisticated. This began the shift to a systems focus, and less on what individual products could do by themselves. For the purposes of this discussion, we'll characterize this second evolutionary wave a focus on "systems".

Notwithstanding the great innovation and substantial progress made in the "stand-alone" products era, end-users became increasingly dissatisfied in dealing with collections of products from different manufacturers that didn't work together. Companies in turn became focused on developing system architectures that would permit sets of products to interface and interact with each other in order to accomplish greater purposes than simply the features and functions that were contained within. This naturally resulted in an increasing need to cooperate across companies in the early planning and design phases of product development (usually via standards bodies) and to share efforts across the industry without giving up too much competitive advantage or early access to undeveloped market opportunities (delicate balance).

At this same time, universities also became integration laboratories for many point products from different companies. As early adopters, they became the testing ground for the latest and greatest advancements that companies were so eager to contribute in order to have the newest product ideas validated and used in interesting ways. As a consequence, universities began to see firsthand the effects of technology feature and function proliferation as they attempted to conduct their research upon a fragmented and ever-changing infrastructure of IT systems, evolutions and upgrades. In some sense, they were caught in the dilemma of both embracing and standardizing on innovations which were essential to support their research work, and at the same time creating the next generation of innovations which would obsolete the very infrastructure stability they so desperately needed.

The underlying modalities upon which research and development were conducted began to shift. Conversations turned to emphasizing cooperation, coordination of activities, and addressing the systems interfacing and integration challenges in the research areas. Standardization and convergence also became a locus for much of the dialogue, and consortia and other cooperative cross-industry structures sprang up as vehicles to focus efforts and give shared context to the multiple independent activities underway. Emerging countries began to challenge the U.S. in specific industries (semiconductors, low-cost manufacturing), and the need to cooperate and orchestrate efforts was felt for the first time across America, in both academia as well as industry.

As funding and investment increased, so did the need to eliminate redundant activities, give more focus to sponsored work, reduce the proliferation of dissimilar architectures and technologies, and to standardize on fewer platforms and infrastructures going forward. All of this propelled government, universities and industries further in the direction of cooperation and set up the conditions for the next wave of innovation.

THE 'NETWORKS' INNOVATION WAVE

The third wave of R & D model innovation can best be seen by looking at the IT infrastructure that resulted from collective efforts. In it, complex "systems of systems" were developed and linked together into "networks of networks", resulting in a broad, highly-capable information infrastructure that is low cost, pervasive, and widely available to individuals as well as companies. Interestingly enough, it is ever-changing, while also being "standardized" at the same time. Many paradoxes which remained unsolved in the second wave (such as how to have both innovation and standardization at the same time, or how to have both quality and low cost in the same item) were solved in the third wave, and the world moved forward tremendously in the development of its compute infrastructure capability.

Probably one of the best examples of this model, though certainly not the only example, was the personal computer. As an extremely useful tool in its own right, it is also both a system that contains components (the processor system, the video system, the memory system, the i/o system, etc.), as well as a component or building block of a larger system (a client, a server, a node, a controller, etc.). In this innovation wave, the understanding of how to effectively make components into systems was developed, as well as how to decompose systems into ever-increasingly sophisticated components. Still, that doesn't paint the whole picture. It is the *networks approach* that makes possible the systems of systems, and the inherent flexibility, coupling and configuration of elements at just the right level in the compute fabric.

In terms of the research and development *modality*, we collectively managed to figure out how to have holographic, recursive development take place at any level in the infrastructure, without impact to either components at the levels below, or the systems at levels above. Without ever making it explicit, unstated agreements were ratified on how to do innovation within standardization, radical change within stability and revolution within evolution.

To further illustrate this new style of value-creation, companies were able to create whole new "sub-industries" in which they fiercely competed with each other while advancing the state-of-the-art for their own "component-systems" and continuing to create new value. Again, using the personal computer as the system-level element for this example, component industries which illustrate this concept would include the video system-component being advanced by companies like NVIDIA and ATI. The processor system world continues to be fiercely fought out by Intel, AMD, TransMeta, IBM and others. Even I/O was split into two distinct sub-industries — disk drives (Seagate, Maxtor, IBM, Hitachi, Quantum), and controller cards (Adaptec, Chips & Technologies, etc.) Without going further, it's easy to see how this unstated, multi-level, stratified architecture provided the framework for intense, distributed, parallel innovation and competition across companies and sub-industries, all the while providing tangible value to the end-users and consumers from the ongoing technological progress and achievement.

What were some of the philosophical orientations that underlie this research and development modality? What were the unstated assumptions that drove this world? It's probably easier to discuss what these were not, more than to identify what they were.

First, consider the interaction model. Independent research explorations, "go-it-alone" product development philosophies and other methodologies which optimize individual activity apart from the whole, did not garner much support in the third wave. The reality was that the world (at least the IT world) had become very interdependent, not independent. The environment would no longer tolerate having unsolved interfacing and integration issues deferred until later from new technologies that were created without some understanding of how they would be used.

Second, each technology player (be they in industry or in academia) knew their place in the multi-level, system-component world. They knew their place and level in the network, and hence where they would focus their research and innovation efforts. They knew who to cooperate with and who to compete with, and they new how to advance their particular part of the ecosystem without causing ripples or claiming territory in other parts.

Third, through the network of human professionals, we somehow learned to "get along" — to both compete and cooperate with each other. This was the age of "co-opetition", where companies both competed and worked together with some of their fiercest competitors at the same time. We also learned how to replace/obsolete and to complement with our technologies, to do research and to do development in the same spaces, and to both lead and to appropriately follow/participate in steering and direction setting. One observer put it this way: "We learned how to humanly interact and sustain the very values that were instantiated into our multi-level infrastructure networked architecture. We learned how to be both 'components' and 'systems' in our own human world of leadership, follower-ship and moving the IT world ahead for all humanity."

This third wave of activity produced the network fabric and know-how that enabled our systems to interact in ways that were previously unavailable in the first and second waves. Not only did it give rise to unparalleled innovation, advancement and prosperity, but it was also highly efficient in this regard. All of this infrastructure innovation set the stage for a fourth wave of advancement which would take us forward into new ways of operating that had not before been recognized.

THE 'INTERACTION AND KNOWLEDGE EXCHANGE' INNOVATION WAVE

The fourth wave isn't so much about raw technology, as it is about thinking, interaction, the flow of ideas and knowledge exchange. Through its networks, the third wave gave us an unparalleled, pervasive global communications capability, which was previously unavailable through telecommunications efforts alone. This in turn provided the foundation on which to develop things like e-mail, voice-mail, file transfer (ftp), and the World Wide Web. As these technology layers were built out, the ability to send almost any information to any place on the planet within a few seconds was created.

Within this information and communications infrastructure, another important capability was instantiated as well. The ability to disjoin space and time emerged. In the old telecommunications world, one had to be at a particular place in space and time to receive a telephone call, a message, or a package. With the advent of e-mail, voice-mail, contact managers, document standards, etc. it has become possible to send a communication or information packet to anyone in the world *wherever* they are, and *whenever* they are. The intended receiver of a message or document, for example, might be travelling to a location on business, yet they can still pick up their messages and documents via the internet from other places remote to where they live, at a time when it's convenient for them to do so.

Simultaneous with these developments, the physical networks underwent major transformation and grew significantly in their capabilities. Companies like FedEx, UPS, DHL and others have effectively dis-intermediated proprietary shipping and receiving, while extending their global reaches in the most competitive of environments. Global supply chains and logistics networks have moved beyond where anyone would have imagined ten years ago, and established companies both large and small now rely on these outsourced, aggregated capabilities for the transportation and delivery of their hard goods and physical items.

Not to be outdone by the advances in other industries, the telecommunications industry made significant strides as well. Cellphone networks improved considerably, prices dropped, 2nd- and 3rd-generation digital data networks came into existence as the underpinnings of cellphone communications and the cellphone boom took off! The desire of humans to communicate with each other frequently and "never be out of reach", together with the technological advances and build-out of infrastructure, propelled the cellphone adoption and subscriber rates to the highest ever. The result was that another building block of the interaction and knowledge exchange wave was put into place.

Through the efforts of the global communication and information interchange networks, the advancement of the physical item logistics and supply chain networks, and the global reach of the cellphone communications infrastructure, the world has indeed become very small and very flat (Friedman, 2005). Packages move around the world almost as easily as information bits and data move over fibre-optic cables. The world is developing along an unrelenting accelerating path to reducing most everything to being transportable, whether it consists of information bits or physical items.

So what does the future hold? What happens when most things of interest either arrive at one's door or are available through the internet? What happens when people can get whatever they want, wherever they are, whenever they are? What will they want next?

One idea is that the focus then moves from information and things to ideas and experiences. People become enabled to interact with things and with each other, with a different purpose in mind and a different intent behind their interaction. As more of the infrastructure gets put into place and global access becomes pervasive, people can become less focused on the mechanics of acquiring and accessing what they want, and become more enabled to reflect on the whys, the wherefores, and the quality of their experiences. Metaphorically speaking, these infrastructure advancements can enable humankind to elevate their attention and focus to have the deeper more personal interactions, the ones about connection, contribution and meaning.

In this new infrastructure-enabled world, human interactions and engagements can become much more personal, simultaneous and parallel. Conversations can focus more on the frequent, synergistic exchange of ideas and concepts to yield new developments and insights. Interactions become much more "real-time" as built-in delays are systematically moved out of the system (for example, not having immediate access to someone because they don't have a cellphone.) And the world becomes much more enabled to literally move "at the speed of thought". So, who will be doing the thinking in this new paradigm?

Another important aspect of this new modality is the non-local nature of human interaction. Given the ability to disjoin space and time in communications, it now becomes possible to have exchanges of thoughts and points-of-view with just about anyone around the globe with whom we have a connection. As an example, an e-mail can be sent from California to the U.K. just before going to bed, and a reply e-mail can be received first thing in the morning after a fresh night's sleep. While people may take time out, dialogue can become almost continuous, and the advancement of thinking and the development of new insights can occur unfettered by the limitations present in the earlier innovation waves. Consider the infrastructure advances in global finance. Due to recent developments in the financial infrastructure, money is now able to move around the world and be invested continuously on a 24-hour basis. The markets of North America, Europe, and Asia provide continuous opportunity for dollars/euros/yen that are seeking to be invested. Why not take advantage of the same opportunity for idea development, for R & D, and in the advancement of research? Somewhere on planet earth, minds are available 24 hours a day to do the thinking that needs to be done.

What has now become possible in this new interaction paradigm is that technological and infrastructure advancement has mitigated distances, has disjoined space and time, has enabled conversations and dialogue to be almost continuous, and has enabled humans to spend less time focusing on the whats and hows, and more time searching out the whys and wherefores. What are the essential characteristics of research and innovation in this world? What modalities emerge as being significant for universities, for industry and for government? And what challenges will we be presented with, as a result?

Given the ability of potentially everyone on planet earth to communicate and exchange information through an inexpensive, global, pervasive information network, access to each others thoughts, ideas, perspectives, energies and efforts becomes radically increased. The world becomes much flatter (Friedman, 2005) and much more of a "level playing field" than at any time previous in human history. Throughout the ages, it used to be necessary to travel to other lands of opportunity to engage in trade, commerce, to be a part of a new social fabric, or access a land of opportunity. Through the infrastructure, these things can now much more easily come to us, wherever and whenever we are. In this emerging paradigm, "goodness" and advancement will be bestowed upon those who can successfully orchestrate greater access to and application of the thoughts and ideas of others that exist throughout the vast world of planet earth. Challenge and difficulty will find their homes with the limited, narrow-scope, protectionist thinkers who strive to draw boundaries around what they already have, and try to keep it from expanding and developing. The future will belong to those who are comfortable with abundance, openness, inclusion, interaction, engagement and diversity.

THE COLLABORATION IMPERATIVE

Given the interactive nature and modalities present in the fourth innovation wave, it's easy to recognize why the need for early-stage collaborative efforts is so vitally important in the research and innovation spaces. Under the modalities of a "flat world", the resource base of human individuals potentially becomes infinite, and the supply of knowledge and information workers becomes unlimited. The community of thinkers and unique perspectives becomes as many as six billion people strong. And somewhere, someone on planet earth is likely to be thinking similar thoughts to mine.

With an advanced global infrastructure it thus becomes possible and even easy to exchange perspectives, share thoughts, synergize concepts and develop thought processes with other like-minded people. Access to and engaging in productive interchanges with other thinkers on a global basis becomes the norm, and accelerates the idea development process considerably. It becomes easier to find the key people through social networks, enabling these people in academia and industry to interact with each other to achieve effective knowledge exchange (Schramm, 2004). After all, isn't that what innovation is all about? The Knowledge Supply Chain provides a high-level understanding of what is possible in this interaction.

What does this mean for those who are reluctant to embrace the open, unlimited flow of ideas and concepts. History has shown, time and time again, that closed systems, protectionist-based ideas, and local-optimizations cannot stand the test of time. While they may provide limited benefits for narrow contexts and relatively short time intervals, ultimately the largest benefits are to be derived from the open, free exchange of information and ideas. In strict competitive terms, those who don't take advantage of the vast supply of knowledge workers, and integrate the best and most innovative thoughts and concepts into their work, will find themselves under-competitive as others pass them by with better concepts, superior innovation, and break-away contributions from their open, collective efforts (Chesbrough, 2003).

Looking back at our four innovation waves, we can now contrast the first wave with the last wave, and make some observations about the underlying paradigm. Technology-transfer was predominantly seen throughout the first innovation wave. It is a serial process that is primarily oriented around the transfer of thoughts and ideas in "relatively finished form", after they are embedded in a technology which is demonstrated as being real or useful. This has both advantages and disadvantages. While the outputs of the technology-transfer process are the most tangible and concrete, they are also only available late in the development process. They are the least able to be targeted at new problems areas (malleable and influenceable), and have the highest probably of being outdated, outmoded or incorrectly aimed.

Collaborative exchanges, predominantly used throughout the fourth innovation wave, are early stage processes that occur at the onset of thought and idea development. While they are the least tangible and least concrete (as they are not yet embodied into a technology), they are also the most malleable, can be aimed at a variety of problems, and are the most easily evolvable. The ideas that are exchanged in collaborative environments usually occur far upstream from technology development, and produce the largest gain and the best match to being applied to many different problems of interest, simultaneously, by multiple independent communities (companies, industries, other researchers, etc.)

The interactions that produce successful innovation and commercialization are not random. It appears that university faculty who are involved in a "cluster" of collaboration, innovation and commercialization also have a high level of experience in industry engagement, consulting and collaboration. While in the earlier waves the knowledge of facts and skills was important, it is in the fourth wave that the knowledge of social relations or networks, the knowledge of "who knows what" and "who can do what" may be of greater importance to innovation than knowing scientific principles (Schramm, 2004). Because of these researchers' involvement in a social network of friends and colleagues who are entrepreneurs, venture capitalists and other experts, their opportunity recognition skills are more keenly developed (Schramm, 2004). Collaboration among researchers with consulting experience and well developed social networks enables them to be more successful as collaborators and entrepreneurs.

Recognizing the forces and contributing factors present in the fourth wave of innovation, the need for early-stage collaboration cannot be overstated. Advances in the global infrastructure, and the increasing migration of innovation into a fourth wave style of interaction and knowledge exchange, necessitates and even demands that people interact early and often, if they are not to be left behind. Without the parallel thought processes, the able to retarget ideas to a variety of implementation and application areas, the ability to access many minds with a global perspective, and the ability to link with and federate with the efforts of others who have been working in the same field, under-competitiveness is the most likely outcome. Go-it-alone idea development, late-stage interactions, serial application of ideas to problems and limited access to a small subset of the vast array of thinkers that are out there, simply won't cut it any longer.

REFERENCES

Bush, Vannevar. (1945). *Science, the Endless Frontier, A Report to the President on a Program for Postwar Scientific Research*. Office of Scientific Research and Development, (reprinted by the National Science Foundation, Washington D.C., 1990).

Chesbrough, Henry. (2003). *Open Innovation, The New Imperative for Creating and Profiting from Technology*. Harvard Business School Press, Boston, MA.

Friedman, Thomas L. (2005). *The World is Flat*. Farrar, Strauss and Giroux, New York.

Johnson, Wayne. (2004). "Globalization of Research and Development in a Federated World", in Weber & Duderstadt (eds), *Reinventing the Research University*, Economica, Paris, pp 159-175.

Schramm, Carl. (2004). Accelerating Technology Transfer and Commercialization, Kauffman Foundation IP Commercialization and Research Spinouts Conference, Boston MA. http://www.kauffman.org/pdf/IPCommercRev.111504b.pdf

Zachary, G. Pascal. (1997), *Endless Frontier, Vannevar Bush, Engineer of the American Century*. MIT Press, Cambridge, MA.

CHAPTER

Global networks and knowledge diffusion: the Quantum physics model of 21st-century University

William R. Brody

Thomas Friedman, in his recently published book, *The World is Flat* (2005), describes ten phenomena that are changing the nature of how and where work is done. One of these — the ability to disaggregate workers from the source of work — has already created amazing economies of production, but also tremendous dislocations of entire geographic segments of the workforce. In much the same way, developments leading to a "flat world" — which Friedman describes as the new world where boundaries of space and time have been largely overcome — are having a profound effect upon the organization of research universities and the diffusion of knowledge. I would like to discuss three of these phenomena that are changing our future in profound ways.

First and foremost among these have been the revolutionary changes in the speed and cost of transporting people and information. Beginning initially with steamships, railroads and telegraphs, then the automobile and telephone, followed by jet aviation and now, the internet, the speed of travel has accelerated to the point that today we have created a global forum for both education and the discovery and dissemination of new knowledge.

The second major change has been the shift in the nature of discovery, particularly in, but by no means confined to, science and technology. At the beginning of the 20th century, most research was mono-disciplinary, often conducted by a single investigator, working pretty much alone in his or her discipline. Around mid-century, fuelled by the explosion of scientific research during and following the Second World War, scientists often worked in teams to conduct research. Yet those teams were still primarily focused within one academic department or discipline. The last two decades of the 20th century saw the growth of multidisciplinary research, where teams of scientists and engineers began working across departmental and even across university boundaries, to tackle the most exciting and challenging problems at the boundaries of science.

And third, the 21st century may usher in yet another fundamental change in information dissemination: the use of open-source networks to meld together entire communities of scientists and engineers. Propelled once again by low-cost communication and the availability of broadband internet connectivity in even the poorest countries of the world, this new amorphous network will allow the assembly of the brightest talent from multiple disciplines to discover literally at the speed of light.

These three factors are overturning the existing order to create what I call the Quantum Physics model of the 21st-century university.

RAPID COMMUNICATIONS ACCELERATE KNOWLEDGE GENERATION AND TRANSMISSION

Lowering the cost and increasing the speed of the transcontinental transport of people and information over the past 100 years have produced enormous changes in our society, and universities have been affected as well. In 1876, Johns Hopkins University was founded as the first research university in the United States. The new university recruited Daniel Coit Gilman, from the University of California, Berkeley, to be its founding president. This in itself was a departure: to move from California to Maryland, a distance of some 3,000 miles, was highly unusual in the 19th century. Most scholars were not so freely mobile. As for faculty, if you were a scholar in, say, Chinese political science at Johns Hopkins, and you knew more than any other scholar between Washington D.C. and New York City, you were in a pretty good position to become a tenured professor. Even if you were not particularly accurate in your knowledge of the subject, the time to discovery of these shortcomings was measured in months or even years. Knowledge diffusion was slow and, as a result, expertise was primarily local.

But today the diffusion of knowledge is measured in milliseconds, and flawed information is quickly exposed. Speeches and papers appear immediately on the internet, providing rapid global sharing of knowledge. Theories are proved or disproved through the international network of scholars who have immediate access to the latest discoveries. The "discovery" of cold fusion in Utah was seriously debunked by physicists in the Ukraine within days of the announcement.

Since international jet travel has become relatively affordable to all, the expertise that generates such knowledge is also mobile, placing a much higher value on global expertise today than a century ago. It is simply no longer possible to rely on local expertise for the discovery of new knowledge. Only if the local "expert" is also globally expert, can you rely on your faculty colleague down the hall. Scholars today are freely mobile.

As a result, global expertise commands a premium position in the academic marketplace. This new reality is what I call the "Michael Jordan faculty" phenomenon. Michael was making $5 to $10 million a year to play basketball with the Chicago Bulls, while the person sitting on the bench next to him — though a very good player in his own right —was only making $500,000 a year. Why? Because Michael Jordan was truly the world authority of basketball and able to command a global audience. The journeyman guard playing next to him may have been fine for the local crowds in Chicago, but was not going to have the drawing power on an ESPN worldwide broadcast. I happened to travel to China the year Mr. Jordan had announced his retirement from the NBA. Everywhere I went, the first question I received from the Chinese people was why was Michael Jordan retiring? The Chinese people I met were mourning his exit from the game.

It's the same thing with academic expertise. We demand and require world-class expertise among researchers. There is a premium on knowledge generation, and no country, no university, no state, no region, can have a monopoly on intellectual capital. Expertise will seek its own level. This has profound implications for the university, as we will see shortly.

Similarly, the student population is global. We need access to the very best students, and so the talent search has moved to the global arena, to those students who need access to top universities. This explains why more than 50% of graduate students studying in U.S. universities are foreign nationals.

Before the information revolution, expertise was confined by university boundaries in the same way that geopolitical boundaries were defined by nation states. Post-internet, expertise flows freely across the globe. No one university, nor even one country, can have a monopoly on expertise.

Speed is important because the half-life of new knowledge is decreasing rapidly in many fields and the pace of innovation is increasing. Call this the "information spiral": the more ubiquitous the access to information, the more bright people that can have an impact on a field. And the more people working in the field, the faster the pace of discovery. In terms of knowledge creation, time is money — and so we're back to the Internet time frame of "dog years" — where a year of internet-driven discovery is the equivalent of seven ordinary human years. Coupling knowledge and skills to opportunities requires a rapid response — it means we must have the ability to put teams of people with the expertise together very quickly.

Universities will therefore have to become more nimble to respond to rapid changes in knowledge generation. We all know about information overload. The interesting thing is that the more information out there, the more job security we have in the university environment, since we are the people who can take raw information, generate signal and remove noise when it is becoming harder and harder to do so. Anybody who doesn't believe that can surf the internet and see the difficulty of getting good information. There's a good reason that Google commanded a multibillion-dollar valuation at its initial public offering.

THE WALLS COME DOWN

Friedman points out that the fall of the Berlin Wall was one of the enabling events leading to the creation of the new flat world. The reduction in the importance of geopolitical boundaries was pointed out some years ago by Peter Drucker, in his important work, *The Post-Capitalist Society* (1993). As geographic boundaries become less important, countries in some respects take on a secondary role to global corporations. And, now, as Friedman indicates through a number of examples, corporations are becoming somewhat secondary to individuals in the flat world.

It should be no surprise, then, that the walls are coming down for universities as well. Not only are the geographic boundaries being blurred by the need for global expertise, but more fundamentally, the walls of academic disciplines are being torn down and overrun. The exciting frontiers of research, whether in the sciences, engineering or in the humanities, are increasingly those in which teams of experts from multiple disciplines come together. Even problems in relatively narrow fields like biochemistry can no longer be dealt with by the biochemist alone: you also need a molecular biologist, a biophysicist and a physiologist. Where then does biochemistry end and biophysics begin, or, for that matter, physical chemistry or even materials science? The old walls have become permeable if not downright porous. We increasingly find that research is conducted in these multidisciplinary teams. Universities will need to develop new skills in forging new partnerships for assembling multidisciplinary expertise.

If you looked at research grants in a typical Hopkins department as recently as 1985, most of them probably involved a single faculty member and/or a single faculty or discipline. Five or 10 years later, grants were often going to groups of faculty members from multiple disciplines, but most of them still at Hopkins. Today, very few grants are given to just a single faculty investigator, and probably 20% of our grants involve one or more faculty investigators who are *not* at Hopkins.

For example, we received a prestigious National Science Foundation grant for robotic surgery that involved a number of divisions at Hopkins, including our Applied Physics Laboratory and the School of Engineering, but also included faculty members from Carnegie-Mellon, MIT and Harvard Medical School. This is the way of the future.

With the availability of transportable curricula and faculty, one can collect world-class expertise to put together a grant. You might say that we need the Michael Jordans of the academic world to assemble all-star teams, not just Hopkins franchises, in order to compete. It's more like putting an Olympic team together than a single state or local team. One needs to draw on expertise as widely as one can. On a trip to Singapore once, by chance I was accompanied by three other Hopkins faculty members: one teaches mathematics during winter semester in Singapore and the other two were doing collaborative research with faculty at the National University of Singapore. Their paychecks may say they are employees of Johns Hopkins, but that is not what is important to their students and colleagues in Singapore — it's their world-class expertise that matters most.

Paraphrasing Thomas Friedman (2005), I would say: "The academic world is flat." Rapid, low-cost transportation and communication, the destruction of the walls of academic disciplines and the globalization of scholarship are combining to change the organization and the culture of research universities.

Which leads me to the **quantum physics model of the university**. We all remember being first exposed to the classical model of the atom: a central sphere with electrons orbiting around it. You can also think of the classical model of the university as this well-defined nucleus — the campus — with faculty and students acting as tightly coupled electrons rotating around the nucleus. The faculty and university were held together by commitment and tenure. Students were there full-time and physically present, and everything was good, except when the students rioted every spring. But the students also felt a lot of loyalty to the university. Again, the faculty members, although loyal to their discipline, only needed to be *local* experts, so in some sense they had a lot more commitment to their institution.

But the classical model has given way to the quantum physics model. Today we have multiple campuses, in fact, more like a cloud-like collection of sites. Hopkins has more than a dozen sites in the U.S., and operates in 80 countries around the world, with significant physical campuses in Singapore, China and Italy. And it will probably have even more in the future. The faculty are no longer in a tight orbit around campus, but now can be described as only loosely bound: the more you try to pin down where they are, both physically and in terms of loyalty, the harder it is to find them. The faculty has to be a collection of international, world-class experts. Their loyalty in some sense is not only to their discipline but to their sub-field, and they need to work with others with the same focus. This association is natural and is made possible through electronic connections or physical moves. Faculty somehow "tunnel" between organizations in some quantum mechanical sense. We may have a faculty member teaching at Harvard in the fall, Singapore in the winter, and Hopkins in the summer. Or we may have faculty members doing collaborative research with Harvard or Singapore.

The loosening of the affiliation between the faculty and the university is an inevitable consequence of the globalization of knowledge. In the quantum physics model, the faculty obey the uncertainty principle. You may know where the faculty are at any given time, or you may know their institutional affiliation. But the more you try to understand the former, the less certain you may be about the latter, and vice-versa. This phenomenon prompted the former president of Boston University, John Silber, to actually propose taking "roll call" to see whether the faculty were on campus. But such goes against the grain of knowledge generation and diffusion in today's information-sharing environment.

It's not hard to predict that our 19th-century university structures will be increasingly stressed by 21st-century realities. One consequence of the quantum model is that the relationship between the faculty and university has become increasingly one-sided. On the one hand, tenure provides a life-time, no-cut contract for our faculty. But their allegiance is necessarily to their discipline and field of study, and they have no requirement to stay to retirement with the university that granted them tenure. And faculty whose field of study becomes obsolete or is no longer within the primary purview of the university's mission cannot be removed.

A second and equally serious issue facing the university is the organization of its faculties. The use of discipline-based departments has many advantages for teaching and quality assurance, but in many cases also serves as an impediment to fostering interdisciplinary research. Whether by culture or by geographic, financial or other bureaucratic barriers, universities are being challenged by the need to quickly assemble interdisciplinary research teams to react to new frontiers. Computational biology and nanotechnology are but two examples of exciting new research areas in which universities are struggling to assemble competitive teams of scientists and engineers.

FROM PROPRIETARY NETWORKS TO OPEN-SOURCE RESEARCH IN KNOWLEDGE DIFFUSION

As discussed above, university research is increasingly conducted by teams of faculty working across multiple disciplines. The requirement for having world-class expertise dictates that these teams will be increasingly global in nature. Formation of these networks may require inter-university agreements, but, most often, they occur without the explicit contractual arrangement for these multi-university affiliations, and sometimes without any knowledge by the university administration that these networks exist — faculty-to-faculty collaboration is in itself the *raison d'être*. Perhaps this is the modern day interpretation of *cogito, ergo sum*, "I think, therefore I exist," which becomes "I, and the network, exist."

Currently, however, these global research networks are proprietary in nature. Membership is by invitation only, as it were, and information developed within the network is retained until the time of official release of the intellectual property generated — either by patent application or by publication of the research in peer-reviewed journals, or both. One can think of these research networks like a "virtual private network", or VPN, that is used by global corporations to share proprietary information across the internet in a way that maintains the privacy of that information. We can call these networks, RPNs — "research private networks".

No doubt that a large number of Johns Hopkins faculty are participating in one or more of these global RPNs, and the number is likely increasing each year. But I have no way of knowing for sure, as my university does not require explicit disclosure by faculty of their research activities, except in situations where government or corporate grants are funding their research.

In the late 1980s, while I was Chair of the Department of Radiology at Johns Hopkins University, our physicians were developing methods to take sets of cross-sectional images from MRI or Computed Tomography (CT) scans to produce three-dimensional rendering. We required additional expertise from mathematicians and computer scientists with expertise in image rendering. Rather than hire a cadre of new faculty, and lacking such expertise within our computer science or biomedical engineering departments at the time, we developed a collaboration with the National University of Singapore, which did have world-class expertise in this area. In this case we signed a bipartite memorandum of understanding to facilitate the collaboration. A particular advantage of this arrangement, adding to the fact that we didn't have to find additional resources to hire new researchers at Hopkins, was that the software development could be done in Singapore during the daytime, 12 hours ahead of Baltimore, and the new versions available the next day for testing by our physicians. Productivity increased almost twofold. And this was achieved before broadband networking was available.

The next logical step in the diffusion of knowledge is going to be the establishment of open-source networks for research. To my knowledge, this phenomenon has not yet occurred to any significant degree. But, based upon the history of the open-source movement for software development, however, I think this form of research networking has much to recommend it and will probably be the wave of the future.

Open-source software development has enabled literally thousands of programmers to work together on the development of complex software that is

put into the public domain. While "freeware" or "shareware" is not a new phenomenon, there are important differences between the open-source movement and shareware. In the latter, the programme may have been written by
only a single person, and only the final programme is made available to others.
In open-source code, many, many people, perhaps even thousands, contribute
to the latest version of the programme, facilitated by the fact that the source
code is published on the web and anyone is free to modify the code, provided
they make their changes available on the internet to others. Through this iterative process, highly refined software code can be developed rapidly and effectively and used immediately by all. That's because there is no owner, per se —
all of the results reside in the public domain.

One would have to ask why software programmers would spend countless
hours developing software that they might otherwise be compensated to
develop. The answers are complex, but point to a new cultural phenomenon
that is extraordinarily powerful. First, there is the challenge of doing something at the peak of excellence, and the global assembly of programmers virtually guarantees the highest level of performance. When IBM decided to
scrap its proprietary web-hosting software and instead join the open-source
consortium that had developed Apache (today the leading web hosting software programme), they committed to supply additional resources, both dollars
and programmers, to support the effort. After a few months, the consortium
told IBM to take their programmers off the project and not to send any more
— unless they were willing to send their very best.

Other reasons why software developers are attracted to open-source software consortia is perhaps an anti-establishment bias — sort of a way to take
down Microsoft (or IBM) a peg or two. Regardless of the motives, it is clear
that open-source software development is both powerful and here to stay.

Open-source research networks for the diffusion of knowledge may seem
like a far-fetched idea, but, in fact, we have a major example of a successful
open-source network that has been in existence for a number of years: the
Human Genome Project. Funded by consortia including the United States
National Institutes of Health, the Human Genome Project (HGP) is
exactly the model of open-source collaboration that could be employed
more broadly across many scientific areas. In the HGP, scientists working
across the globe have sequenced various gene segments and placed those
data into the common human genome database. The consortia established,
early on, a common data format that enabled tens of thousands of workers
to contribute successfully to the database, as well as to access the information for their own research. The result was a much more rapid sequencing
of the human genome than was predicted by the experts at the outset,
enabled by the peer-to-peer collaboration through an open-source research
network.

There are many challenges posed by open-source research collabora-tion. Most of these are not significantly different from those already faced in the open-source software development arena: intellectual property rights; quality control; loss of credit to individual contributors, to name a few. However, these issues have been successfully resolved in the software field and in the Human Genome Project, so I would predict that the use of open-source networks will grow to be an important mechanism for sci-entific discovery.

There are already projects underway in several disciplines that point the way to this new future. One of the most exciting is Bioconductor (2001), which describes itself as "an open-source and open development software project for the analysis and comprehension of genomic data." This project, modelled deliberately on the Linux software development template, started in the fall of 2001 at Harvard's Dana Farber Cancer Institute. Four years later, its core team of 23 developers consists of five Harvard faculty, a Johns Hopkins biostatistics professor and colleagues from Austria, France, Germany, Italy, Switzerland, the U.K. and elsewhere in the United States. I am told that Bio-conductor is sweeping through the bioinformatics world and is rapidly becom-ing one of the most powerful and important tools in this field, and the nexus of the international research effort.

At Johns Hopkins, a team of researchers in the Bloomberg School of Public Health has been pioneering another facet of the open-source trend in an effort they call "reproducible research". Concerned with measuring the health effects of low levels of ozone and other air pollution, the Department of Bio-statistics, supported by the Environmental Protection Agency's Health Effects Institute, has created the internet-based Health and Air Pollution Surveil-lance System that puts custom-tailored regression analysis software and com-plete health and air-quality data sets on line in an effort to encourage other researchers both to check and confirm the results of the team's own studies, and to customize the data sets and software to reach research conclusions of their own.

At the Johns Hopkins Whiting School of Engineering, Civil Engineering professor Ben Schaeffer is advancing new building design through the use of thin-walled structures, a wide and growing field of engineering applications which seek efficiency in strength and cost while minimizing the use of mate-rials. To promote new uses of materials like very thin cold-formed steel, Pro-fessor Schaeffer created an open-source, academic free licence programme called CUFSM that calculates the buckling stress and modes of arbitrarily shaped, simply supported, thin-walled members. Researchers and, increas-ingly, designers and builders from around the world are using the software and contributing to its expanding capabilities as a vital desktop tool used to create the next generation of highly efficient buildings.

CONCLUSION

Universities, along with churches, are one of the two institutions of society that have survived almost unchanged for centuries, while all others have fallen prey to social, political, geographic and environmental forces. By their design, universities are slow, if not sometimes downright immutable, to change. This inertia has been their intrinsic survival advantage. Yet today the research university is subject to the same forces of globalization that confront all other aspects of society, and is facing similar stresses.

Foremost among these stresses is the changing relationship between the faculty and the university brought about by the interdisciplinary nature of research. The implicit and ages-old contract between the faculty and the university has become skewed by the forces of globalization. Increasingly, there are serious disputes revolving around who should own the rights to the intellectual property generated by the faculty, by the increasing mobility of faculty, and by the obligatory responsibility of the university to its tenured faculty. Productive faculty of today may be rendered less relevant to the research agendas of tomorrow as the pace of discovery quickens. Stem-cell research, now the hottest area of biomedical science, was mostly an unknown area less than a decade ago. Ultimately, the ability of the university to reconfigure its research efforts depends upon the agility of its faculty and the porousness of its traditional boundaries.

Finally, for nearly three quarters of a century, scientific research was largely the province of the United States and Europe. Now, emerging countries — especially in Asia — are increasingly significant contributors to science and technology, and this trend is likely to continue for the next half-century or more. The leading role of existing research universities is likely to be diminished unless they are able to form, or join, worldwide networks of researchers working at the frontiers of knowledge creation. The world, as Thomas Friedman (2005) suggests, may be becoming flat. It will be the research universities' challenge, in the process, not to get flattened.

REFERENCES

Bioconductor. (2001). http://www.bioconductor.org/
CUFSM. http://www.ce.jhu.edu/bschafer/cufsm/index.htm
Drucker, Peter. (1993). *The Post-Capitalist society*. HarperBusiness, New York.
Friedman, T. L. (2005). *The World is Flat*. Farrar, Strauss and Giroux, New York.
Health and Air Pollution Surveillance System. http://www.ihapss.jhsph.edu/

CHAPTER 10

Innovation and Wealth Creation

Dennis Tsichritzis and Michael-Alexander Kreysel

INTRODUCTION

Over the years there has been enough evidence of a correlation between scientific achievements and the well-being of nations and regions. Places with strong economies produce remarkable scientific achievements. The other way around, scientific progress often gave rise to industrial and military strength which created and maintained strong economies. It is, therefore, tempting to equate thus: Science = Wealth. This is a good reason for scientists in every region to demand and expect more resources with a vague promise that eventually the stakeholders will be paid back directly or indirectly. For example, there is a current debate about the Lisbon goals in the E.U. and the lack of progress in implementing them.

In our view, Science is definitely interesting, but not necessarily lucrative. It is true that strong economies have outstanding Science. It would have been surprising otherwise. People who can afford it develop intellectual curiosity which eventually is channelled to the Arts, Music and, why not, Science. It is also true that some, though not all, scientific results can produce unique opportunities for enrichment. The problem is to predict which ones. The temptation is to pump enough money into Science and hope that statistically and eventually there will be a huge payback. That approach fits well the interests of scientists, but unfortunately not finance directors and finance ministers.

To improve the success rate of the investment in Science one can concentrate efforts in specific areas. Over the years the "hot areas" are redefined, with a current emphasis on Info/Bio/Nano. There is always a large effort to pinpoint the most promising areas in scientific programmes which eventually guide the distribution of resources. That approach is in itself too static to be successful. First, during the execution of research programmes, prospects can

121

change dramatically. Second, scientists are very clever and they relabel rather than reinvent their efforts. Third, the definition of what is "hot" is very subjective, and is influenced by the people who are themselves beneficiaries. In short, the Research Programme definition process is time-consuming and has limited success. It is better than random choice, but far from efficient.

To really be efficient we need to link scientific effort with economic activity. That Scientific Innovation = Wealth Creation is not controversial. Everybody believes that when science is applied to real world problems, then there are economic benefits. The goal is uniformly accepted. Scientists love to see their results work in practice. Alternatively, industrial activity draws decisive advantages from specific scientific results. It leaves us with the problem of organization and implementation. Mount Everest is known and visible. The difficulty is to find the way to the top. We will call the way of achieving wealth creation by scientific innovation simply Innovation. This problem is not new. History has many successful examples of enlightened leaders who through scientific achievements became rich and powerful.

The issue of Innovation has become very actual lately mainly for three reasons. First, Science has become much more expensive. It is normal that stakeholders want value for money. Second, timing is critical. There is ferocious competition for economic advantage which translates into time pressure to produce and exploit results. Third, globalization allows transfers of capital, know-how and people. It becomes important to reap the benefits locally and not give them away to potential competitors.

In the rest of the paper we will sketch different ways to Innovation and explore their relative advantages. In the whole discussion we should not forget: The goal is to create wealth, not only to advance Science.

THE RESEARCH UNIVERSITY MODEL

The most traditional and well accepted model for Innovation is through people. When students in universities are well educated in the most modern, advanced methods and techniques, they in turn bring the necessary Innovation to the economy. This gave rise to the linking of research and education and the role of the university professor as a truly independent thinker in the modern research university. The goal of such a university is always to produce well educated people. Research, and especially its application to the economy, are important funding opportunities, but are often considered secondary.

This Innovation model has three problems. First it does not scale easily. In many countries there is an effort to produce more well trained people by increasing the number of students and/or increasing the number of universities. This approach has many shortcomings. Elite universities cannot grow indefinitely, nor be established overnight. Second, it takes too long for progress in Science to be introduced in educational programmes and then for the trained people to find their way in the economy. Third, educated people are becoming very mobile. They will go to work where they can optimise their own personal and professional life. This, in turn, creates long-term opportunities for a region if they come back. Short and medium term, the costs are real and the benefits virtual.

We do believe in the important role of elite universities. Educating the best people is necessary for Innovation. We believe, nevertheless, that it is not sufficient. We sometimes see the phenomenon that regions can chronically lack in Innovation, although they still retain a high level of university education. Educating the best students does not imply Innovation.

THE RESEARCH CENTRE MODEL

To focus and accelerate Innovation in specific areas, countries and companies have created research centres. In this way, experienced and talented scientists can get together and share knowledge and infrastructure in specific, well defined areas. The research centre model works analogous to cooking:

1) Get excellent people   (the best ingredients);
2) Give them what they need   (prepare);
3) Provide local/global competition (heat);
4) Monitor and focus   (cook);
5) Disseminate widely   (serve).

It is clear that such a model produces the best scientific research and usually the best results. It is not clear, however, that these results have any direct relation to Innovation. First, there is often a mismatch between produced results and exploitation potential, especially locally. Second, research centres are often concentrated thematically. It is difficult to combine different scientific areas to bring to bear on real world problems. Third, technology transfer is notoriously difficult. Excellent scientists want to talk to other excellent scientists and not to unwashed company developers.

We do not argue against research centres. We believe that excellent research centres are a necessary condition for Innovation. They are not, however, sufficient. Doing first-class research does not imply Innovation.

THE TURBO MODEL

Most countries already have a university and a research centre infrastructure. To achieve Innovation there is the temptation to use it as a platform to pump in a tremendous amount of money. This model works in the following steps.

1) Focus on specific areas.
2) Hire the best research management talent.
3) Network with the best worldwide.
4) Invest in extravagant infrastructure.
5) Get the best young people worldwide.
6) Overspend for a sustainable period.

This results in extraordinary achievements within a short time. In addition, a brand name is obtained, which is necessary to attract further excellent people. The costs, however, are also extraordinary.

The problem with such an approach is its inherent instability. When the interest of the stakeholders wanes, whether companies or countries, things turn around. A short period of under-investment or disinterest results in undermining the whole effort. The best people are also the most mobile. The real difficulty is nevertheless technology transfer. Excellent researchers, well funded in universities and research centres, become very arrogant. They are pushing for Nobel prizes and they consider any other activity very marginal. Innovation requires long hours of field work and there is nobody willing or able to undertake it.

The turbo model works like a hotrod car. It accelerates fast in a straight line, but cannot take curves and it does not win races.

THE FORMULA 1 MODEL

To achieve Innovation a more global, all encompassing, approach is needed. Most of the preceding models are preconditions. We need a strong elitist university system. We need excellent visible research centres. We need to turbo-charge the university and research infrastructure to achieve brand name and global reach. In addition, we need a whole series of other very important steps:

1) We need to finance cooperative projects between industry and research. In this way we strengthen the existing national champions.
2) We need to create clusters between universities, research centres and companies large and small.
3) We need to actively manage IPRs and put the accent on exploitation.
4) We need to finance new ventures and start-ups with seed capital.
5) We need to promote innovative markets with national programmes.
6) We need to give tax breaks for venture capital to attract risk-taking investors.
7) We need to help exit strategies in terms of IPOs and trade sales for investors.
8) We need flexible bankrupt laws to protect small entrepreneurs.
9) We need to attract international investors.

10) We need media coverage that we are seriously embarking in a new direction to obtain local support and global interest.

We claim that without an all-round strategy we cannot win. This is the reason that we call it the Formula-1 Model. It is not about having the best motor, or best tyres, or best aerodynamics. It is about having the whole car performing. If one link in the innovation chain is weak, the whole thing does not work.

There are examples of countries and regions that have achieved this model. The areas of intervention are known. The difficulty is to match them to local conditions. One cannot imitate Silicon Valley. One has to create its own version. There are already many developed countries committed to intensifying their efforts for Innovation, e.g., Sweden, Finland, Germany, Singapore or France. They are using mainly two instruments: agencies and institutions. Here we present two examples, Vinnova as agency and Fraunhofer as institution.

Example 1: The Swedish Agency Vinnova (www.vinnova.se)

Scandinavian innovative action was determined by the question of how to change the whole innovation system efficiently. While modifications in innovation policy, e.g. in Finland, occurred rather incrementally, the innovation structures of the other Nordic countries, especially Sweden, underwent far-reaching changes. However, all activities were affected by the rationale of systemic innovation.

The most obvious effect of this change in Sweden was the establishment of the Swedish Agency for Innovation Systems (VINNOVA) in 2001, which currently has around 150 employees and a total budget of 1 GSEK (€100 million). The goal was to promote sustainable economic growth by developing effective innovation systems in Sweden and by funding problem-oriented research towards the needs of society and industry, primarily at the universities. It is one of the most important agencies of the Swedish Government for financing research.

The system-based approach is the guiding principle for all initiatives. Hence, they address failures in the innovation system, strengthen innovative capacity of Swedish industry and help transform knowledge into technology. The various programmes address national, regional or sectoral innovation system issues.

Example 2: The Fraunhofer Model in Germany (www.fraunhofer.de)

Most German R & D which is financed by the public sector is conducted by public research institutions, about half of which are universities. Knowledge transfer between Science and Industry is promoted by a highly organized division of labour between research institutes, mainly oriented towards basic research and others with an applied research focus. Fraunhofer is the largest organization focused on applied research. It employs roughly 13,000 people in 58 institutes across Germany, and has a R & D-Budget of more than €1 billion. Fraunhofer is active in different fields of technology, e.g. Life Sciences, Information and Communication Technology, Microelectronics, Materials and Components. This broad technological expertise makes Fraunhofer's research particularly strong in cross-section fields. Fraunhofer is run according to a decentralized management concept, in which the otherwise independent institutes share the same basic aims and a common organizational structure.

Fraunhofer receives base funding from the public sector (approx. 40%) and contract research earnings (approx. 60%). As a consequence, Fraunhofer operates in a dynamic equilibrium between application-oriented research and innovative development projects. Fraunhofer develops products and processes right up to commercial maturity. Individual solutions are sought in direct contact with its more than 3,000 customers.

Fraunhofer's designated role is to intermediate between business enterprises and science based institutions and facilitate knowledge and technology transfer to industry. The volume of base funding is linked to success in obtaining research contracts from the private and public sector, allowing the institutes to engage in basic research and in technology transfer to private sector enterprises. Because of this infrastructure and corresponding funding schemes, comparatively few enterprises in Germany report a lack of technological knowledge as a factor limiting their innovation activities. SMEs are important customers of Fraunhofer and are simultaneously actors of technology dissemination.

The intensified commitment to innovation of the developed countries is accompanied by many national innovation initiatives which recently have been established with different configurations and goals. For instance, the German innovation initiative intends to increase the awareness within the population and therefore tries to realize different innovative pioneering projects. Even in the U.S. well known experts wrote the report "Innovate America" showing paths to increase innovativeness.

Developing countries also have no good reason to complain and stay out of the Innovation game. There are steps which prepare the ground and eventually enable every dynamic country to participate. As a first step, it is necessary to develop the economy and infrastructure. We need at least the following actions:

1) Bring in manufacturing and service industry with tax laws, low costs.
2) Generate enough economic activity to feed the Innovation chain.
3) Buy some time to upgrade universities and research centres.
4) Become known to the global players.

Later on we need to bootstrap the expertise and join the global innovation activity. This can be achieved by exploiting existing potential. For instance, we need the following actions:

1) Repatriate talent and give benefits for global players to establish R & D locally.
2) Leverage your manufacturing facilities.
3) Get the necessary local/global recognition to attract/keep top talent.
4) Link to the global R & D effort.
5) Get ready for a general mobilisation with Innovation as a goal.

Countries like China and India show very clearly that this path is feasible.

CONCLUSION

In this paper we made the following points: The benefits of Innovation are well known and accepted (*Everest*). However, to get there you need a careful plan and many years of sustainable efforts (*expedition*). It should be promoted and accepted widely as national goal and kept outside parochial political interests (*you play to win and not to explain failures*). For every region and country the plan has to fit local strengths and weaknesses (*no uniform strategy for everybody*). Getting half way through has no benefits (*reaching halfway up Everest brings nothing*). The whole plan should be visible, known and accepted to the people shouldering the burdens (*role of politics, media*).

We should mention in closing that many countries have already realized the importance of Innovation and are taking appropriate action. This situation puts in turn enormous pressure on the rest. Globalization has created competition and a level playing field for all regions. In a flat world every person or region has chances, but has also the great responsibility to exploit them.

PART III

•••••••••••••

The European Experience

CHAPTER 11

The EPFL approach to Innovation

Hervé Lebret, Jan-Anders E. Månson and Patrick Aebischer [1]

Innovation has become a major subject of discussion in developed countries. From the European Union's Lisbon Strategy (2000) to the contribution of Beffa (2005) in France, the number of studies on how to improve innovation has not only been high, but the quality of the authors is also noticeable. Switzerland is no exception to the situation, and the political and economic decision-makers have been very sensitive to the Swiss challenges and opportunities, e.g. Avenir Suisse (2002). As in any developed country, academic institutions are and will be even more important contributors to innovation in the future. A description of the innovation landscape in Switzerland and of the Ecole Polytechnique Fédérale de Lausanne's (EPFL) unique strategy is developed herein.

Silicon Valley is the example of what developed countries would like to achieve: a hugely successful technology cluster, where corporations, which were once little start-ups, renowned academic institutions, and individuals who have become role models for an entire country. Investors, lawyers as well as established companies also contribute to the wealth of a region not larger in km^2 than Switzerland. Need we mention Intel, Cisco Systems, Genentech, Apple Computers, and Oracle? Stanford University and UC Berkeley? Steve Jobs, Larry Ellison? Names such as Kleiner Perkins, Sequoia, or Wilson Sonsini may be lesser known, but were as instrumental in the development and success of the Bay Area. As innovation is complex and requires a variety of

1 The authors would like to thank Pierre-Etienne Bourban, Pascal Vuilliomenet from the vice-presidency for innovation and valorization, Gabriel Clerc, delegate to valorization and head of the EPFL's TTO, for their contributions to the new EPFL strategy in innovation, as well as the College of Management of Technology, Technology Transfer Office (SRI) and Industry Liaison Program (CAST). Additional thanks to Virginia Picci, Hélène Herdt and Christina Deville Salmgren for their valuable comments on the drafts.

people and experiences, technology clusters are the right models. Though Silicon Valley will probably remain unique, original approaches should be developed to favour innovation.

ABOUT INNOVATION

"Anything that will not sell, I do not want to invent." Thomas Edison

There is sometimes confusion about the definition of innovation. It is different from invention. Innovation is the successful commercialization of inventions; it is the development and application of new ideas to create value. Coming from an innovator, it is obviously his main motivation. "However, there is another side to innovation at a university — Cambridge University, England, in 1855 — if you had asked what its biology department would look like in 1880, you would have missed the Darwinian revolution. So we don't know exactly which of the things we're working on at Stanford today are going to be the ones that have terribly important relationships to human welfare, indeed, to human survival a hundred years from now." Donald Kennedy, former president of Stanford University, from Whiteley (2002).

Innovation is not and will never be the main mission of universities, even of institutes of technology. To reassure those who are sceptical, let us look at numbers: Stanford with all its successful ventures in innovation is generating about $40 million in royalties per year, a small 2% of its annual budget. The figure of 2% is probably a good average number for most American universities. However, in a rather striking study, Stephan (2005) has shown how Ph.D. students trained in the very good universities of the U.S. Mid-Western states often relocate to the East and West Coast. It seems that some discussions do occur about the efficiency of state funding in high education as a good local investment. The Swiss universities are all state funded. Their budget should be guaranteed and increased, not just for the beauty of science, but also for the benefit of their students and as a good investment for Switzerland and its future.

SWITZERLAND AND INNOVATION

Switzerland has discovered with awe that it is not good at innovation, e.g., Avenir Suisse (2002), Volery (2004). The country may be wealthy with a sound economy and global infrastructure, as numerous reports show, however the trend is negative and many countries are catching up. In the same reports, it has been widely agreed that "future growth will be through the ability to innovate". A detailed analysis of Switzerland reveals that productivity has fallen drastically, new product development is moving out and new venture creation is too small. However, Switzerland is and will be more and more a knowledge-based society; if it wants to grow, it will have to show that the money spent in innovation is a good investment from which society also benefits.

The reasons for such apparent challenges are difficult to assess and the determining criteria are not yet clear. However, the studies mentioned seem to converge on the same points. It does not seem that political will and decisions, the lack of money or infrastructure are critical. In a small survey on Switzerland, Avenir Suisse (2002) itemized more specifically the following barriers:

Table 1: Barriers to innovation in Switzerland

Category	Category Type	Weight
Risk Aversion	Cultural Issue	10.28
Public Complacency	Cultural Issue	10.28
Innovation Is Not Highly Valued	Cultural Issue	9.66
Existing Education Does Not Provide Tools for Innovation	Educational Issue	8.41
Access to Appropriate Financing	Political Issue	7.48
Closed Networks	Cultural Issue	6.54
Legal Barriers	Political Issue	6.54
Limited Manpower	Educational Issue	5.92
Lack of Vision and Policy Growth	Political Issue	5.61
Innovation and Education	Educational Issue	4.98
No Role Models	Educational Issue	4.36
Lack of Entrepreneurial Mindset	Educational Issue	4.36
Existing Infrastructure and Mind Resources Under-Utilized	Political Issue	3.43
Critical Mass	Size Issue	2.49
Human Potential Exits	Success Factor	2.49
Limited Internal Market Size	Size Issue	2.49
Ivory Tower	Educational Issue	1.87
Positive Business Climate	Success Factor	1.25
Too Many Restrictions on Innovation	Political Issue	0.93
Provincialism	Cultural Issue	0.62
Total		**100.00**

Interestingly enough, if we summarize by category type, we obtain:

Table 2: Barriers to innovation in Switzerland by categories

Category Type	Total
Cultural Issues	37.38
Educational Issues	29.91
Political Issues	23.99
Size Issues	4.98
Success Factors	3.74
Total	100.00

This table illustrates clearly that cultural and educational issues constitute the main barriers to innovation. This paradox will not be easy to resolve. In his very interesting keynote speech to the Thought Leadership Forum, Kurtzman (2002) states: "Innovation and competitiveness are not national issues. They are corporate issues. Companies compete. Countries don't compete. Yes, a country has to provide the infrastructure, the educational superstructure and health care. But, that is not where competitiveness lies. Competitiveness and economic benefit lie in companies, in the economic engines of that economy. From my standpoint, the most important thing to think about is not the country, but it is how you create economic value within companies. That alone will give the country benefit.... Therefore, I look at innovation and define innovation from a very narrow perspective. From the perspective that the purpose of innovation is to create value — measurable value." The paradox lies in the fact that academic institutions will be asked to be strong contributors to innovation but the measure of success or failure will probably be outside the universities, i.e. within corporations.

SWISS UNIVERSITIES AND INNOVATION

The innovation infrastructure of Switzerland is sound. To focus just on academic innovation, let us try to briefly describe how innovation can be ideally supported. Surlemont (1999) explains the necessary infrastructure for academic spin-offs. His very exhaustive analysis is interesting for many reasons but one of his best achievements is a description of the infrastructure needed to support ambitious innovation. He classifies such support in six different areas: government, universities, entrepreneurship and innovation education, poles of excellence, incubators and coaches, and industry and financial partners. Figure 1 also illustrates their respective weight from idea generation to development and success.

Figure 1: EPFL innovation actors

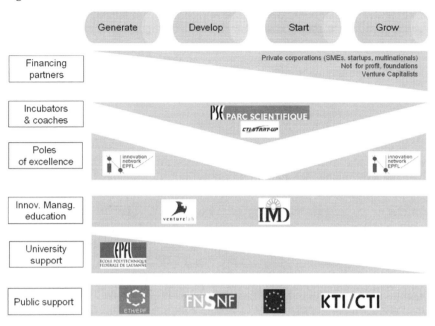

The description made below corresponds to the EFPL situation; it has the advantage of giving concrete examples, which can be easily generalized to Switzerland as a whole. Let us begin with external support, i.e. government, industry and financial. The government support begins with the fact that EPFL is a federal school within the ETH/EPF domain. For more than 150 years, Switzerland has been playing a critical role in science policy combining high quality standards in education and research. The ETH/EPF domain today is a very strong support which guarantees a world-class level that enables EPFL in particular to attract the best professors and students. Innovation begins with such prerequisites. Two other agencies, the Swiss National Science Foundation (FNS) and the Swiss Innovation Promotion Agency (KTI/CTI) support research and innovation on a project-based format similar to the American model. Finally, the European Union becomes a major actor in the funding of research. There is one major difference to be noticed: Switzerland does not fund the private sector with public money in the same way as the SBIC program (http://www.sba.gov/INV) in the USA or Ozeo in France, the merger of ANVAR and BDPME (the bank for the development of small and medium size enterprises — SMEs).

At the other end of the spectrum, the private sector is also a major player in innovation: established companies contribute more and more to innovation with direct collaborations with universities and indirect ones in partnerships with the KTI/CTI. Another feature of Switzerland is its dense network of SMEs. Historically, the country has always been very strong with such companies in the mechanical, electromechanical, chemical and health industries.

More recently with the development of a new generation of start-ups, a decent number of venture capitalists, accounting and law firms have developed around companies spun-off from academic institutions. Professional associations, foundations and also awards supporting entrepreneurships followed. A foundation, dedicated to innovation, is providing personal loans with very good conditions to entrepreneurs linked to local academic institutions. Finally, as anywhere else, and sometimes with more success thanks to the flexibility of the Swiss federal system, legal and fiscal advantages contribute to making Switzerland an attractive area.

Swiss universities did not stay inactive during these sustained efforts. As American universities following the Bayh-Dole Act (1980) which gave universities the responsibility to manage the intellectual property (IP) generated by their staff, most European universities have developed technology transfer offices. EPFL's Technology Transfer Office (TTO) has been in the forefront as it has been managing IP for more than 15 years. EPFL is also allowed to take equity and royalties in technology licensing deals with private companies. Figure 2 gives some indication of EPFL's data of technology transfer. On the incubator and coaching side, a science park, the PSE, was built starting in 1993. Today, this independent legal structure welcomes more than 100 start-ups on the campus. The PSE also provides coaching supported by KTI/CTI and an incubator for entrepreneurs and early stage companies. The region has also been lucky to see the recent creation of other incubators and numerous coaching programmes.

Education in entrepreneurship and management of technology may have been less developed in the past. The College of Management of Technology at EPFL, a new college founded in 2005, is dedicated to train engineers in the economic and business aspects of innovation and technology. It exemplifies the recent important decisions taken in the area of teaching entrepreneurship and management. With these initiatives, EPFL will be able to attract students with a strong innovative and entrepreneurial mindset that will be further stimulated during their education. It would be terrible not to encourage scientifically brilliant students to develop also their potential in innovation.

To quote Kurtzman (2002) again: "Creativity often happens at the edge of chaos....It has been my contention that the edge of chaos is important, and yields results. Innovation is not a clean process. Innovation has a lot of failure built into it, and innovation is about tolerating those failures. The best venture capital firms in the world have about a 20% success rate — admittedly much worse in the current environment. Innovation means tolerating the fact that failure is a part of the game. Innovation means celebrating failures as the

Figure 2: EPFL technology transfer activity

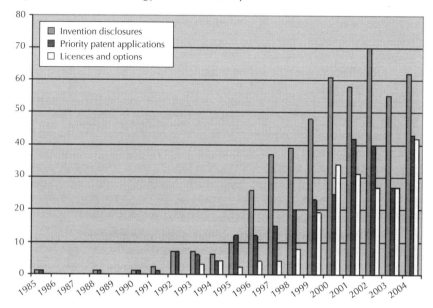

first step in the process.... Innovation is an unnatural act for many organizations and is often not part of the culture. Many of Russia's best-trained minds were stagnant for decades until they came to the U.S. or to Israel where innovation was something that was valued. Innovation is not just a matter of intelligence."

THE INNOVATION GAP STILL PREVAILS – PART I

Despite all these efforts, the difficulty to innovate — that is the difficulty to successfully market products coming from the inventive activities of technologists — has been recognized. This "Innovation Gap" remains as ever a real challenge. This is not to say that all the past initiatives have failed. It would certainly be quite easy to show that without such support, Europe and Switzerland may have been in a more difficult situation. All efforts in this field can only give long-term results, with their positive outcome only to be seen as positive in the future.

Numerous studies explain the difficulty to innovate: fear of risk-taking, reduced funding, disconnection between academia and industry, lack of university focus on commercialization. These are generally accepted as the main obstacles to innovation. Remedies include actions on culture and education, a more flexible funding scheme, closer links between universities and industry, and a system of rewards inside the universities to facilitate innovation.

The linear approach considering that education, research, development and industrialization follow each other in a natural manner, is arguable. A more integrated framework is certainly necessary.

There are many books about the challenges of innovating, for example, Lester (2004) or Haour (2004). Innovation has never and will never be simple or mechanized, neither will entrepreneurship. Looking again to the other side of the Atlantic, MIT has made a similar analysis: in 2002 it created the Deshpande Center, with the idea of bridging the Innovation Gap by better connecting all innovation actors and diminishing risk taking.

Individual willingness to achieve something, with or without the fear of taking risks, is critical to innovation and entrepreneurship. In the will to achieve, there may or may not be any technology content: innovation is not always about brilliant scientific breakthroughs. It has often been noted that (unfortunately) scientific quality and entrepreneurial mindset are seldom found combined in one individual's brain. Is there a myth in combining Bill Gates and Paul Allen, Steve Jobs and Steve Wozniak, Bill Hewlett and David Packard? Certainly to some extent, but it is the illustration that teams may be stronger than isolated individuals.

EPFL'S NEW INITIATIVES IN INNOVATION – PART I

This analysis is certainly too short, but we are convinced that more can be done to improve innovation. To assist individuals to better connect in a complex network of actors and to convince established companies that better links can be created with universities, EPFL decided in 2004 to create a new Vice-Presidency for Innovation and Valorization (VPIV). The VPIV encompasses EPFL's TTO and industry liaison programme and in mid-2005, it also created its Innovation Network — a Network, and not a Centre, to emphasize that innovation will not be improved by being centralized. As has been shown by all experts, innovation is about creating open spaces where creativity is first encouraged and then streamlined.

EPFL's strategy to improve innovation will focus on addressing key issues: better communication channels, an effort to change the culture and internal support to encourage innovative projects. Innovation has its roots in research and therefore this effort begins by encouraging trans-disciplinary activities between the different laboratories, to enable the exploration of new fields. Such so called "Strategic Initiatives" should help eliminate the traditional barriers between research domains. Trans-disciplinary centres have been and are being set up linking disciplines such as biology and computer science, chip design at the hardware and software level, material science and bioengineering among others.

Two unique examples of Strategic Initiatives are the collaborations with Alinghi (2001) and Solar Impulse (2003). In the case of Alinghi, the Swiss challenger and winner of the America's Cup, R & D collaborations have been in place since 2001, with particular focus on fluid mechanics, materials and visualization. The more recent Solar Impulse project for a round-the-world solar airplane flight will draw upon intellectual and scientific resources from more than ten diverse research domains. These will focus on the following technological challenges: ultralight materials, novel energy storage and retrieval systems, and new types of human-machine interfaces. The original motivation here is not only to address trans-disciplinary collaborations, but also to create unique and highly successful role models for students and researchers through the visible nature of these two challenging projects.

Figure 3: EPFL innovation strategy

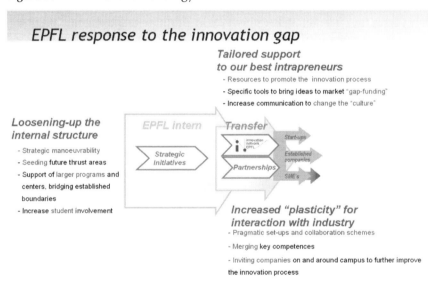

Poles of excellence, as defined by Surlemont (1999), unite universities, research centres, companies and professional associations to facilitate contacts, to animate and promote skills linked to the pole, so as to create a sufficient critical mass. They also create a top-down clustering access (and not to only one laboratory) with a better use of resources. FNS has created at the federal level such areas of expertise (NCCRs), notably around EPFL, on molecular oncology, mobile communications and quantum photonics and in more than 10 other fields in Switzerland. This programme, initially dedicated to high quality research, is now experiencing a second phase in which it focuses more on technology transfer and Partnerships with the private sector. EPFL will give strong support to follow the early results of the NCCRs, in particular by inviting companies to join the university's efforts. Discussions to create new efficient models for industry-academia Partnerships have been launched. Corporations have been too cautious in funding research which lacked a strong focus on the applications. Mixing strongly university labs and corporate R & D has not always been optimal. The creation of more neutral joint-ventures near university campuses will be one way to promote the open innovation which is seen nowadays as the only way to efficiently innovate. As big corporations have reduced their basic R & D activity, they will rely more and more on university research to innovate. Hybrid structures will be a model to build confidence between universities and corporations. They can innovate together without preventing high quality research in the university labs and without forgetting corporations' main priority: innovation.

SMEs represent a huge proportion of the Swiss economic network: SMEs, those with up to 250 employees, represent 99.7% of the country's 300,000 companies and account for well over two thirds of employment. SMEs are sometimes known as those squeezed in the middle with fewer resources to innovate: on one side, start-ups in their early phase are totally dedicated to the development of new products coming from breakthrough inventions; on the other side, bigger companies, including multinationals, have the resources and flexibility to plan the long term even though their R & D capacity has been under more pressure than it was 15 to 20 years ago. SMEs, on the contrary, due to more limited resources, focus more and more exclusively on their existing customers and have strong dedication to provide the best possible products. This gives little time to look at the future product development. Their research capability is also limited. Bigger companies have specialists who can communicate with innovators outside, such as those in university labs. A unique and potentially very rewarding effort that will benefit the Swiss economy is the launch of a new initiative facilitating SMEs-university communication. This especially supports translating functional technology needs into scientific issues suitable to university research level.

THE INNOVATION GAP STILL PREVAILS – PART II

As it has been shown earlier, the infrastructure for supporting innovation is solid, well in place and it does not lack any tool. Despite this, in the last ten years, not many companies have grown and few inventions made at EPFL have been licensed with an interesting financial return for the school. Why so? It is certainly just a question of time as it must be remembered that successful U.S. universities in technology transfer have often counted on a very small number of "home runs". The Cohen Boyer patent in the 1970s and Google recently are the two big success stories of Stanford. Most other technologies generated less than $10 million whereas these two extreme cases have gener-ated more than $200 million each.

Let's try a simple exercise. Whether the reader is interested in high tech (semiconductor, communications,...) or life sciences (biotechnology, medtech,...), he certainly knows the most famous and successful companies which were start-ups maybe as early as in the 1970s. The same exercise can be done to build a list of American companies and a list of European companies. We would be ready to bet that, for any reader, building a U.S. list is quite easy and a European list much more difficult. We would even be surprised if he could mention 10 European companies. Let's provide the list we built. The numbers are subject to errors as we did the exercise very quickly. Table 3 shows a comparison for hi-tech companies; Table 4 considers the life-science sector.

Table 3: Successful hi-tech start-ups in the USA and Europe

USA				Europe			
Company	Creation	IPO	Market cap ($B)	Company	Creation	IPO	Market cap ($B)
Microsoft	1975	1986	266	SAP	1972	1988	52
Intel	1968	1971	163	Dassault Syst.	1981	1994	5.4
Cisco	1984	1990	120	Bus. Objects	1990	1993	2.5
Dell	1984	1988	95	Arm	1990	1998	2.2
Google	1998	2004	80	Kudelski* [+]	1951	1986	1.7
Oracle	1977	1986	68	Logitech [+]	1981	1990	1.4
Yahoo	1994	1996	47	Gemplus	1988	2000	1.3
eBay	1995	1998	45	ASML	1984	1994	0.8
Apple	1976	1984	30	Soitec	1992	1999	0.8
Amazon	1994	1997	13	* company is not a pure start-up, [+] roots at EPFL			

Source: Yahoo Finance web site, Sept. 05

Discussions may occur about the validity of such an approach, but undeni-able conclusions can be drawn. First, the difference in the number of compa-nies cannot be argued. Finding U.S. names was easy, and tens of names could be added with big market capitalizations. Finding European names was not as easy, and the market capitalizations are lower. It might also be that time from creation to IPO is shorter in the U.S. than in Europe, but this would require a very serious study.

Table 4: Successful life-science start-ups in the USA and Europe

USA				Europe			
Company	Creation	IPO	Market cap ($B)	Company	Creation	IPO	Market cap ($B)
Amgen	1980	1983	99	Serono*	1906	1987	14.5
Genentech	1976	1980	94	Shire	1986	1996	6.4
Gilead	1987	1992	19	Elan	1969	1992	3.6
Genzyme	1981	1986	18	Actelion	1997	2000	2.5
Biogen	1978	1983	14	Qiagen	1986	1996	1.9
Chiron	1981	1983	8	Crucell	1993	2000	0.9
Medimmune	1987	1991	7	Genmab	1999	2000	0.6
Invitrogen	1987	1999	4				
App. Biosystems	1981	1983	4				
Affymetrix	1991	1996	3	* company is not a pure start-up			

Source: Yahoo Finance web site, Sept.05

Let us come back to EPFL. In the last 15 years, and thanks in part to the nearby PSE, more than 100 start-ups have been established near EPFL. In recent years, 10 companies on average were created per year. Let us also add that both Logitech and Kudelski can trace their roots to EPFL. Universities such as Stanford or MIT create about 15 to 20 start-ups per year, so EPFL is certainly among the most dynamic European universities.

However, Surlemont (1999) classifies start-ups in two categories: individual projects and enterprise projects with the characteristics described in Table 5. Could it be that the reason why companies do not grow big in our area but also elsewhere in Europe is linked to a higher ratio of lifestyle companies vs. "hi-potential" ones. One element is clear, not many start-ups after 5 years of existence have more than 10 employees in Europe. An interesting study by Zhang (2003) shows in fact how Silicon Valley differentiates itself from other regions in the U.S. such as the Boston area in the nature of its start-ups. One key fact is that the number of start-ups with more than five employees at some point in their history is proportionally much higher in the Bay Area than anywhere else. This weakness in growth is certainly a character of European and Swiss start-ups.

Innovation is about value creation and we are in a competitive world. Lifestyle start-ups should exist. They do in fact make a large majority of the start-ups in any area (Zhang, 2003). They also can be considered as the seeds for hi-

Table 5: Type of start-ups

	Individual project (lifestyle)	Enterprise project (hi-potential)
Founders	One (two) individual(s)	A team
Initial investments	Low	High
Financial needs	Low	High
Equity structure	Closed	Open
Growth potential	Low	High
Export potential	Low	High
Main goal	Short term profits	Growth
Dependency on founders	High	Low
Activity	Consulting	Product development and sale
How should university support project?	Moderately	Strongly

Source: Surlemont (1999).

potential start-ups; sometimes they will also become the hi-potential start-ups once they have found their growth niche. But competition is about speed. Your competitors will take your customers if you are not strong, fast and versatile enough. Will you take theirs if you are too small? Innovation is also about speed and efficiency. There is a need to be ambitious and aggressive when one believes in the value of one's venture.

Finally, it is often said that start-ups should be able to convince friends, investors and local customers first. If they cannot do so, they will never be able to sell. But in technology innovation, your markets may not even exist in your backyard; and even the experts, who will convince potential investors that your project has value, do not always live in Europe.

EPFL'S NEW INITIATIVES IN INNOVATION – PART II

The final tool in EPFL's new strategy to support innovation will try to address the challenges analysed in the previous section. EPFL needs to support its best entrepreneurs, the young people who will become tomorrow's entrepreneurs with the ambition to create hi-potential companies. EPFL also needs to help established companies with their intrapreneurs. These are two different types of support that EPFL will address with a new tool, its INNOGRANTS.

INNOGRANTS have been created independently of what MIT launched in 2002 as the Deshpande Center. The similarities in the model are sufficiently striking to convince us of the validity of the approach. EPFL put in place in mid-2005 the INNOGRANTS as a financial as well as an advising tool to help EPFL people with innovative projects. The fear of risk-taking as well as the difficulty of convincing possible partners (investors, industry) in the early stage of an innovation are reasons why some incubation may be profitable inside the school before any external partner is solicited. Page (2002) stated in a video document that he worked for many years at Stanford before launching Google. The two founders became real experts, understood all aspects of search by talking to search companies and worked cheaply on this, as the real cost was only their time — not hundreds of people's time. He also adds that it is absolutely compulsory to work with the right people. It appears that the initial backers of Google were outstanding people. The INNOGRANTS managers do not have the arrogance to believe they will initiate the next Google, but their ambition should be to create great companies with great people.

INNOGRANTS also have the ambition of inviting the local industry, the rich network of SMEs as well as bigger companies to dialogue more with EPFL. Innovation is about sharing ideas to help innovation arise; it is also about creating the right climate and environment which facilitates innovation. Christensen (1997), in his famous approach about innovation dilemmas, explains how great companies fail to identify the disruptive technologies, which will destroy their existing businesses. As a solution, one of his proposals is to let intrapreneurs develop promising technologies outside their existing environment, possibly in a newly created spin-off. EPFL will offer companies with such projects to consider INNOGRANTS as a way to match their collaboration proposals. EPFL also proposes bigger companies to jointly create poles of excellence in areas where EPFL and its partners see very promising development.

Everywhere in Europe, the innovation ecosystem is very fragile. Innovation cannot be done inside EPFL as in an ivory tower. Advisors, friends, experts, business angels with good will and some resources will be needed. They are not easy to find locally, and this is another challenge U.S. technology clusters do not face. The MIT mentoring service involves more than 100 business angels and experts who offer their experience for free. Founders from Logitech, Serono or Kudelski (some of the rare success stories near Lausanne) cannot always be asked to help our entrepreneurs. It might be that experts and early investors have to be found outside Switzerland and even sometimes outside Europe. EPFL's recent successful spin-offs (in terms of their ability to fundraise with venture capitalists) such as BeamExpress or Innovative Silicon had to find some of their managers and investors in the U.S. It is both an opportunity and a challenge. The good news is the companies did not have to move to the U.S., an argument which was often heard a few years ago when investors and high-calibre individuals were asked to join ambitious European start-ups.

A SIMPLE CONCLUSION

EPFL has the ambition to bridge the innovation gap with its own tools and culture. A key ingredient is a greater flexibility in its relations with its partners as well as with its staff. Better communication channels, better networking with all innovation actors are actively promoted. The culture of trying and risk-taking is encouraged so that our entrepreneurial and risk-taking people can enlarge their vision and ambition. Role models illustrating this philosophy will prove the validity of these beliefs.

A good infrastructure has been set up in the last decade. However it must not be forgotten that innovation is people-centred. A nice physical infrastructure, without the right people to use it will fail. It is therefore a very fragile ecosystem given the rare species formed by entrepreneurs and intrapreneurs. As has been emphasized, our main barriers to successful innovation lie in culture and education. It is easy to change laws and build infrastructure, but it takes time to change people.

REFERENCES

Alinghi. (2001). "Science Goes Sailing", *Science*, 21 March 2003, vol. 299: 1841.
Avenir Suisse and MIT Enterprise Forum of Switzerland. (2002). *Success Factors and Barriers to Innovation in Switzerland,* http://www.softxs.ch/innovation
Bayh-Dole Act. (1980). See, for example, the web site of the Association of University Technology Managers, www.autm.net/aboutTT/aboutTT_bayhDoleAct.cfm
Beffa, J. L. (2005). *Pour une nouvelle politique industrielle,* http://www.rapport-jeanlouisbeffa.com
Christensen, C. (1997). *The Innovator's Dilemma. When New Technologies Cause Great Firms to Fail,* Harvard Business School Press, Boston, MA.
European Union's Lisbon Strategy. (2000). http://www.etuc.org/a/652
Haour G. (2004). *Resolving the Innovation Paradox: Enhancing Growth in Technology Companies,* Palgrave Macmillan, New York.
Hardy, G. H. (1940). *A mathematician's apology,* Oxford University Press.
Kurtzman, J. (2002). In *"Thought Leadership Forum: Switzerland: Fit for Innovation?"* pp.16-21. http://www.firsttuesdayzurich.com/thoughtleadership/
Lester, R. & Piore, M. (2004). *The Missing Dimension,* Harvard University Press.
Page, L. (2002). Stanford Technology Ventures Program. Educators Corner, http://edcorner.stanford.edu/
Solar Impulse. (2003). *Popular Mechanics.* Sept. 2005, pp. 98-103.

Stephan, P., Sumell, A. & Adams, J. (2005). "Capturing Knowledge: The Location Decision of New PhDs Working in Industry", working paper.

Surlemont, B. (1999). *Les spin-off universitaires; contours et enseignements des pratiques exemplaires internationales*, Centre de Recherche PME et d'Entrepreneuriat, Université de Liège.

Volery, T., Leleux, B. & Haour, G. (2004). *The Global Entrepreneurship Monitor. Rapport 2003 sur l'Entrepreneuriat en Suisse*, University St Gallen and IMD.

Whiteley C. & McLAughlin, J. (2002). *Technology, Entrepreneurs and Silicon Valley*, Institute for the History of Technology, WV.

Zhang, J. (2003) *High Tech Start-ups and Industry Dynamics in Silicon Valley*, Public Policy Institute of California.

CHAPTER 12

Developing ongoing Research and Learning Relationships between Business Firms and Academic Institutions

Sigvald J. Harryson and Peter Lorange

INTRODUCTION

We have looked at a dozen relationships between business firms and academic institutions when it comes to ways of cooperating on research and learning. Our primary focus, which is reflected in this chapter, is to examine learning from the company's viewpoint. Thus we have not examined this phenomenon from the academic institution's viewpoint. By implication several such views will, however, become apparent. Firms may typically see academic institutions as attractive, brain-driven organizations that thus might possess relevant knowledge for them. A key question will be how to get access to this in a cost- and learning-efficient way. How does one find efficient, appropriate organizational ways to achieve this today? What are new trends in such learning collaborations? How can this be contrasted with more traditional ways?

Traditionally, many academic institutions have been predominantly supply-oriented. They have focused on what might be seen as axiomatic teaching and research reflecting many academicians' conventional disciplinary focus and interests (Lorange, 2002). This has often also led to a rather "top-down", or "in-out" mode for conceiving cooperation with business, mainly as a supplier of the more-or-less finished research outcuts. While individual researchers have been sporadically engaged in more interactive consulting, the aca-

147

demic institutions have typically provided final research findings more as a one-way delivery.

Today however, a more demand-oriented direction seems to be becoming more of a norm — and offer a clear contrast to the "old way". This involves "listening" more effectively to the customers, regarding what *they* find to be relevant — both in research and in teaching. This would, in the end, open up for a more realistic learning agenda based on more of a two-way collaboration — with inputs from firms and academia alike. We shall not exclusively review the literature in this field, but also report on our empirical research and related emerging research reports (Harryson & Lorange, 2005; Harryson, 2006). As far as we can see, there is an increased orientation toward the "business dimension" of publicly funded research, with increased industry collaboration based on factors like: rapidly growing costs of conducting fundamental science; decline in the costs of travel and communication; a much more widespread spreading of formal as well as informal collaboration links; increasing need for specialization within certain scientific fields; and the growing importance of interdisciplinary fields of cooperation. Thus, collaboration on research and learning seems much more widely adapted than ever, while taking fundamentally new forms. Above all, our findings strongly suggest that new forms of co-location and job-rotation are driving better effectiveness of industry-university collaboration, which therefore still remains a global business. Let us discuss this further.

KEY-LEARNINGS FROM OUR OBSERVATION

Based on in-depth research with 12 companies representing best practice in university collaboration, we shall articulate the following observations regarding how effective learning challenges in the academic-business context now might look.

First, it seems key to emphasize that one might devote relatively more attention to the development of personal contacts as a means to establish mutual trust. This personal chemistry seems key. Effective cooperation thus seems to be based relatively more on personal chemistry than on abstract rational logic! This also means that one might devote more attention to selecting the right individuals (professors and students), say, by applying a more professional recruiting process. A related issue, to be discussed later, would also mean that one should try to always keep the students within one's own company.

Second, we find that every external cooperative project needs to have an internal fund- and time-budget allocated for steering the project towards business needs and supporting internalization of the results. This might at times be further enhanced by actually establishing a separate company, with its own resource-based budget and its own milestones to more easily secure systematic selection and development of corporate university-based ideas for cooperation — before the results are transferred into the mother-company. It should be clear, however, whether an independent unit is established or not, that one should have clear and mutually understood definitions of milestone-focused success when establishing a cooperative project.

Third, one should be careful when trying to understand the geographic dimension. It appears that a partner's geographical closeness is key — physical proximity still seems to be a major advantage for smooth learning, despite all the progress that is being reported regarding the virtues of virtual organizational forms (Beise & Stahl, 1999; Katz & Martin, 1997; Lindelöf & Löfsten, 2004; Mansfield & Lee, 1996; Harryson, 2006).

RELATIONSHIP MANAGEMENT APPROACH

Taking the above considerations into account, we will now outline a more comprehensive framework and decision-making scheme to propose how business firms can articulate and manage their university relations in more systematic and efficient ways. Based mainly on discussions with leading practitioners, in particular the CTOs and University Collaboration Officers of a dozen companies actively working with universities, we can define and propose six dimensions that seem particularly critical to manage carefully for immediate innovation impact of university collaboration:

- **Scanning:** Identification of the most relevant opportunities for R & D cooperation with universities. How can strategic intelligence help to find all possible opportunities — especially in research areas beyond the well mastered core business?
- **Screening:** Selection of the "best" external units in terms of universities and their leading faculties. What evaluation and selection-criteria to apply (e.g., Citation index of the leading professors, patents awarded, research budgets, business-rankings)?
- **Involvement for Knowledge Transfer:** How to become sufficiently involved in the joint programme and build the required relationships to acquire, transfer and utilize the results back home?
- **Steering Towards Business Objectives:** How to secure appropriate steering of direction if any?
- **Exclusivity and IPR:** How to manage possible competition for results in non-exclusive programmes, in particular, how to share IPR and other intellectual assets?
- **Globalization:** How to manage across distance without losing control?

In order to explore new knowledge in the area of I-U collaborations, we established research partnerships with Stora Enso and SCA from the world of pulp and paper. From the wireless world, we have the three leading mobile operators in Sweden, Switzerland and Poland — as well as the recent Born Global Anoto in Lund. In food processing and medical equipment, Alfa Laval and Gambro are other well-known Born Globals from Lund. Porsche in automotive, Hilti in fastening equipment and SIG Combibloc in packaging offer unique examples of networked innovation in advanced engineering and mechanics. Finally, Bang & Olufsen in Denmark offers a compelling example in consumer electronics of how to spin out a core technology and turn this into a new platform for university collaboration to accelerate innovation-driven growth. We also found that Porsche has developed an equally unique and distinct model for university collaboration, which deserves particular attention.

Although all 12 companies held the six dimensions as the most critical ones to manage successfully for immediate impact on their innovation activities, these dimensions have only been presented in fractions in previous research. The main contributions are reviewed below:

Scanning: Fritsch & Schwirten (1999) suggest that scanning for innovation-related I-U relationships is primarily based on existing personal contacts between companies and research institution employees (39% of responses referred to this factor). Other frequently mentioned answers were specific temporary search initiatives conducted by companies (29%) and conferences and fairs (14%).

Screening: According to Burnham (1997), companies should consider a series of criteria before entering a collaboration agreement with an academic institution, such as IPR policy; overhead charges; calibre of the graduate students; supervision/interaction time with faculty members and dissertation committees. Research by Mansfield & Lee (1996) regarding factors determining which universities major U.S. firms in various industries support find that "second-tier" universities and departments more often act as a valuable and frequently used source of research findings for industry than the first-tier players. Their main explanation is that much of the applied R & D supported by industry can be done satisfactorily at less prestigious departments as these are more prone to focus immediately on industry problems than highly ranked universities are.

Interestingly, a study of the German market by Beise & Stahl (1999) reveals that the top four German research institutions received almost 30% and the top ten got 43% of the citations as the most important institutions involved in business-academic collaboration. Similarly, a study of the Japanese market by Wen & Kobayashi (2001) suggests that highly ranked universites are the most active participants in joint research with companies, and play the more significant role in the formation of collaborative R & D networks for the country as a whole.

At first glance and based on only a few studies, it would seem that a broader range of universities — including the top-tier players — are active partners of corporate innovation in the German and Japanese markets. Conversely, it would seem that U.S. companies are limiting their collaboration to second-tier universities as these are claimed to be more prone to focus immediately on industry problems than highly ranked universities are. In this context, Audretsch & Stephan (1996) found that the status of being a scientific "star" reduces the need and incentive to commute outside the region in which the scientist is located and thereby also reduces the degree of collaborative links with industry.

Knowledge Transfer: Owen-Smith & Powell (2003) hold that successful technology transfer relies on access to evaluations provided by commercial contacts. These evaluations enable universities to assess their invention transferability and act accordingly. One of the most effective methods of collaborative research and knowledge exchange between academic and industrial researchers resides in a temporary secondment of university-based researchers to industry (Schmoch, 1999) — ideally involving joint supervision of Ph.D. and Master theses (Schartinger *et al.*, 2001).

Steering: Numerous authors [1] propose to establish a high degree of engagement and trust through frequent face-to-face communication, thus mitigating the risk of conflict. Several authors (Goldfarb & Henrekson, 2003; Friedman & Silberman, 2003; Siegel *et al.*, 2003), mainly related to the German market, hold that perhaps the most critical steering mechanism is a reward system for faculty involvement in technology transfer — issued as clear compensation and staffing practices by the technology transfer office of the university in question. Our observations suggest that this practice is as common in the German-speaking world as it is uncommon in Scandinavia.

IPR and Exclusivity: The output of a university can be licence agreements which permit the use of university IP by private firms, usually combined with royalty payments received by universities in exchange for the use of IP (Thursby & Kemp, 2002). Santoro & Chakrabarti (1999) and Thursby *et al.* (2001) agree that many universities prefer not to grant exclusive licenses to their industrial partners, since exclusive licensing to one firm restricts the dis-

---

1 See, for example, Bloedon & Stokes (1994); Davenport *et al.* (1999); Kogut & Zander (1992); Rappert *et al.*, (1999); Rogers *et al.* (1998); Santoro and Chakrabarti (1999); Santoro and Gopalakrishnan (2001); Schartinger *et al*, (2002); Zander and Kogut (1995).

semination of knowledge to the general public. Surprisingly, in a cross-sectoral analysis conducted by Rappert et al. (1999), only very few companies considered formal protection of IP to be essential — mainly technology-driven firms in the material sectors. Similar findings are proposed by Thursby & Kemp (2002) and Harabi (1995). In contrast, all of the companies in our sample put strong emphasis on IP ownership in the context of university collaboration.

Globalization: Sporadic meetings between disparate teams are not enough to effectively share tacit knowledge (Nonaka & Reinmoeller, 2002). Trust and mutual understanding can only be developed through frequent and long-lasting cooperation, which necessarily involves geographical proximity (Leonard-Barton, 1995; Davenport & Prusak, 1998). It is true that advanced ICT tools can facilitate global industry-university collaboration. Still, such collaboration will only give mediocre results if attempts to build a common foundation for trust and understanding among all global R & D team members are neglected. In line with the dogmatisms of knowledge-creation, organizational learning and knowledge transfer theories (Kogut & Zander, 1992; Nonaka, 1994; Von Krogh et al. 2000), a large number of authors [2] on I-U collaborations find geographic proximity to be a crucial factor in the knowledge transfer process. For example, in a study of three German regions, Fritsch & Schwirten (1999) found that geographic proximity constitutes a clear advantage for establishing or maintaining cooperative relationships, and that a disproportionate share of I-U cooperation partners come from within the same region. Our own sample of 12 companies fully confirms a strong focus on proximity to the university collaboration partner. In fact, most companies in our survey limit their main academic interaction to those universities that can be reached within two hours of travelling.

The six steps outlined above may seem rather self-evident. Let us now, however, attempt to fame them into a more general scheme for positive learning enforcement, see Figure 1.

The model is based on our strong conviction that there is a need to have a purposeful network when it comes to a firm/university learning relationship. The proposed purposeful network can have four different distinctive roles/ tasks, with interaction along all six management dimensions. The key is that this network encompasses both the firm and the academic institution together, as if they were one entity! Only by having cooperative activities involving all positional aspects — including also interaction along each of the

---

2 Beise & Stahl (1999); Fritsch & Schwirten (1999); Katz & Martin (1997); Lindelöf & Löfsten (2004); Mansfield & Lee (1996); Santoro & Gopalakrishnan (2001); Schartinger et al. (2001).

Figure 1: Research and Teaching: A positive reinforcement Cycle

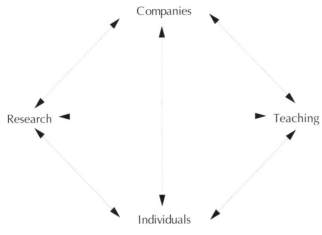

six dimensions, will there be full benefits from the cooperation. Speed of inter-action will of course be key also. The appropriate formation process is there-fore critical — with the right people focusing on appropriate tasks. And, clear delineation of resource — and time-line budgets must be behind it.

TWO EMERGING COOPERATIVE OPTIONS

Based on our case study analysis, we distinguish two basic options for cooper-ation between business firms and academic institutions — and both seem to be workable! One is what we shall call *The In-Sourced Model*. An example of this, to be discussed, is Porsche (Harryson & Lorange, 2005). The other is what we shall call *The Spin-Off Model* and exemplify through a brief case on Bang & Olufsen.

The In-Sourced Porsche Model

Porsche's in-sourced model seems primarily to be driven by cost-efficiency considerations, but also with a clear view of achieving even more creative technical approaches. The approximately 2,000 internal engineers at Porsche are augmented by about 600 Master students, who are temporarily "insourced" each year. On average each of these students is dedicated for 4-6 months to very specialized research tasks. Indeed, many of the tasks are so focused and narrowly defined that it would be hard to motivate an employee to do them. How about devoting six months to searching for new raw material sources for magnesium? Would an employee have embraced this task with such passion that the possibility of buying old submarines from Russia would have been identified? The main benefits might be: on the cost, eight Master students cost approximately as much as one engineer! Clearly a lot more can thus be achieved, even though the student can never be substituted for good, permanently employed engineers! On the focus side, this is typically driven by the high speed and motivation by the students. It is seen as a great honour to be recruited to Porsche. To be a member of this prestigious high-technology group induces extraordinary inspirational efforts!

There are also negatives, of course: the major one seems to be the potential risk of leakage, particularly when the Master students leave Porsche. It is hard to avoid this, even though Porsche is putting a lot of effort into creating solutions and approaches that are broader than what individual students would work on, i.e. "black boxes". Much in contrast to what we seem to find at Porsche, most peer car manufacturers have developed a strong internal infrastructure, and employed resources that typically cover most or the whole range of R & D process. Porsche, on the other hand, employs only a small group of specialists in the research area, who seem to be given broader freedom to cooperate with individual external providers of expertise — other industrial companies to some extent, but even more with academic institutions. They clearly seem more open to going outside, sometimes in unconventional ways, whenever they require additional brainpower and new solutions. Porsche seems to build more of a broad collaborative network among professionals and academics than the more typical company-to-company research project cooperation one tends to find in the traditional automotive industry.

To make this work, the selected candidates tend to be fully based within the Porsche premises throughout the duration of the collaboration. We observe that they typically work hard — often spending 60 or more hours per week on the assignment! Half the students typically write their master theses in close collaboration with the R & D department staff, who thus act as coaches, also for the academic part of their thesis work. The other half of the 600 students also perform a highly focused R & D task, but without writing their thesis in parallel. From Porsche's viewpoint this helps create a certain degree of protection — the company maintains the overall focus, while each thesis is focused on the specifics. Accordingly, Porsche currently "produces" around 300 diploma theses per year in their R & D department. Non-disclosure considerations can be relatively easily handled when it comes to the specific themes of diploma projects and/or Master's theses. In contrast, this is harder when it comes to Ph.D. theses — they tend to be broader! Porsche thus "has" less than 10 Ph.D. theses per year! Intellectual property rights and non-disclosure aspects are thus the main reasons for not cooperating to the same extent with Ph.D. students. Above all, it is typically harder for Porsche to create a "black box" protection when it comes to the broader Ph.D. theses, which typically cannot be phrased to focus on their specific issue — as is the case for the Masters theses. In this latter case it is Porsche that keeps the overall integrative view!

The Bang & Olufsen Spin-off Model, driven by innovation flexibility

The spin-off model is adapted by several firms including Bang & Olufsen. It seems to be primarily driven by striving towards more innovation flexibility. Bang & Olufsen, headquartered in Struer, Denmark, has spun off a separate organizational R & D unit — located in Copenhagen (which is also close to the university-city of Lund). There are 35 internal employees, as well as 25 Masters — and Ph.D. students from universities working as fully co-located "temporary unpaid employees" in this unit. The benefits primarily seem to be again, in part on the cost side — relatively low or even no salary to the students. Regarding the scope of innovations, however, it is interesting to see that the students explore ideas that might have been killed if they have been part of the internal R & D, above all due to internal risk resource considerations. In line with this, B & O has also become known for establishing a new breakthrough standard through proactive teaching at selected universities, bringing the research "back to the classroom" at the cooperative institutions.

Here too, of course, there are negatives. Students who do not join the company will walk away with a lot of valuable knowledge at the end of the thesis project. However, B & O is highly proficient at patent-protecting the knowledge as soon as it starts to get business-relevant. However, due to the new patent legislation in Denmark, patent results generated by Ph.D. students in Denmark will now belong to the university partner. As a consequence, B & O has been forced to limit its collaboration to the Bachelor and Master levels in Denmark. In Sweden, these "new" IPR regulations seem to be less restrictive, at least for now. In the longer run some countries may gain an advantage due to less restrictive IPR rules, when it comes to providing a basis for graduate students — having a context for more cooperative R & D networks. Sweden and Finland still seem to fall into this category. This would be important for the present cooperative model to work, since the "black box" protection of the firm will be largely based on owning the IPRs that emerge out of the collaboration.

In the case of B & O, hence, it holds the rights to the patent results (IPRs) — perhaps above all to secure its own stream of recurring royalties. But, as partly attended to, due to the new patent result rules in Denmark which were issued in 2000, universities have became more aggressive in pursuing their own patent strategies. Thus, employees of Danish university now have to file their patents at the university, and that university will own the patent. If the university is not interested in commercializing the patent, then the student might be free to start a business, but the university will even then get one third of the company stock for free.

As a consequence of this, B & O is now looking more proactively for university partners in countries with less rigid legal constraints, such as Sweden, which is only a few miles away right across the bridge!

SOME TENTATIVE CONCLUSIONS REGARDING INDUSTRY-UNIVERSITY COLLABORATION

The perhaps most cited challenge of I-U collaboration is that scientific knowledge produced by companies is short- and medium-term oriented, aiming at appropriating research results as much as possible, whereas the strength of public research is claimed to prevail in basic research, providing important new theoretical findings with high spillovers, but seldom coming up with specific inventions or products ready for commercialization. Our empirical research is revealing how two emerging management models help to bridge the time and appropriability gap.

The two models also represent excellent recruiting mechanisms. The companies get a chance to "test" out the graduate candidates before they might get actually hired — often exposed to situations of "intensive stress" to perform extremely focused tasks that would be hard to motivate internal employees to do.

Limiting Scanning to Existing Social Networks: Our empirical research largely confirms previous findings that scanning is primarily based on existing personal contacts between companies and research institution employees, sometimes complemented by temporary search initiatives and conferences and fairs.

Most of our case-companies rely on their existing network of trusted colleagues as a human search-tool to scan for new collaboration partners. We also find that our case companies rarely look for a new university as such, but rather for the actual researchers within an already selected university or institute to reach the required expertise.

Screening – Reversing the Benefit of Being a Star: The literature review suggested that, especially in the U.S., companies are limiting their collaboration to second-tier universities as these are claimed to be more prone to focus immediately on industry problems than highly ranked universities are. It is also quite intuitive that the status of being a scientific "star" reduces the need and incentive to commute outside the region in which the scientist is located and thereby also reduces the degree of collaborative links with industry. Indeed, most of our benchmarking partners view high numbers of patents and publications of a professor more as a reason to avoid collaboration than the opposite. Perhaps the most critical screening criterion can be summarized by the term "reliationshipability" — or, the ability and natural willingness to participate in a collaborative network. Relationshipability is critical for partners to rapidly understand the company needs — ideally based on prior experience in industry cooperations.

Knowledge Transfer Only Through Co-Location: Most literature argues that proper involvement for knowledge transfer requires a joint laboratory operating on a clear framework agreement with complementary research relationships. A method with similar effect is the temporary secondment of university-based researchers to industry — ideally involving joint supervision of Ph.D. and Master theses. Another critical mechanism is a reward system for faculty involvement in technology transfer — issued as clear compensation and staffing practices by the technology transfer office of the university in question, or paid directly by the sponsoring company.

Our empirical cases highlight the importance of having a clearly dedicated knowledge "receiver" with a strong personal reason and interest to obtain and integrate the knowledge by bridging the two worlds of science and practice.

Steering Through Co-Location or Financial Incentives: The obvious advice from literature is to establish a high degree of engagement and trust through frequent face-to-face communication and on-site demonstrations. Gambro illustrates in several ways that the steering of "external" Ph.D. projects may sometimes be quite challenging — in particular if the Ph.D. student is not based in the corporate-lab. In such situations, close and frequent interaction with the researchers who actually do the work is required. Relying on the Professor of Liaison Officer rarely guarantees good steering. Rather, it seems essential to have a transparent university team structure to clearly see who is doing what and have direct contact with the knowledge contributors. It is also important to keep the areas of investigation well defined in an area of specialization that is fully mastered and understood by the selected institute or specialist.

Personal financial incentives as steering mechanisms to get the desired results were as rare in the Nordic countries as they were common in Central Europe. This mechanism may spread more widely in years to come. It is also reasonable to assume a continued focus on exclusive collaborations — away from multi-member projects, or consortia research.

Destructive IPR Laws: Collaboration with Ph.D. students seems to be problematic in many countries. This includes issues in IP ownership; the difficulty in keeping the thesis confidential; and longer lead-times from problem-definition to completion of the results. However, in some increasingly rare exceptions, such as Sweden and Finland, it is still possible for companies to work with Ph.D. students while maintaining full ownership of the IPR.

It also seems to be an important learning-point that I-U collaborations do not yet tend to be globalized. These seem to work well in geographically close co-locations, enriching both for the companies (financially) and for the students (intellectually). Above all, this seems to be an impressive innovation choice.

Let us now conclude with one major point of concern. We know that for creativity to thrive we cannot apply too strict mechanisms of control. However, much literature and many observations in practice relate to steering and control. Are we possibly in danger of strangling the dog by pulling too hard? Can we identify further approaches and models to strike a better balance between exploration and exploitation? Clearly, more research is required in this exciting area!

REFERENCES

Audretsch, D.B. & Stephan, P.E. (1996). "Company-Scientist Locational Links: The Case of Biotechnology", *The American Economic Review*, 86(3), pp. 641-652.

Beise, M. & Stahl, H. (1999). "Public Research and Industrial Innovation in Germany", *Research Policy*, 28, pp. 397-422.

Bloedon, R.V. & Stokes, D.R. (1994). "Making University/Industry Collaborative Research Succeed", *Research Technology Management*, 37(2), pp. 44-48.

Burnham, J.B. (1997). "Evaluating Industry/University Research Linkages", *Research Technology Management*, 40(1), pp. 52-55.

Davenport, S., Davies, J. & Grimes, Ch. (1999). "Collaborative Research Programmes: Building Trust from Difference", *Technovation*, 19, pp. 31-40

Davenport, T.H. & Prusak, L. (1998). *Working Knowledge. How Organizations Manage What They Know*, Harvard Business School Press, Boston.

Friedman, J. & Silberman, J. (2003). "University Technology Transfer: Do Incentives, Management and Location Matter?" *Journal of Technology Transfer*, 28, pp. 17-30.

Fritsch, M. & Schwirten, Ch. (1999). "Enterprise-University Co-Operation and the Role of Public Research Institutions in Regional Innovation Systems", *Industry and Innovation*, 6(1), pp. 69-83.

Goldfarb, B. & Henrekson, M. (2003). "Bottom-up Versus Top-down Policies toward the Commercialization of University Intellectual Property", *Research Policy*, 32, pp. 639-658.

Harabi, N. (1995). "Appropriability of Technical Innovations", Research Policy, 24, pp. 981-992

Harryson, S. (forthcoming 2006). *Know-Who Based Entrepreneurship: From Knowledge Creation to Business Implementation*, Edward Elgar Publishing, Cheltenham, U.K.

Harryson, S. & Lorange, P. (2005). "Bringing the College Inside", *Harvard Business Review*, December 2005.

Katz, J.S. & Martin, B.T. (1997). "What is Research Collaboration?", *Research Policy*, 26, pp. 1-18.

Kogut, B. & Zander, U. (1992). "Knowledge of the Firm, Combinative Capabilities, and the Replication of Technology", *Organization Science*, 3, pp. 383-397.

Leonard-Barton, D. (1995). *Wellsprings of Knowledge: Building and Sustaining the Sources of Innovation*, Harvard Business School Press, Boston, MA.

Lindelöf, P. & Löfsten, H. (2004). "Proximity as a Resource Base for a Competitive Advantage: University — Industry Links for Technology Transfer", *Journal of Technology Transfer*, 29, pp. 311-326.

Lorange, P. (2002). *New Vision for Management Education: Leadership Challenges*, Elsevier.

Mansfield, E. & Lee, J.-Y. (1996). "The Modern University: Contributor to Industrial Innovation and Recipient of Industrial R & D Support", *Research Policy*, 25, pp. 1047-1058.

Nonaka, I. (1994). "A Dynamic Theory of Organizational Knowledge Creation", *Organization Science*, vol. 5, no. 1, February, pp. 14–37.

Nonaka, I. & Reinmoeller, P. (2002). "Knowledge Creation and Utilization: Promoting Systems of Creative Routines", in Hitt, M.A., Amit, R., Lucier, Ch.E. & Nixon, R.D. (Eds.) *Creating Value Winners in the New Business Environment*, Blackwell Publishers, New York.

Owen-Smith, J. & Powell, W.W. (2003). "The Expanding Role of University Patenting in the Life Sciences: Assessing the Importance of Experience and Connectivity", *Research Policy*, 32, pp. 1695-1711.

Rappert, B., Webster, A. & Charles, D. (1999). "Making Sense of Diversity: Academic-Industrial Relations and Intellectual Property", *Research Policy*, 28, pp. 873-890.

Rogers, E.M., Carayannis, E.G., Kurihara, K. & Allbritton, M.M. (1998). "Cooperative Research and Development Agreements (CRADAs) as Technology Transfer Mechanisms", *R & D Management*, 28 (2), pp. 79-88.

Santoro, M.D. & Chakrabarti, A.K. (1999). "Building Industry-University Research Centers: Some Strategic Considerations", *International Journal of Management Reviews*, 3 (3), pp. 225-244.

Santoro, M.D. & Gopalakrishnan, S. (2001). "Relationship Dynamics between University Research Centers and Industrial Firms: Their Impact on Technology Transfer Activities", *Journal of Technology Transfer*, 26, pp. 163-171.

Schartinger, D., Rammer, Ch., Fischer, M.M. & Frohlich, J. (2002). "Knowledge Interactions between Universities and Industry in Austria: Sectoral Patterns and Determinants", *Research Policy*, 31, pp. 303-328.

Schartinger, D., Schibany, A. & Gassler, H. (2001) "Interactive Relations between Universities and Firms: Empirical Evidence for Austria", *Journal of Technology Transfer*, 26, pp. 255-268.

Schmoch, U., (1999). "Interaction of Universities and Industrial Enterprises in Germany and the United States — a Comparison", *Industry and Innovation*, 6(1), pp. 51-68.

Siegel, D.S., Waldman, D. & Link, A. (2003). "Assessing the Impact of Organizational Practices on the Relative Productivity of University Technology Transfer Offices: an Exploratory Study", *Research Policy*, 32, pp. 27-48.

Thursby, J.G. & Kemp, S. (2002). "Growth and Productive Efficiency of University Intellectual Property Licensing", *Research Policy*, 31, pp. 109-124.

Thursby, J.G., Jensen, R. & Thursby, M.C. (2001). "Objectives, Characteristics and Outcomes of University Licensing: a Survey of Major U.S. Universities", *Journal of Technology Transfer*, 26, pp. 59-72.

Von Krogh, G., Ichijo, K. & Nonaka, I. (2000). *Enabling Knowledge Creation: How to Unlock the Mystery of Tacit Knowledge and Release the Power of Innovation*, New York, Oxford University Press.

Wen, J. & Kobayashi, S. (2001). "Exploring Collaborative R & D Network: Some New Evidence in Japan", *Research Policy*, 30, pp. 1309-1319.

Zander, U. & Kogut, B. (1995). "Knowledge and Speed of the Transfer and Imitation of Organizational Capabilities: An Empirical Test", *Organization Science*, vol. 6, no. 1, pp. 76-92.

CHAPTER 13

Best practice in Business-University Collaboration

Richard Lambert

Academics and business people are not natural bedfellows. They talk in different languages. They work to different timetables, and are driven by different incentives. Whereas business people are primarily held to account by a single group of stakeholders — the owners of their firm — academics are accountable to a much wider range of interest groups — including their colleagues and students, the institutions for which they work, and the providers of their funding.

Developing constructive relationships between such disparate groups of people is a challenging exercise. And yet efforts to build business-university collaborations are gathering momentum throughout the developed world, and for obvious reasons.

Governments everywhere are putting universities at the centre of their economic development strategies. As global competition intensifies, it is becoming increasingly clear that future economic growth will rely on knowledge-intensive industries, and that university teaching and research have a crucial part to play in this process. The obvious model is the U.S., where the innovative application of new scientific knowledge has been the key to economic success for at least the last quarter century. As the nation's principal source of basic scientific research, universities have made a substantial contribution to this competitive advantage (National Academy of Engineering, 2003).

At the same time, the nature of innovation and business research is changing in a way that gives a much more prominent role to university research departments. Businesses everywhere are cutting back their big corporate laboratories and seeking to build research partnerships with talented outsiders. And breakthroughs in new products and services are com-

161

ing increasingly from inter-disciplinary research — computer scientists, say, working alongside biologists — as opposed to the narrower focus of a traditional corporate laboratory. These trends favour universities, which are by definition multi-disciplined in character, and which are constantly being refreshed with new brains. As businesses cut back, a growing proportion of fundamental research is flowing from universities (Chesbrough, 2003).

There are now enough examples of good, and bad, practice in business-university collaborations to be able to draw some general conclusions about the ingredients of success. There are three main groups of participants in the process, and it is worth examining each of them in turn.

REGIONAL AND NATIONAL GOVERNMENTS

Governments have several important incentives for helping to build bridges between the higher education sector and the world of business.

- They want to push their economies up the value chain and build a competitive advantage in knowledge-intensive industries. High quality teaching in a wide range of disciples at university level is an essential ingredient of this process.
- They want to maximize the return on the public funding of research. In Europe, German, British and French universities have high quality research outputs, but a poor record of translating this achievement into commercial success. Governments in all three countries see this as a problem that needs to be addressed.
- They want to attract and retain research-intensive multinational businesses at a time when business research is going global. Big companies are increasingly locating their research centres in their most important markets, especially if those markets happen to contain centres of outstanding research. Their home country is no longer the automatic first choice for this investment, and with the help of its strong university-based research the U.S. is taking an increasing share of the world's investment in business research and development.

Nowhere are these challenges more important than in Europe. Its businesses are much less research-intensive than is the case in the U.S. or Japan in 2002, business financed 56% of domestic R & D spending in the E.U., compared to 63% in the U.S. and 74% in Japan.

This means that universities *have* to play a large role in the E.U.'s research and innovation effort. They employ more than a third of all researchers in Europe, and in countries like Spain or Greece the proportion is very much higher even than this.

Europe also has an urgent need to raise the quality and breadth of its human capital. Only about a quarter of young people aged between 18 and 24 were enrolled in higher education in the E.U.25 in 2002, compared with nearly two fifths in the U.S. (OECD, 2005).

Governments can support business-university collaboration in a number of important ways.

The first is by creating the conditions in which universities can cooperate with outside partners. This means giving them the authority to take on a rather more entrepreneurial role than has been traditional, in order that they can themselves work with entrepreneurs. They need enough autonomy to build areas of comparative strength and to form strategic partnerships. And improved systems of governance are necessary for the university to handle complex relationships with outside partners (Clark, 1998).

Among other things, universities need much more sophisticated financial management than most have been used to in the past if they are to make sensible decisions about collaboration. An institution that cannot produce a clear statement of its annual revenues and costs is in no position to negotiate terms for contract research. Indeed the reality is that a great deal of such work, especially in Europe, has been poorly costed and has subsidised business research at the institution's expense.

The second key support provided by the state comes in the provision of funding for high quality teaching and research. Much the most important form of knowledge transfer from the campus to commerce comes in the form of well-educated students completing their studies and moving into the work place. And universities are accounting for an increasing proportion of fundamental research as businesses cut back on their in-house laboratories.

There is a very wide range in investment per student among OECD members. Top of the list come Switzerland and the U.S., with annual spending of $20,000 or more. At the other end of the table are countries like Italy, Spain and the E.U. accession countries, with well under $9,000 per student. They will find it increasingly difficult to hold their own in what has become a globally competitive marketplace for research (OECD, 2005).

As well as providing funds for teaching and research, governments also need to create financial incentives for collaboration. For example, most now provide some form of R & D tax credit, but these are not always made available to collaborative research programmes. It is important to have in place a clear and consistent policy covering the management and ownership of intellectual property. Denmark, Germany and France all brought in legislation in the late 1990s to allow institutions to claim ownership of IP created by their researchers.

Governments need to make sure that public funding for collaborative research is available on the same basis as money that is provided for work which is driven entirely by academic curiosity. In the U.K., research funding is allocated on the basis of peer review, which finds it easier to recognise excellence when it takes the form of academic citations as opposed to commercial success. The intention is to correct this anti-business bias in future reviews, but it will be a challenging task (Lambert, 2003).

The higher education systems that are likely to be the most successful in collaborating with business are those that contain a diverse range of institutions. The type of business collaboration that would make sense for one kind of university might be either impossible or irrelevant for another — for example, a less research-intensive institution can play an extraordinarily valuable role in working with local business in a way that might make no sense to one of the big research universities.

Moreover, proximity matters when it comes to business collaboration, especially for small and medium-sized enterprises. Informal networks cannot easily be sustained over long distances, and even large companies often find it more efficient to work with research departments in their own locality. Successful large economies need to contain both world-class research universities and a strong spread of regional institutions. This helps to explain why Germany is now determined to create a number of elite research-intensive universities to complement its strength in regional institutions.

The fifth area in which government support makes an important difference lies in building the infrastructure needed to support successful collaboration. Examples include the establishment of technology transfer offices and corporate liaison offices on the campus; the provision of seed funding to support pre-competitive research or early stage spin-out activities; or the provision of subsidies for students to spend time in industry.

Universities do not usually have the funds available to initiate such programmes. And businesses find it hard to justify investments which may not bring direct benefits to their shareholders. This is the kind of market failure that merits modest public funding, and such support is available in one form or another in many developed economies.

The U.K. is probably the example of best practice in this respect. The government introduced a specific stream of funding to support knowledge transfer in the university sector in 1999, and this money has now been consolidated into a permanent source of finance allocated on a competitive basis and approaching £100 million a year. The result is that successful entrepreneurial universities can plan ahead rather than having to adjust their knowledge transfer activities to match short-term funding incentives. This so called "third stream" funding (coming on top of funding for teaching and research) has contributed to a significant culture change on U.K. campuses over recent years, and has given academics real incentives to reach out to commercial partners.

Another obvious way in which governments can help or hinder collaborative efforts lies in the way they set targets for this kind of activity. One example of a perverse target: government ministers in a number of countries, including Japan and the U.K., have from time to time suggested that success can be measured by the number of spin-out companies created by university departments. But whereas establishing a spin-out is a simple process, sustaining such a business over time is a very different exercise. As a result, public funding has been wasted by too much effort being devoted to this particular activity.

The main role of universities is to create and distribute knowledge and they do not exist for the convenience of the corporate sector. But wise government policy-making can help to channel commercially relevant knowledge into the marketplace, to the benefit both of the university system and the national economy.

UNIVERSITIES

Universities must be clear about their motives for collaborating with business. Unless they are very lucky, such partnerships are not going to provide them with the resources that most of them so badly need to support their existing activities. The experience of the U.S., which is longer than that of other countries, demonstrates that technology transfer is not usually a large revenue earner. A number of U.S. universities started out with that aim, but found it impossible to make significant amounts of money and so changed their objectives. MIT, Stanford and Yale all now state that their main aim in pursuing commercial activities is the public good — they want to create the greatest possible economic and social benefits from their work, whether they accrue to the university or not (Bok, 2003).

This is an entirely proper approach. Public funding for university research is intended to create a public good, rather than to make universities rich. The public interest lies in the results of university work being widely distributed, rather than being used to maximize the economic returns for the exclusive benefit of the institution.

Of course this is not to say that collaboration does not bring economic returns. Working with outside partners may allow an institution to cover some of the overheads of a research laboratory. It may well give academics access to equipment that could not otherwise be afforded. Consultancy arrangements can provide a badly needed supplement to academic salaries. And from time to time, a licensing arrangement or a successful spin-out may bring a valuable boost to the university's income.

But there are other potential benefits for the university. There is an intellectual pleasure to be derived when ideas are translated into commercial activity. Some academics have distinct entrepreneurial flair, and enjoy the idea of commercial engagement. Companies like Du Pont and Rolls-Royce have demonstrated the ways in which academic and business researchers can work alongside each other over a period of time, to their mutual benefit.

Moreover rapid expansion in student numbers across the developed world over the past 30 years means that universities have for the first time become important economic entities in their own right. They are among the major wealth creators in many European cities, and they are by far the biggest employer of researchers in a good number of European regions. Universities lie at the centre of most of the successful business clusters around the world. For all these reasons, they have a much clearer role to play in economic life than in the days when most of them were nothing more than small communities of scholars.

Successful entrepreneurial universities have the following characteristics. They have sound and well established systems of governance. As universities become more involved in commercial activities of one kind or another, they have to develop clearer ideas of their mission and firmer rules for dealing with potential conflicts of interest. They need to build new kinds of relationships, and have a highly proficient approach in areas like financial control and human relations (Clark, 2004).

How much time are they prepared to let their academics spend on commercial activities? What are the rules for publishing collaborative research results? How far, if at all, are they prepared to let commercial sponsors shape their research programmes?

The U.S. provides examples of both the best and the worst practices in these sensitive areas. U.S. universities tend to be much more precise than their European counterparts about how academics can allocate their time. For example, MIT's faculty employment contract only covers nine months of the year: the rest of the time can be filled by consultancy work.

European universities, by contrast, tend to turn a blind eye to outside consultancies, regarding such activities as a useful supplement to often inadequate wages. This approach ignores the potential conflicts of interest that can tempt academics to spend a disproportionate amount of their time on commercial work.

But there are also well documented cases of governance failures in the U.S. — for example, where commercial sponsors have sought to suppress research that reflects badly on their products, or where universities have allowed the shape of their research activities to be distorted by commercial demands. These represent serious reputational risks, which university leaders have to recognize (Washburn, 2005).

Successful entrepreneurial universities have invariably set up systems to help businesses find their way around the campus. Business liaison offices are established to act as the interface with the corporate sector: their job is to market the research strengths of the university; to develop business networks; to advise on consultancy arrangements; and to help arrange collaborate agreements and other joint ventures.

There is no single model for such offices. Some take in technology transfer activities, while other universities have established specialised companies to manage technology transfer.

But experience shows that at least three qualities are essential for success in this area.

- First, corporate liaison and technology transfer offices need trained staff with commercial experience. Such people are hard to find and to retain. This is why it usually makes sense to set up separate companies to manage these activities, not least to get away from academic pay structures and incentives.
- Second, the university needs to have an agreed and clearly understood approach to the management and ownership of its intellectual property. Disagreements about IP are the biggest single stumbling block in commercial collaboration, and lack of clarity about who owns what is the main explanation. In the past, German academics built their own relationships with industry: recent legislation means that their IP is now shared with their institution which — once the new system is properly established — should encourage stronger and longer lasting partnerships.
- Third and most critical, academics must have trust in the competence and effectiveness of their university's technology transfer arrangements. Otherwise they will not cooperate with the university authorities, whatever the rules may say. Examples of best practice in this respect include Oxford, Stanford and MIT.

Innovation processes are complex and non-linear. It is important to understand that the best ideas and the great product breakthroughs emerge out of all kinds of feedback loops, development activities and sheer chance. And inter-disciplinary research is becoming increasingly important — with social scientists, for example, making an increasingly important contribution to information technology.

So the most successful entrepreneurial universities are those which succeed in building dynamic networks both among their own academic researchers and with their business counterparts. If you walk around the campus of universities like Loughborough, Monash, or Twente you will often come across groups of like-minded people from different backgrounds discussing common problems — and sometimes coming up with innovative solutions. Some of these networks are formal, others are completely casual — where, for example, alumni have have built lasting relationships with their former teachers and colleagues.

Universities' relationships with business will depend on their location, mission and size. But networks that go across disciplines and functions are an essential ingredient of success in all cases.

BUSINESS

There are six related ways in which businesses around the world have gained competitive advantage from working with universities.

- Access to new ideas of all kinds. The best academic researchers are in touch with knowledge breakthroughs in their area of activity wherever they may be happening in the world.
- The ability to tap into a wider range of disciplines and a much larger intellectual gene pool than even the biggest company could possibly create on its own.
- The ability to overage the research dollar by working in partnership with institutions that have access to public funding.
- The opportunity to identify and recruit the brightest young talent.
- The ability to expand pre-competitive research. By working with universities, businesses can widen the range of their research horizons and spread the risk.
- Access to specialised consultancy (Lambert, 2003).

Not surprisingly, the evidence suggests that companies which use universities and other higher education institutions as a source of information or a partner tend to be significantly more successful than those that do not.

However, a good number of business-university collaborations fail to meet their objectives. Half the companies responding to a U.K. survey said they had difficulties in managing the relationships with academe (The Confederation of British Industry, 2003), and for their part universities complain about the problems that can arise from frequent changes in corporate strategies, or from personality changes in the boardroom. These collaborations require careful and consistent management by both sides: without that, they will fail.

Experience shows that it is critically important to get the relationships right from the very beginning. A whole range of questions has to be answered, including:

- What are the arrangements for the ownership and control of the resulting IP?
- What are the academics' publication rights?
- How important is exclusivity to the business sponsor?

- Who are the key individuals with responsibility for success on each side, and how will they work with each other?
- How will the recruitment process work?
- What are the financial and time commitments of both sides, and how will they be spread over the life of the project?
- What are the mutually understood definitions of success in this project? How can these be reviewed over time as the work moves forward?
- What are the appropriate milestones against which progress can best be measured?
- How much access will the business partner have to the campus?
- Remembering that proximity matters in building these relationships, how are the partners distributed geographically?

Once the initial agreements have been signed, the collaboration will need careful management and continued commitment from both parties if it is to succeed over time.

An increasing number of large multinationals are concentrating their collaborative efforts on a small number of research led universities around the world: examples include BP and Schlumberger. Advantages of this approach include the opportunity to relate to the university at many different levels, so that collaboration does not rest entirely on a small number of individuals. If things go wrong, it is much easier to resolve the problem if the partnership is broadly based. There are also real advantages in establishing a continuous relationship, in order to develop a shared sense of purpose and of trust.

For example, Rolls-Royce has established a number of University Technology Centres in the U.K. and elsewhere, each dealing with a specific piece of engine technology. The university researchers benefit from long-term funding, and from working alongside corporate researchers on practical challenges. These strategic partnerships encourage long-term working relationships and trust and, the company says, have proved to be substantially more effective than its previous approach of more ad-hoc relationships with academia.

Small and medium-sized companies are more likely to work alongside university departments located close to their plant, but the ingredients for success are much the same as with large multinationals. They include a strong and shared sense of purpose, a common strategic vision and detailed planning from the beginning. Each side must feel that the other is making a genuine contribution to the collaboration, and researchers need to get together often enough to discuss problems and establish trust.

Business-university collaborations are difficult to initiate and to sustain. But there are now enough examples of best practice around the world to show the ways in which governments, universities and businesses can work together to their mutual benefit.

REFERENCES

Bok, D. (2003), *Universities in the Marketplace*, Princeton University Press.

The Confederation of British Industry (CBI), 2003. London.

Chesbrough, Henry. (2003). *Open Innovation*, Harvard Business School Press, Cambridge, MA.

Clark, B. R. (1998). *Creating Entrepreneurial Universities: Organisational Pathways of Transformation*, Pergamon/Elseveier Science, Oxford.

Clark, B. R. (2004). *Sustaining Change in Universities*, Society for Research into Higher Education and Open University Press, London.

Lambert, R. (2003). *Lambert Review of Business-University Collaboration*. HM Treasury, London.

National Academy of Engineering. (2003). *The Impact of Academic Research on Industrial Performance*, Washington D.C.

OECD. (2005). *Education at a Glance*. OECD, Paris.

Washburn, J. (2005). University, Inc. *The Corporate Corruption of Higher Education*. Basic Books, New York.

CHAPTER 14

Obstacles to University-Industry Relations

Horst Soboll

THE MISSION OF UNIVERSITIES

The future of our universities — the traditional higher education institutions — is often subject of discussion and careful analysis, as can be seen at the fourth Glion Colloquium 2003, "Reinventing the Research University" (Weber & Duderstadt, 2004).

It seems to be widely agreed that there are three main activities that universities on all continents — with varying emphasis between them — are engaged in. These three fields are:

- I education;
- II research;
- III service to society.

These three goals — in this particular order — certainly reflect the expectation that industry has of modern universities.

Back in medieval times, the first universities were established to distribute knowledge and to educate students, and even today this continues to be the main task of a university from an industry perspective — to prepare students for a career as professionals in the various areas of economy and society.

Only in the following centuries was an additional function, which we know as research, established. It is seen as the basis for the development of science and technology, which have progressed impressively since then and are influencing our lives and our society today more than ever.

The universities' task of research continues to grow in importance today as more and more enterprises — even the large multinational high-tech companies — cannot afford to rely on their own research activities alone anymore in order to create innovative products and services — as many of them used to do in the past (e.g. SIEMENS, DAIMLER, IBM etc.). Today the creation of a successful network of cooperating research partners from industry and academia is considered a prerequisite for a future-oriented, innovative company.

The third role of the "university of the future" — service to society — is the most recent one.

It may be of a purely economic nature and aid the development of a region, as seen in Silicon Valley. It may include supporting governments in the role of "neutral advisors", providing the subject-matter knowledge needed to make informed political decisions. It will almost certainly involve educating the public and the media about the benefits of modern technology and the impact of scientific results on society.

In all three core activities the relationship between university and industry is an important element. Now, what are the current obstacles to those relations between universities and industry? How can the interactions between players as different as a university and an industrial enterprise be improved?

Obviously, there is no single simple recipe that will solve all problems in a community as heterogeneous as modern universities. Besides, there are outside factors to consider, like the significant influence that regional and state governments still have on the majority of universities.

Some recommendations applicable to some institutes don't work for others. However, some of the following issues — ranked by priority — are seen as relevant to a wider range of universities.

INTELLECTUAL PROPERTY RIGHTS

If asked to name the most pressing obstacle in the relationship with universities, industry representatives will mention most frequently the area of intellectual property rights (IPR). This applies to both sides of the Atlantic Ocean and for small and large companies alike.

Especially in recent years of reduced university budgets, government or university officials realized that some universities manage to gain significant income through the licensing of technology to companies. As a consequence, more and more universities are being urged to strengthen their efforts to produce licensing fees when transferring research results to companies.

But this analysis overlooks the fact that patents play a completely different role in industry than they do in the world of the university. They serve as a protection of industrial investment in R & D, in one case, and as a potential new revenue stream, in the other case, developed by newly gained knowledge from the universities.

Patent applications — first they cost a lot of money and it takes a long time to get a break even if patents are considered to be an additional financial source for universities.

Looking at some known examples of where significant income could be made through licensing, it is hard to imagine that those very few can be generalized and applied to other universities. In most cases these licences were generated in a very specific small sector — like life science — and are based on a unique time window constellation or a specific situation hardly duplicable.

As a consequence of a new IPR policy, many technology transfer centres are now established at universities, or at least the IPR activities of a university are centrally run by a professional patent unit. Their first objective is often seen to be earning money and to finance themselves, rather than to encourage university-industry cooperation per se.

Therefore, negotiations between industry and their cooperation partners at university institutes are now often delayed and complicated through the involvement of those services resulting in less productive research collaborations with industry.

It is an interesting fact that in the U.S. the Bayh-Dole Act has the unintended consequence that U.S. industry now is often approaching non-U.S. universities for collaborations due to faster and simpler IPR negotiations with them compared to their U.S. counterparts.

In this decade of globalisation and modern communication technology, industry is free to collaborate with any university worldwide, rather than being limited to just the regional contenders.

Industry's IPR principle is clear: if a company has paid for 100% of a specific piece of knowledge generation, they want all the results and IPR for their own use. It is their view that they have paid for the infrastructure already with their taxes. Also any pre-existing background knowledge of the institute is seen merely as a selection criterion when choosing one university over another.

If both partners, university and industry, jointly participate in publicly funded research programmes, or if the industry partner pays only part of the research activity, then the IPR of any knowledge generated may be owned by both depending on the individual shares.

The universities' IPR activities described above are often considered to be based on some misunderstandings in the IPR area and are seen as main obstacles in the cooperation. But they should always be seen in the broader perspective of the overall goal of cooperation rather than trying to maximize IPR at the expense of further cooperation.

If both parties — universities and companies — try to understand each other better and mutually agree on the overall goal to strengthen research collaboration as a whole, a major obstacle to relations between the two will be reduced.

COOPERATION CULTURE

On the whole, the **cooperation culture** as a basis of university-industry relations has improved significantly over the last years.

Nevertheless in certain sectors and in certain countries, close cooperation of a university scientist with industry — perhaps based on a strategic cooperation agreement — is sometimes suspected to undermine their scientific reputation and as a consequence they might avoid such cooperation altogether.

The goal instead is an open situation, as exists in some of the top-ranking U.S. universities. There signing a strategic agreement with industry and researching for the Nobel prize run in parallel, and both are based on scientific activity. **Both activities are fully accepted** and seen as complementary activities undertaken in the same institute.

Some private universities in Europe have already successfully reorganized their research activity by aligning it with the research strategies and the needs of their industrial partners.

This is not in contradiction to conducting cutting-edge research and excelling in basic science if the university institute treats the industrial strategy merely as additional input only in order to broaden their research portfolio, and if they keep full freedom and responsibility in directing and orienting their own independent university research.

In addition there may be **special incentives** needed to strengthen the research collaboration, depending on the specific level of a particular nation's innovation system.

For instance the Federation of German Industries (BDI) proposed that the German government should provide an **additional financial bonus to those university institutes** which successfully closed an industry contract — the research activity selected by both partners would be doubled and the results (IPR) would be owned by both partners. This way universities would have an incentive to initiate industrial collaboration and the public money spent by the university would be allocated in areas of interest for Germany's industry — the expectation being to boost both employment and economy.

Even if such incentives are applicable to a limited number of research sectors only (e.g. engineering and life sciences) and even if they don't cover the whole wide spectrum of academia, it may well serve to improve the relations between industry and universities as such.

EDUCATION

As mentioned before, the most important task of a university is **education,** and here the relation with industry is very successful — potential for improvement can only be seen in a higher flexibility and responsiveness to industry's demand and to market requirements — examples include upcoming new disciplines in research (e.g. biotechnology or information and communication technology) or new interdisciplinary education. The new Bologna process and the European Education Area are not yet homogeneously interpreted across Europe, due to a heterogeneous environment and varying degrees of government support.

The ambitious objective to reach mutual acceptance of equivalent university degrees (bachelor/master vs. diplomas) across European nations has yet to be implemented in order to meet the requirements of today's global industry.

SERVICE TO SOCIETY

In universities' "service to society", special attention should be paid to the regional development — especially the development of small and medium businesses in the region, which incidentally in many cases are high-tech spin-offs started on university campuses.

It is quite obvious that the region — its economy as well as its cultural environment — may benefit greatly from successful university activities and vice versa. Well known examples include MIT, Cambridge or Munich. But often such successful symbioses are not based on regional strategies, but were created from a personal network or even happened by chance.

The regional component of supporting the local economy and industry may even be part of a top-down strategy from universities in general — at least for those parts or institutes in which the research fields indicate such relevance.

Universities as a breeding ground for new start-ups have a significant multiplier effect as well, at least for specific technology disciplines in which the universities are able to support growth and employment — electronics or biotechnology.

In some nations, like Finland, such a third dimension for universities' objectives is already being discussed and is close to being introduced as an explicit responsibility of university management and it should be seen as equally important as the other two objectives — education and research.

UNIVERSITY MANAGEMENT

All of the four obstacles mentioned above may be discussed by all stakeholders of the universities, but even if they were to be agreed on by university management, it is a long way to go until they will be successfully implemented. There are various hurdles to overcome, not least of which is the traditional freedom and independence of university employees.

Therefore, if any of the obstacles discussed above is supposed to be overcome, special attention must be paid to how the envisaged solutions are to be implemented. Unlike in industrial enterprises, there is no hierarchy at a university that could guarantee to pass a strategy from top management down to the working level. There seems to be a need to develop professional leadership, based on academic traditions that could be inspired by structures and culture in the private sector.

Even in the attempt to gradually improve some of the issues discussed, several specific measures combined with communication activities have to be undertaken in order to achieve the expected results — this may also include a further development of the university's governance structure.

REFERENCES

Weber, L. E. & Duderstadt, J. J. (eds). (2004). *Reinventing the Research University*. Economica, Paris.

CHAPTER 15

University-Industry Collaborations: a Source of Continuous Mutual Stimulation and Inspiration

Klaus Müller

INTRODUCTION

I n a small country like Switzerland, close contacts and collaborations between industry and academia have a long tradition. They have been and continue to be essential for research-based healthcare companies like Roche. With increasing globalization such collaborations are considered with groups all over the world. They are always sought on the basis of clear win-win situations with groups of best technological competence and scientific excellence. Roche has a particular impressive record of many very successful collaborations of mutual benefit to both Roche and the academic groups.

Close contacts, cooperations and collaborations with academic groups have been a constant source of mutual stimulation in science and technology, new discoveries and joint learning, and ultimately creation of true innovations by transforming novel ideas into successful solutions.

In order to ensure mutually beneficial collaborations with academia, there are a number of critical issues to be carefully observed on both sides, which will be discussed below. Interestingly, even with all the positive experiences over long periods of time, there are occasional misconceptions, some recurrent, others of more recent origin due to changing politics or modes of operation. They tend to counteract good collaborations and need to be addressed accordingly.

177

DIFFERENT AGENDAS

Due to their different missions and mode of operation, academia and industry are subject to intrinsically different agendas (Figure):

Table 1: Some key differences between industrial and academic research due to intrinsically different agendas and focus.

Academia	Industry
novelty/curiosity-driven	Goal/target-driven
novelty, publication	Impact in Drug Discovery
Satisfaction of curiosity	Decision-critical data
Education on projects	Experts in charge
Volatile expertise	Continuity of expertise
Struggling for funds	Struggling of approval
Long project approval times	Prompt start on needs
Continuity/project life cycle	Flexibility to change or stop
Research alone	Research in teams
Teaching to next generation	Peer knowledge exchange

While academic groups may be largely curiosity-driven, industry is primarily focused on preset tangible targets. This does not necessarily imply that basic research is performed solely in academia, while industry is the place for applied research or engineering only; nor does it mean that basic research, applied research and engineering always follow in a linear sequence from an idea to a practical solution. These are recurrent misconceptions, particularly regarding research and development in the Life Sciences and Medicine, where much fluctuation between fundamental, applied research and development is the rule and indeed mandatory for success. It goes without saying that purely curiosity-driven approaches can be perfectly legitimate for academia, while a tightly target-focused attitude without lateral explorations may have to be imposed during certain phases of industrial research in order to ensure success.

New discoveries, advanced knowledge, improved understanding and publication thereof, as well as education on frontier research, are the primary goals of academia. This should not preclude the possibility and often desirability for academic groups to explore opportunities to convert their discoveries into novel practical applications or technology developments. Depending on the nature and the actual stage of a discovery, this can often be best done in collaboration with a suitable industrial partner who can offer a broad technology base, experience and application environment in order to perform the necessary evaluations and required feasibility studies quickly, thus guiding successful further developments. For the healthcare industry, on the other hand, the leading principle must be sustained significant innovation in health care; scientific publishing is not the primary goal, although it is a regular, essential and desired activity of industry that can contribute much to the advancement of science and strengthening of contacts to academia. Accordingly, an industrial group will always strive for research activities that promote the project towards its set goals and provide validation- and decision-critical data as early as possible, whereas the academic group may have more flexibility to explore other scientific directions that promise novel discoveries, independently of an originally set objective.

In industry, a group of senior experts is collaborating on a given project. This contrasts the typical situation in academia where projects have to be carried out with undergraduate, graduate, or young postdoctoral fellows, i.e., collaborators who are still in education and learning on projects. It should be emphasized that frontier research is an exquisite vehicle for best education of young scientists. This important aspect must not be ignored by a potential industrial partner. Therefore, the latter must not expect or push for important results too quickly and, should even be prepared to offer additional education or training of young collaborators of the academic group by the experts in its industrial environment.

In most cases, the academic research supervisor represents one major discipline, and the multidisciplinary aspect of a complex project has to be managed through collaborations between groups in different institutions or universities. The establishment of a multidisciplinary research group in academia is the exception. In the healthcare industry, it is the rule. Thus, collaboration with an industrial partner may offer a particular benefit to an academic group. This aspect should be clearly recognized by both parties.

Another important difference concerns the continuity of expertise established by the collaborators. Typically, young collaborators, after concluding their Ph.D. thesis or postdoctoral research period, are expected to leave for a further training stage abroad in complementary fields. Rarely does a collaborator stay on in the same group for many years, even if his or her departure represents a major loss of competence for the research group. Thus, technical or methodological expertise in an academic group tends to be volatile. It is essentially maintained only by its supervisor and, in lucky cases, senior group members in permanent positions. Industry, on the other hand, takes all efforts to maintain its expertise and skill set in key scientific and core technology areas and can do this by an appropriate personnel policy.

Research groups are used to struggling for approval; there is always competition between good ideas. Academic groups are used to quite long approval times; however, on top of this, even best projects may receive an "approved, but not funded" verdict or still face a substantial reduction of the requested support, which is often totally unrelated to the quality of the project. Such measures slow down or render a project ineffective. In general, industry cannot accept such non-competitive measures. Once a project is recognized as being of high priority, everything is done to ensure that it starts promptly and with sufficient resources.

Scientific projects often develop their own dynamics, spawning sub- and side projects, establishing frameworks of internal reference that tend to maintain longevity irrespectively of external points of reference or peer review. In an industrial environment, projects have a clear target and are logically structured into shorter phases with defined deliverables and assessment points. Decision-critical experiments are performed in due course to address all relevant aspects of the project in each phase in order to guide towards possible solutions and to re-assess the validity of the project at each stage. If such a reassessment leads to an overall negative conclusion, a given project is stopped promptly in order to free the resources for other, more promising tasks. The situation is often quite different in academia, where each project also has an important educational function. This is particularly true for Ph.D. theses which often cannot be stopped abruptly or radically shifted into other directions. Rather, the initiated work would continue along related sub-projects that could still produce publishable results and finally lead to a successful wrap-up of the thesis, however, without ever reaching the goals originally set. This attitude may be fully justified and should be recognized as such by the industrial partner in a given collaboration. Likewise, the academic group should also understand the mechanisms of industrial project management with its regular assessments, decisions and prompt actions on new critical results.

Industrial projects are typically driven by a project group that involves many experts from different scientific and technology backgrounds, thus ensuring full and timely support from all required disciplines. This contrasts most settings in academia, where a research group spans essentially one major scientific discipline or technology area. The integration of several disciplines and technologies within one and the same academic group is the exception, and is encountered only with relatively large and fully established research groups. Even for such groups, it is quite common to seek collaborations with other academic groups to complement their own expertise and skill set, in order to make sure that a given project receives the necessary multidisciplinary support typically required for cutting-edge life science projects. Interacademic collaborations may suffer from proper task allocation, timing and other coordination problems, as an academic partner typically would not favour "service support" to other groups, but needs to focus on collaborating contributions that can lead to first-author publishable results as well as work efforts that can be rounded up in Ph.D. theses of its collaborators. The situation is quite different with an industrial partner, where the multi-disciplinary environment may be fully established and the concept of (expert) service provision to a project is a well established mode of operation. A collaboration with an industrial partner may thus provide a number of significant benefits to an academic group. In order to foster cross-disciplinary collaborations, academic research networks and centres of competence have been established in recent years. These are interesting new developments. However, it remains to be seen to what extent such largely top-down implemented schemes will succeed in overcoming intrinsic barriers to unconditional collaborations.

Academia has a prime responsibility in teaching next generations. Scientific and technological training is best provided by involving young talents in research programs at the cutting edge. In industry learning is a constant and lifelong requirement, which is facilitated through permanent involvement in multi-disciplinary project teams. Apart from this, there is a need for more formal knowledge transfer, which is being addressed by courses at different levels, regular or ad hoc organized seminars with internal or external experts, or more recently by elegant web-based knowledge management tools. The unique feature of all these teaching activities in industry is their peer-to-peer nature, differing from the senior-to-junior teaching in academia. In collaborations between industrial and academic groups this should be recognized, and special efforts should be undertaken by the involved industrial experts to provide adequate teaching to the junior partners involved from the academic side. Most often this can be and is being done "through the project". Interestingly, most often this is not seen by the industrial expert simply as a time-consuming and painful obligation, but rather as a most rewarding and motivating exercise bringing young interested talents "up to speed" in novel technologies and concepts required in a given project.

ADDRESSING THE DIFFERENCES

These differences in environment, concept and operation need to be properly recognized and respected by both partners in collaborations between academia and industry. Interestingly, it appears that in general good solutions can be found that equally satisfy the needs on both sides. Under such circumstances, these collaborations are most rewarding and a continuous source of mutual stimulation and motivation, regularly leading to significant scientific advancements and interesting innovations.

It is worth noting that in the majority of all such collaborations, comparatively little money is involved from the side of the industrial partner, i.e., ranging from a one-time paid-up fee for some specific materials, (unpublished) procedures or key data sets, to fellowships for one or more junior collaborators in the academic group over a limited period of time. Yet the benefits for academic groups can be enormous and multi-faceted. They often lie more on the immaterial side, giving access to key technologies to the academic group, opening new research opportunities, providing insights into new scientific and technical problem areas of high actuality, significance and impact. Therefore, many academic research groups actively seek and receive this type of collaboration.

There has been a good tradition for such collaborations to be set up easily and with lean conditions. However, more recently, academic institutions have come more and more under financial pressures, being forced to seek substantially more funding from non-governmental sources. To the extent that governments are not recognizing the prime value of higher education of its young generations, as well as the eminent importance in promoting science and technology, this forces academic institutions to seek more financial returns from their research through collaborations with paying customers. Whether the concomitant commercialization of science is a viable concept in the long term remains to be seen.

In principle, nothing is wrong with the imposition of science and technology politics that foster the entrepreneurial attitudes of professors and their academic research groups, provided this does not jeopardize the prime missions of academia to guarantee excellent modern education and knowledge transfer, independence of decision-making, as well as advancement of science and technology ultimately for the benefit of its paying society and eventually mankind at large. Along this philosophy, most if not all larger academic institutions have established special technology transfer groups with a two-fold responsibility. On the one hand, they should assist the academic research group to better assess their possibilities in seeking intellectual property protection and, on the other hand, help them in negotiating the most favourable conditions for collaborations with industrial partners. If properly done, such technology transfer groups can be truly helpful also for an industrial partner to set up a good collaboration, since their expertise in formal aspects of technology transfer and intellectual property protection may simplify the negotiations with an industrial partner.

However, in many cases and in spite of best intentions by technology transfer groups, their activities have negative impacts on intended collaborations of academic groups with industrial partners. This is particularly true when their primary focus is on a short-term maximization of the financial income for a whole research institute, rather than on the actual needs of and the many immaterial benefits for a specific academic group through collaboration with an industrial partner. The often overestimated value of an offered technology or exaggerated projection for a potential outcome from a given collaboration further contributes to unrealistic financial requests and stiff legal formalities which tend to undermine easy collaborations on a step-by-step, exploratory and mutual-benefit basis. The technology transfer groups often also underestimate the possibilities (and needs) of a globally operating enterprise to select collaborating partners from academic institutions all over the world. Industry will always look for the best collaborative partner, not only in scientific and technological terms, but also regarding open and lean ways for cooperation on a true win-win basis for all involved partners.

SPIN-OFF START-UPS

Another remarkable development is the tendency of academic staff members to spin off some of their research discoveries into start-up companies for further development and commercial exploitation. This has become quite common in the U.S. over the last two decades and has also been advocated in Europe as a means to accelerate technology transfer from early discovery to tangible applications with commercial impact. While this is certainly a viable modality for entrepreneurial researchers in academia and may offer interesting new job opportunities for young scientists, there are several critical aspects that have to be carefully observed.

Starting a new enterprise around a promising discovery or technology may be comparatively easy, although the efforts, particularly in Europe with its partly over-regulated and financially not overly abundant environments, must not be underestimated. Likewise, the rapid and successful development into a truly selling product is often not easily achieved. However, even if the initial hurdles are mastered successfully, the maintenance of the enterprise by a sustained flow of innovations to keep it ahead of its competition is considerably more difficult, and this is where most successfully started enterprises still eventually fail. All this takes a heavy toll in energy, time and effort from the founding scientist in academia and may detract too much from prime scientific and teaching responsibilities. More importantly, the founding and running of a private enterprise requires an established intellectual property base and its continuous development. Accordingly, patenting has become more widespread for academic research groups compared to the past. This, however, keeps them from early publication, which may adversely affect young scientific collaborators whose further career development may critically depend on timely publications, as well as the possibility of presenting their research at international symposia or in front of recruiting bodies. Furthermore, it can lead to serious conflicts of interest when the founder wishes to enter further collaborations with other industrial partners that may be considered competitors in some of the activity areas of the small enterprise. Furthermore, it may counteract the easy exchange of scientific results both within the research group of the founder itself and with other academic research groups, which may be quite disruptive for an academic research environment. It is often not easy, but absolutely mandatory, to find an acceptable balance between the potentially positive and negative consequences of running start-up companies in parallel to one's prime academic responsibilities.

CONCLUSION

In spite of all these developments, we have witnessed a continuous flow of highly rewarding collaborations with academic research groups and are quite confident that this mode of close, lean and open industrial-academic interactions can be maintained in the future. They are a valuable source of much mutual stimulation, inspiration and discoveries. They represent a most effective way for academic groups to sense the rapid developments of science and technology in industry and to see new needs and opportunities for basic and applied research. They also offer the industrial partner possibilities to spin out research questions of fundamental interest that regularly emanate from applied research and development activities. Thus, both academic and industrial partners may profit much from such collaborations, which ultimately advance science and technology to the benefit of the science community at large.

PART IV

•••••••••••••

The American Experience

CHAPTER 16

Universities, Businesses and Public Authorities — and the Inclusive Development of Society

Marye Anne Fox

EARLIEST HIGHER EDUCATION IN THE U.S.

American higher education has reinvented itself many times since its founding in the 18th century. Originally conceived as a vehicle for educating clergy and for the evangelization of indigenous native tribes to Christianity, America's oldest private institutions were religious and focused on studies of the Old and New Testament, complemented by studies of Latin, Greek, rhetoric and arithmetic, as was fashionable in Europe at roughly the same time. Indeed, the seemingly benevolent outreach to the soon-to-be-displaced Native Americans persists to this day in the seal of Dartmouth College, which was founded in 1769. Despite such images, very few Native Americans or freed slaves, and certainly no women, were admitted to such institutions, which were populated almost exclusively by upper-class white males. Teaching was emphasized, with faculty members often called upon to act as tutors.

As American higher education entered the public realm with the establishment of the University of North Carolina at Chapel Hill in 1789, the religious focus of the private institutions/seminaries began to wane, and a roughly common curriculum focused on secular studies was adopted at public and private schools alike. Reflecting the broad interests of Thomas Jefferson, its founder (as well as the third American president and author of the Declaration of Independence), the University of Virginia offered practical studies appropriate for the gentleman farmer or the upper-class architect from its founding in 1819. However, top-quality higher education was limited to only a few such institutions.

Not until after the American Civil War (1861-1865) was serious consideration given to educating the masses beyond primary or secondary education. Given that higher education was generally considered a luxury, it remained broadly accessible only to the upper classes. But even in this unsettled period of American history, the value of education and training for practical careers was becoming increasingly apparent in a local context. However, most public higher education that was available was typically of poor quality and was narrowly focused on preparation for a career as a schoolteacher, doctor, lawyer, military officer or minister. And in a nation lacking easy transportation, only unusually highly motivated students would be able to travel the very long distances that separated their homes from the existing high-quality colleges.

LAND GRANT COLLEGES

Nonetheless, in facing the hardships associated with opening the American frontier, groups of citizens in largely rural American towns began to recognize the importance of developing an appreciation for evolving technologies. This was especially true for those advances related to improved crop yields and to the use of the newly developed tools that made efficient manufacturing possible. In the oldest of American traditions, such groups organized themselves into political alliances and took their pleas for distributed access to practical higher education to the national legislative bodies. Some of these local advocacy bodies persist to this day: for example, the Watauga Club of Raleigh, N.C., led the political charge for applied higher education in North Carolina through the founding of North Carolina Agricultural and Military College (now North Carolina State University) in 1887, and still meets monthly in Raleigh. To this day, it still counts among its members the most highly placed political figures, business leaders and higher-education presidents and chancellors in the state.

In the mid-19th century, such groups from around the nation joined forces to lobby for a new kind of higher education based on economic development of the sponsoring state. With the passage of the Morrill Act by the U.S. Congress in 1862, each state was empowered to establish a college or university dedicated to addressing the needs of local communities by applying these new and evolving technologies in solving practical local problems. To be financed through a generous donation of federal land to each state (30,000 acres for each elected member of the U.S. House of Representatives), these land grant institutions were to educate the populace in "agriculture and the mechanic arts". In this way was born the land grant college which, together with the "normal school" for teacher training, provided for the first time broad access to higher education by the working class. From their beginnings, land grant colleges have represented the best in collaboration and cooperation between the university and its state-wide community. The land grant model has prospered and continues to this day as an accessible route for practical-minded students to achieve upward mobility through higher education. In this model, service to the community and strong interaction with private concerns became valued as complements to the dominant teaching mission.

Land grant institutions have grown significantly in size from these early models, and now educate a large fraction of American students seeking baccalaureate and advanced degrees. In some states, one institution carries the land grant responsibilities (e.g., Texas A&M or North Carolina State), whereas in others the land grant tradition is shared within a state system (e.g., the University of California Berkeley, like all of its sister U.C. institutions, considers itself a land grant institution, although U.C. Davis acts as home institution for most of the state's agricultural programmes). In still others, the land grant tradition is secondary to another primary mission, e.g., at Massachusetts' land grant college, MIT, a private university.

Land grant schools emphasized two of the core values most cherished by the American people: openness to new ideas and social egalitarianism (Kellogg Commission, 1997-2000). Not only were enrolled students educated to become civic leaders and successful entrepreneurs, but the faculty were rewarded and recognized for service inside and outside the university community. University faculty engaged freely with the local agriculture and technical communities flourished, and strong contributions to problem solving for farmers and businessmen became routine, with an improved quality of life and enhanced productivity as the accepted performance criteria.

Most land grant institutions also established an institutional support unit, referred to as Cooperative Extension, with the explicit task of providing problem-based assistance free of charge to the individual who sought its assistance. Cooperative Extension, so named to emphasize the effort of the university to extend its expertise to the community in a true collaborative spirit, soon reached into many sites, with expert university employees, both faculty and research staff, being stationed in different regions of the state. University employees would take the results of agricultural research conducted at associated agricultural experimental stations which were federally funded through the Hatch Act of 1887. In North Carolina, for example, Cooperative Extension opened offices or research field stations in every one of the 100 counties and in the Cherokee Indian reservation in the western part of the state to provide easy access to farmers and small businesses.

So successful were these institutions in improving agricultural and manufacturing efficiency and productivity that even in those days of nearly ubiquitous racial segregation, Congress approved a second Morrill land grant act in

1890, designed to bring segregated states in the South to the educational standards of northern land grant institutions. With this act, a state became eligible either if race was not an admission criterion or if a "separate but equal" facility was available to non-white students.

This second land grant act made possible the establishment of historically black land grant schools, with a parallel Cooperative Extension service. Later Congress extended the concept to Native American tribal colleges. Often these minority-focused programmes operate collaboratively with operational Cooperative Extension offices already existing in each state. Furthermore, funding for all of these institutions has become formulaic within the purview of the US Department of Agriculture (USDA), making continuity a reasonable expectation, but forcing annual political lobbying by higher-education groups for maintaining the Cooperative Extension budget.

Within the last decade, the land grant concept has been applied as well to small business start-ups, whose requirements for technical advice usually involve engineering expertise. Accordingly, the Industrial Extension Service provides an infrastructural basis for the Manufacturing Engineering Partnership (MEP), which in turn is funded by the National Institute for Standards and Technology (NIST), which requires matching funding from each state. Unlike Cooperative Extension, the MEP requires annual evaluation of proposals focused on innovative technologies likely to be successful in the creation of jobs. MEP programmes have been very effective in helping academic scientists and engineers understand real-world problems that require creative applications. These, in turn, have been the basis for collaborative research at the university conducted in partnership with private sector businesses. They have also provided a forum for important continuing/executive education in many business/management colleges.

RESEARCH UNIVERSITIES

The founding of Johns Hopkins University in 1876, America's first research university, represented the next step in American higher education, emulating the German model of graduate education in which scholarly investigations are conducted within a group working under the supervision of an expert professor. The research university model emphasized the creation of knowledge over other institutional missions. Thus, teaching and professional/community service were overtaken by an emphasis on scholarly research. Ira Remsen, a professor of chemistry, became a model faculty member in advocating for strong collaborations with an emerging chemical industry. Academic rank and career progress for faculty began to be linked to research productivity, and peer review emerged as a reliable, fair and convenient means by which the quality of faculty research could be judged.

If research productivity was to be a primary measure for academic success, the value of apprentice researchers within the research group soon became apparent (Kunhardt, 2004). Accordingly, graduate education became an important component of the portfolios of the nation's best universities. In order to bring such institutions together for discussions of best practices in graduate education and to advocate for national policies that support such institutions, the American Association of Universities (AAU) was founded in 1900 by 14 institutions offering the Ph.D. degree. To this date, AAU continues its traditions of facilitating research collaborations and of acting as a forum for discussion of policy issues affecting the nation's research universities.

Because the success of an institution depended on research quality, so too would the ability of faculty to attract graduate students and to provide the resources and instrumentation that would allow them to conduct state-of-the-art investigations. This, in turn, required financial support which was best available at the time either through sponsored research conducted with industry or through philanthropic contributions. Wisely, private institutions worked energetically to accumulate endowments that would ultimately be used in support of faculty scholarship. Public institutions, in contrast, continued to rely on support from state legislative sources.

The growth of land grant universities was based upon a practical response to national needs. Likewise in the 1960s, the nation responded to the threat embodied by the Russian launch of Sputnik by recognizing broadly the need for broad and deep American expertise in science and engineering. Major new investments from federal sources, especially through the National Defense Education Act, enhanced the U.S. position in technical fields. For new public universities, founded in order to accommodate the "Baby boom" children, i.e., those born in the years immediately following the end of World War II, such funds were a lifeblood and a motivation for focus on top-quality scientific research of vital importance to the nation.

It was in this milieu that the University of California at San Diego (UCSD) was founded. Building on the excellent reputation of her sister schools within the University of California System and upon the unique coastal community present in San Diego, UCSD evolved in less than four decades from a single facility on a barren bluff overlooking the Pacific into one of the top universities in the world (7th in U.S. R & D and 13th in the world on the Shanghai Jong Tao University list). Its success was driven by generous state support, by the highly entrepreneurial culture of southern California and by the clarity of the research focus inherent in the California Master Plan for Higher Education. It is, perhaps, the most compelling example of the revolutionary effect of federal investment on producing world-class knowledge in a public setting. Its success is closely aligned with the development of world-class commercial clusters of technical excellence in wireless communications and in biotechnology that have followed from this model.

RESPONSE TO SCIENCE AS THE ENDLESS FRONTIER

Before World War II, many of the most prestigious universities in the U.S. funded research through their own resources. A chemistry professor now retired from an Ivy League institution told me anecdotally several years ago that when he sought permission to seek financial support for his research from the federal government, he was rebuffed by his president who told him it would be insulting to the institution to even suggest that the school would not or could not meet the research funding needs of its faculty. Nowhere in the U.S., I can assure you, would comparable advice now be offered.

This situation changed dramatically when the U.S. government during WWII recognized that research contributions critical to the war success were made by university faculty, e.g., radar, quinine, the atomic bomb, etc. Vannevar Bush (1945), then science advisor to President Truman, persuaded federal decision-makers to accede to a compact in which the nation's research universities would be identified as the primary sites for federally supported basic research. Unlike Europe, where national laboratories were the primary sites for research, U.S. basic research would be conducted in universities, with funding deriving largely from the federal government, either in support for projects proposed by individual investigators or through scholarships or fellowships for students.

And there were plenty of students, many of whom had never seriously considered a university education, much less the possibility of pursuing a graduate degree. These options became possible only because of the opportunity afforded returning soldiers through the GI Bill, which paid full tuition costs for qualified students, regardless of family resources. Support for science and engineering was significant during the Cold War years, and the launch of the Russian satellite Sputnik in 1957 shocked the nation so thoroughly that Congressionally mandated investment took off. The National Defense Education Act was so generously funded that many female Americans began to join with their male counterparts in studying science, mathematics and engineering. Not only were technical careers considered as stable and well-paying, but proceeding toward a career in science or engineering was considered patriotic. And with President Kennedy's announcement in the early 1960s that the United States would put a man on the moon before the end of the decade, interest in applied science and engineering soared.

RESEARCH FLAGSHIP INSTITUTIONS

Top-quality science and engineering would be conducted at the best universities which would be staffed by the most productive and most creative faculty. Typically, each state's leading public institution (occasionally more than one)

would concentrate its research resources, including expensive instrumentation, in the so-called flagship (Ayers & Hurd, 2005). Research would be
emphasized strongly at such institutions, even at the cost of teaching quality,
and a major requirement of faculty at such institutions became securing external support for their research efforts. In the 1960s this source was typically the
federal government, with additional funds available from the state. Indeed,
about 2/3 of national R & D was funded by the government and about 1/3 by
private industry.

Interdisciplinary research and the construction of core facilities attracted
outstanding scholars, and access to researchers from non-flagship institutions
and from nearby industrial research centres became more common upon
establishing cooperative agreements with the centre directors. By rubbing
shoulders with academic researchers, industrial scientists began to collaborate
much more frequently and groups of industries began to form industrial consortia centered on research problems around which major academic research
centres were founded. The federal government responded by shifting a portion
of research support away from individual investigators to engineering research
centres, science and technology centres, etc., virtually all of which were university-based, led and managed by a university professor with world-class
expertise in a focused area.

Unfortunately, as these research parks arose, general academic support of
state universities began to decline, as did federal support (in constant dollars)
for the physical sciences. Only funding from the National Institutes of Health
(in areas ranging from basic life sciences through translational medical
research in clinics) experienced continued substantial growth. The share of
national R & D shifted from the government toward the private sector, with
about 2/3 of R & D (mostly development) being funded by industry by the
early 1990s.

Many U.S. public institutions began to receive only a small portion of their
budgets from state appropriation: for example, in 2003-04, UCSD received
only 14% of its budget funding from state appropriation. The financial advantage to cooperation with industry became obvious.

RESEARCH PARKS

As relationships improved between university and industrial scientists, many
universities made land available adjacent to or at least nearby the campus.
Typically, an established company would sign a multi-decade land lease, with
the right to sublease or sell the facility under certain conditions. A laboratory/
office complex would be built, with the intention of encouraging collaborative work with the university. After expiration of the lease, the structure
would revert to the university, presumably to be remodeled and reused for aca-

demic purposes or collaboration. The university would benefit immediately in deriving income from the land lease and the future expansion of company-sponsored research at the university was anticipated.

Many such parks appeared, but usually there were only a small number of tenants, and often of different interests. The financial benefit from the land lease was soon subsumed into the university budget, and the anticipated sponsored research rarely materialized at the projected level. Concerns about ownership of intellectual property inhibited the free exchange of ideas.

Michael Porter of the Harvard Business School later rationalized the muted success of such ventures, as having failed to develop a cluster of innovation, i.e., a critical mass of overlapping expertise to make the research park a site sought by new graduates as a feasible career accelerator. Richard Florida (2002), in his book *The Rise of the Creative Class*, argued that talent, technology and tolerance are key in developing such a cluster, and that geographical proximity to the university was not enough to assure the success of the research park model.

CENTENNIAL CAMPUS

An alternative model was pursued on the North Carolina State University research park. In the university's centennial year in 1987, the North Carolina Governor, James Hunt, transferred 1,000 acres of green agricultural land to the university with the intention of fostering collaborations between fledgling businesses and the university. University R & D would be a major driver for identification of partners, and, after an appropriate period of growth, the model would encourage the evolving businesses to step-up to Research Triangle Park (RTP), a cluster where large information technology and telecommunication business clusters had been developed in partnership with the N.C. Department of Commerce. The start-up businesses located on the Centennial Campus were housed in buildings constructed under several different arrangements: university buildings constructed with state appropriations; research buildings, constructed on state-guaranteed loans to be repaid from indirect costs earned on collaborative research grants; partner buildings, constructed with university bonds paid by lease payments by university or private sector tenants; and venture buildings, constructed by a third party for-profit investors who agreed to lease only to tenants approved by the university as continuing research partners. Although those businesses that located on the Centennial Campus paid full market-rate leases, their employees were also eligible to participate in university life, with benefits ranging from use of the library and fee-for-service access to instrumentation to the use of university recreation facilities and access to reduced admissions to some intercollegiate athletic events.

With this model, collaborations with the private sector flourished, with more than 60 small businesses choosing to co-locate with faculty researchers. Faculty were able to learn of practical applications and marketable products made possible by their basic research, and often served as co-principal investigators with company scientists and engineers in seeking research sponsorship. Skilled employees with advanced degrees offered to teach upper-division undergraduate classes and freshman seminars as adjunct faculty, an option that many of the industrial researchers found energizing. Students benefited by having on-campus access to well-paying part time jobs, internships within their academic interests, co-op experiences, or academic credit for faculty-sanctioned research projects supervised by business employees who qualified as adjunct faculty.

TECHNOLOGY TRANSFER: UNIVERSITIES AS ECONOMIC DRIVERS

Because most of the collaborative research was fundamental and because publication in the open literature was the expected course for student work, most collaborative projects avoided intellectual property (ip) concerns. When research was sponsored by companies, the disposition of ownership was negotiated before work was undertaken, and both parties were well aware of the agreement. Typically, these agreements involved exclusive or non-exclusive licensing, depending on the level of financial support being proposed, with the university retaining ownership of the patentable work. They usually also agreed on disposition of legal fees and on responsibilities for legal defence against infringement. Occasionally, such agreements would entail the university accepting equity in the start-up. The negotiations were sometimes difficult, especially if the sponsoring research organization sought sole ownership of the sponsored research or if the company wanted background ip rights or a protracted (longer than 90 days) publication delay (Lovett, 2004).

If a U.S. federal government agency, rather than an interested company, was the primary research sponsor, the provisions of the Bayh-Dole Act (1980) were applied. This Congressional law was designed to encourage more frequent utilization of intellectual property produced with federal funding. Specifically, it allowed for the transfer of inventions or intellectual property from the owner university to a partnering business for further development, including commercialization. The contracting university would typically offer a restricted licence to the invention, but would retain "march-in rights," defined as the ability to retract the disposed intellectual property if the university or the federal government determined that it was not being commercialized or made available to the public on a reasonable basis. In practice, agreements were nearly always reached if a company was serious about the intent to commercialize, but often only after a prolonged period of legal manoeuvring that could be distasteful to either party. Thus, even with the clarifications of Bayh-Dole, American universities and private partners still continue wrangling over details and shared ownership and responsibilities for every new invention.

CONNECT

An alternative method for assisting in commercialization was proposed at the University of California at San Diego (UCSD) in 1985. As part of its Extension offerings, UCSD convened over 200 private sector members, including research and academic institutions, life science and technology companies, service providers and government entities. Called UCSD-CONNECT, the organization initially focused on educational programmes on entrepreneurship. Over 100 events have been produced each year, making UCSD-CONNECT the most successful business accelerator in the country, with over 1,000 new companies with over $10 billion in financing having participated. UCSD-CONNECT has offered continuing education on evolving technologies through its Frontiers in Science and Technology programmes and through its Financial Forums and has provided invaluable recognition for new start-ups and large successful companies through its awards programmes.

A major programme of importance to efficient technology transfer is a series of confidential presentations, referred to as Springboards, which provide local inventors and technology. Recognizing that the key components of a successful technology cluster are: science and technology, talent and invested money, the officers of UCSD-CONNECT assemble representatives from each of these components to effect smooth technology transfer. Not only UCSD, but also San Diego State University and major research institutions located within walking distance of the UCSD campus (e.g., Scripps Research Institute, Salk Institute and the Burnham Institute) have benefited.

Springboards assemble the interested parties for confidential evaluations at five levels. In the first stage, Ideas/Concepts, inventors seek to obtain a candid opinion regarding marketability of their new technology and advice on how to construct a viable business plan. In the second Springboard, appropriate seed or angel financing is attained to implement the plan. At the third stage, Series A financing is identified for full product development, and at the fourth stage, the company will have reached a mature stage in which series B or C financing is required for product testing and marketing to take the company to an initial public offering (IPO) or to a stage that can lead to being acquired by a larger company. Finally, at the fifth stage, the officers of the new company engage with the business community to become contributing intrapreneurs, thus perpetuating the Springboard cycle. This sequence has had a dramatic positive effect on the local economy, particularly in telecommunications and biotechnology. It has also contributed significantly, as a consequence, to the extremely positive goodwill with which the university is regarded by local business leaders.

More recently, members have called on UCSD-CONNECT to act as well as an aggressive political advocate on behalf of research and innovation. Since political lobbying lies outside the university's educational mission, a sub-set group, to be called CONNECT, will soon split away from UCSD-CONNECT as a public non-profit entity. This group will seek to provide an independent voice for the San Diego technology community on legislative matters of concern to these members. Among these issues being addressed in the coming year are: quality of K-12 education, state funding for university outreach programmes focused on academic preparation, proper levels of investment in public higher education, state and national R & D tax credits, government restrictions on stem cell research, handling of H-1B visas, easy entry restrictions for foreign graduate students, and more narrowly interpreting the deemed export restrictions.

OPEN SOURCE AS AN ALTERNATIVE MODEL FOR TECHNOLOGY TRANSFER

Many of the problems arising from partnerships between universities and private sector research collaborators ultimately rest on adaptable intellectual property policies. An alternative to owned/licensed intellectual property has arisen within the last decade within the information technology community. Thus was born the open source movement that posited that when information is publicly viewable and modifiable, a better product will result than if a restricted set of knowledge workers attempt to solve a problem.

The open source movement grew from an increasing frustration with a limited number of options in managing and adapting commercial computer operating systems (i.e., Microsoft products) for special or local applications. Without access to code, as a result of protected ip, software evolution is thwarted, according to this philosophy. Linus Torvalds began this movement by writing and making available Linux, a variant of the UNIX operating system that could run on his home personal computer. His belief is that when many people work on a common serious problem it can be more easily solved when the source code is available to the general programming community. In this approach, individuals can modify, evaluate, improve and release publicly an enhanced source code, thus facilitating the evolution of the code itself. When such improvements are shared over the internet, better software is rapidly produced compared with that attained with a traditional closed model for software development. Access is typically available through a GNU General Public License (1991) intended to guarantee freedom to share, change and distribute free software without warranty or unlicensed patents.

Two examples of the open source movement are found in Red Hat, a publicly traded open source software company, and Wikipedia, an open source encyclopedia providing information contributed by users (Wikipedia). Red Hat's philosophy is to take open source software to the enterprise market through purchased subscriptions that deliver ongoing service, product updates and performance reassurance to commercial enterprises. Wikipedia is a free-content encyclopedia that anyone can edit. Available in over 50 languages, the English language version contains over half a million contributed entries.

If comparable arrangements can be devised between universities and industrial consortia, a new era in information exchange might be expected. Participation by individual academic personnel has been broad and deep, so a future where the open source philosophy more prominently figures in university technology transfer and commercialization seems likely.

GUIRR

As such alternatives evolve, an open platform for discussion among affected groups becomes apparent. By sponsoring periodic gatherings of high-level representatives of government, industry, and research universities, the Government–University–Industry Research Roundtable of the U.S. National Academies addresses such topics as training a science workforce for the U.S., the effect of globalization on cutting-edge research, the impact of government policies and regulations, etc (Government–University–Industry Research Roundtable). In many ways, GUIRR provides a forum analogous to the early interventions into practical dimensions of higher education as provided by the land grant colleges.

CONCLUSION

Recently, many instances have appeared that challenge the American science community's compact with the American people as described by Vannevar Bush over a half century ago. A perplexing disdain for the scientific has emerged: for example, science illiteracy evidenced by widespread American curiosity about "intelligent design" as an alternative to evolution; the title of a recent *New York Times* magazine supplement article "How does the Brain Work? Who Cares?" (Holt, 2005); publication of a book by journalist Jennifer Washburn (2005), entitled *University, Inc. The Corporate Corruption of American Higher Education*, that asserts the financial corruption of the public mission of public research institutions cries for equal distribution of university funding across all schools, irrespective of mission, and hence away from research flagships; and the lackadaisical political response to cries from the science community for in-depth explorations of the effects of globalization on the free movement of scientists.

Even with such concerns, the unsurpassed achievements of American research universities in driving a technological future are based on excellence in basic research. And this excellence in turn is based on flexibility in proposing and collaborating on exciting research directions across sectors. From the initial contributions of land–grant universities to today's efforts to devise productive means by which international collaboration and competition will drive innovation, university education, enhanced through flexible new technologies, has never been so important. New and innovative ways to handle intellectual property by evolving universities will contribute toward achieving excellence in higher education.

REFERENCES

Ayers, E.L. & Hurd, N.F. (2005). "Flagship Universities Must Pursue Excellence and Access". *Chronicle of Higher Education*, 22 April 2005, p. B-12.

Bayh-Dole Act (1980). *(35USC 200-212)*, Library of Congress, Washington D.C.

Bush, V. (1945). *Science the Endless Frontier*. Office of Scientific Research and Development, reprinted National Science Foundation, Washington D.C.

Florida, R. (2002). *The Rise of the Creative Class*, Harper Business, New York.

The GNU Public License (June 1991). Free Software Foundation, Boston.

Government–University–Industry Research Roundtable. *US National Academy of Sciences*. www7.nationalacademies.org/guirr/

Holt, J. (2005). "Of Two Minds". *New York Times Magazine*, 8 May 2005, p. 11.

Kellogg Commission on the Future of State and Land Grant Universities. "Returning to Our Roots", First Report, "Student Access". Second Report, "The Student Experience". Third Report, "The Engaged Institution". Fourth Report, "A Learning Society". Fifth Report, "Towards a Coherent Campus Culture". Sixth Report, "Learning, Discovery, and Engagement in a New Age and a Different World". NASULGC Press, Washington D.C., 1997-2000.

Kunhardt, E.E. (2004). "Necessity as the Mother of Tenure?" *New York Times*, 14 Dec.

Lovett, C.M. (2004). "Prestige, Power, and Wealth". *Educause*, Dec. 2004, p. 10.

Washburn, J. (2005). *University, Inc. The Corporate Corruption of American Higher Education*. Basic Books, New York.

Wikipedia. http://en.wikipedia.org

CHAPTER 17

Lessons about Regional Economic Development from the Austin Story

Larry R. Faulkner [1]

O ver my professional lifetime, economic development in the region of Austin, Texas, has been, by any measure, spectacular. In 1960, the Austin metropolitan area had a population of 300,000, according to the U.S. Census Bureau, and almost no industry. The Texas state government was the primary basis of employment. Today, Austin is a metropolitan area of 1.4 million people and has become an internationally recognized centre of creative activity, not only in technology, but also in the fields related to the arts, such as advertising and film-making. In real terms, the Austin region's gross product has multiplied more than fourfold since 1980 and is now about US$65 billion per year. This represents a growth rate above 6% per year on an inflation-corrected basis, impressive even by Chinese standards.

The University of Texas is, without question, the single most important reason for this transformation.

Some have called the city's economic growth "the Austin Miracle". But like every secular miracle, it took more than 40 years to happen "overnight". How and why did it happen? What preconditions and environment led to the opportunity? What steps brought the opportunity into reality? What can one learn from this history about the influence that a strong university can have on the economic and cultural development of its environs?

---

1 The author is grateful to Mr. Thomas Zigal for assistance in the preparation of this article.

THE CITY AND THE UNIVERSITY

Austin, Texas, is remarkable on its own. Richard Florida, in his widely read book *The Rise of the Creative Class* (2002), names Austin as the second most creative city in the United States, right after San Francisco. Austin likes to call itself "the Live Music Capital of the World" and it does harbour a lively environment for the arts and culture. But it has also become a place of inventive technology and entrepreneurial activity.

Within this city, the University of Texas has evolved into one of the largest and most powerful teaching and research centres in the United States, with a faculty recruited in competition with other top institutions in America and around the world. The university has been historically the most important institution for developing leadership in Texas society across the gamut of human activity in science and engineering, politics and government, media, literature, business, the arts and so on. Its governing board is very powerful in the larger life of Texas. And Texas is important in the life of the nation and the world. It is the second largest of the American states, both in population and geographic area. It is the largest exporter of all the states and its "gross domestic product", if compared internationally, would come in just behind Spain's and South Korea's (both with nearly double the Texas population). The Texas public looks to the University of Texas at Austin to provide knowledge and expertise for solving public problems of all kinds, especially those related to the educational challenges associated with the state's demographic shifts. All of these elements conspire to define the university's relationship to its region, which in turn is central to an understanding of its role in regional economic development.

Over the past 45 years, the University of Texas at Austin has become much larger and more sophisticated. In 1960, it employed about 7,000 faculty and staff members. Today it is Austin's largest employer with 22,000 members. The university budget in 1960 was slightly less than $30 million. Now it is 55 times larger at $1.65 billion. Of course, a large part of that arises from inflation, but the real growth is in the range of eight times.

In fact, a university as large as ours is an economic engine of significant magnitude. Our current students contribute, in direct personal expenditures, more than $800 million into the Austin economy each year, nearly all of it brought in from outside the city. The local economic activity derived from the university's own expenditures multiplies to about $7.4 billion per year. The university generates 82,000 jobs throughout the state both by direct employment and by indirect means, through construction, purchasing, and economic multiplication. A recent study indicates that the university manifests a multifaceted economic impact through its large research enterprise, for which UT Austin receives about $400 million in research grants every year. This is all very stable activity, rather insulated from the business cycle, and with good annual growth.

But the economic activity originating in the University of Texas is not the main reason for the outstanding economic development of the Austin region. That has come from interactions between the university and the larger society of the region.

A CHRONICLE OF DEVELOPMENT

The foundation of the development in Austin is in the powerful College of Engineering developed at the university under consistently superb leadership over decades. By the early 1960s, the college was strong enough to be hosting some excellent, large research programmes in advanced electronics, and it was producing large numbers of well educated engineers. A seminal technology-based business named Tracor spun out of the research programme. And not long afterward, Texas Instruments and IBM — attracted by the availability of engineering talent — built facilities in Austin.

The technological talent found Austin attractive as a place to live and wanted to stay. By the early 1970s, a new company named Radian had spun out of Tracor, and quite a few entrepreneurial engineers from Texas Instruments and IBM had left those companies to begin smaller enterprises of their own.

Perhaps the most important single event in Austin's development was its success in attracting the Microelectronics and Computer Corporation — MCC — in an intense national competition in the 1980s. With American electronics and computing industries under heavy competitive pressure from Japan, the U.S. government sponsored MCC as a richly funded, government-industry consortium to conduct leading-edge, pre-competitive research. Metropolitan leaders across America saw MCC as an enterprise that would define the future of microelectronics and computing, so they bid fiercely for it to be located in their areas. Austin was the successful bidder. There were five important parts to the package:

- Financial inducements offered by the Governor of Texas and the civic leadership of Austin. (A good example of how government and the university, working as partners, can benefit everyone.)
- A commitment by the university to locate MCC in a building to be constructed specifically for MCC's needs on university land. (A good example of how the business sector and the university, working as partners, can benefit everyone.)
- The strength and scale of the university's science, mathematics and engineering programmes.

- Commitments by the State of Texas and by private donors to recruit additional top-level faculty talent into those programmes.
- The attractiveness of the Austin area as a place to live.

The university was a major factor in all five of these elements. In the late 1980s, there was a similar success when the Austin area won another national competition for a second government-industry consortium dedicated to leading-edge, pre-competitive research in the semiconductor industry. That one, called Sematech, was intended to support the development of the tools and materials needed for advancement of technology into new generations. The same five elements used to attract MCC were used to bring Sematech to Austin, including a new facility on university land.

Through the 1980s and into the 1990s, a great many major companies in the semiconductor and computer fields placed large facilities in Austin because MCC and Sematech were in town. They typically drew heavily on the talent and expertise available to them at the university.

During this period, a remarkable entrepreneur named Michael Dell went into business making computers at the age of 19, after just one year as a student at the University of Texas at Austin. His company, Austin's largest corporate success story, has become a global powerhouse in the computer industry.

By the middle and late 1990s, software had also become a significant part of the commercial mix, and Austin became a major centre for development of systems, web-based applications and services, and games. Of course, this sector suffered greatly during the "dot-com bust" in the years after 2000, but there is new vitality in it now. Evidently the dot-comers have not yet been swept into the dot-compost heap of history.

The Austin area now hosts corporate headquarters for four Fortune 500 companies. The largest is Dell. Second is the recently spun-off Semiconductor Division of Motorola, which is now called Freescale Semiconductor. The third is Temple-Inland, a major forest products, paper and financial services company. Just having joined the Fortune 500 is Whole Foods, which has built an empire, in typical Austin fashion, on organic peanut butter, brown rice and tofu.

Did the university assist in the creation of this scene? You bet! (as we say in Texas). Dell was founded by and is led by an ex-student of the university. Temple-Inland was brought to Austin by a UT graduate who built its financial services arm to a substantial degree on Austin-area real estate opportunities extending from the technology-driven growth. Freescale is in Austin because Motorola headquartered its semiconductor division there after MCC and Sematech came to town. Whole Foods built its business concept on the cultural independence of Austin, which has its roots in the university. All four of these companies have relied on the flow of educated talent from the University of Texas at Austin.

And there is more:

- The Austin Technology Incubator, which is part of the university, has graduated 65 technology-based companies. These companies have generated nearly 3,000 jobs in the Austin region and have raised $1.2 billion in capital.
- Scores of companies have been spun off from the university, including Tracor, Radian, National Instruments, Evolutionary Technologies and many smaller enterprises.
- About 2,000 business managers per year are trained in our executive education programme at the university's McCombs School of Business. Many of the programmes are tailored to the individual needs of the companies employing the managers participating in them.
- The university is committed to developing transnational business partnerships. We are especially interactive with Mexico, our neighbour across the Rio Grande River, in industry and educational exchanges. For example, we have ongoing research agreements with PEMEX, the Mexican national oil company, in which our university's geological, environmental and engineering expertise is put directly at the service of Mexico. The North American Free Trade Agreement (NAFTA) has dramatically increased the volume and variety of business between Texas and Mexico, and the University of Texas at Austin has set a priority on facilitating positive mutual development on our border.

GENERAL ATTRIBUTES OF RESEARCH UNIVERSITIES SUPPORTING ECONOMIC DEVELOPMENT

Because universities harbour brain power, ambition and expertise, they are natural partners in building a strong regional economy. In regional economic development, knowledge is indeed power. All sound universities make important, economically significant contributions to the regions that host them. Here are some of the ways that are common to all:

- Universities are magnets that draw young people of talent from a large area and concentrate them into an interactive, creative community. Much of this talent is retained in the home area of the university.
- Universities develop knowledge and skills in their students, so that their graduates are capable of making much more valuable contributions to their families and their society.
- Universities recruit and sustain a talented faculty, who contribute to the creation of a vibrant community outside the university itself and

can bring expertise to the solution of public problems or, as inventors and consultants, to the service of commerce and industry.

- A university has great power to influence the attractiveness of its region as a place to live and work, through the ability, leadership and creativity of its graduates, through its effect on the intellectual life of its community, through cultural and artistic events that it sponsors, and through its ability to build identity.
- Universities also have convening power. They can bring people together from all sectors of society to address the issues of the present and future. In this way, and in others, universities become seen publicly as places where the future is created. The reputation and the reality are both valuable for the economic development of the region that hosts the university.
- Finally, all universities are sizable, stable economic engines in themselves. They bring employment to a community and generate income for many supporting businesses.

With properties such as these, it is no surprise that virtually all regional economic development teams in the United States are placing a strong focus on their local colleges and universities. They are right in doing so, because their educational institutions add value of a kind that cannot be obtained in other ways.

SPECIAL CONDITIONS FOR EXTRAORDINARY GROWTH

Even so, a story like the development of Austin is a rare case, and it rests on more than the basic list of contributions made by universities. To realize the kind of university-aided development that has occurred in the Boston area, or Silicon Valley, or the Research Triangle of North Carolina, or San Diego, or Austin, the assets of one or more exceptionally strong universities must come together with special assets of the region itself. For growth of that kind, four particular conditions must all be satisfied:

- First, the university must host a superb faculty and truly exceptional research programmes, as measured by international standards.
- Next, the university must have high social importance and public credibility.
- Third, the region must be a competitively attractive place for talented people to live.
- Finally, the university leadership must be well engaged with the business and political leadership of the region, and all must be interested in fostering economic development.

Extraordinary university-assisted growth must be built on the basis of a substantial advantage in some specific portion of the world of ideas. This means that the region must host a commanding presence in critical supporting fields, manifested in resident expertise and respected, intensive research at the very edge of knowledge. Experience suggests that these elements can be brought together only in a university with a top-quality faculty and a large volume of internationally respected research. Unless there is broad strength in the institution, it is practically impossible to recruit academic talent at the level and in the numbers required to produce the focused expertise needed for strong economic development. Because such development typically arises from new forms of economic activity rooted in technical advances, the critical areas are likely to be in science or engineering. However strength in other disciplines is also important, not only to the overall reputation and capability of the university, but also for their impact on the larger community.

A close observer may note that Austin's technology base began to develop before the University of Texas at Austin could have laid much of a claim to a top-quality faculty or a large base of research. This is true, but the real take-off in Austin's development as a technology centre did not occur until the early 1980s, when the university was rapidly establishing itself as a leading academic institution.

In a region that has already achieved much knowledge-based development, neither the expertise nor the research will be confined to the academic institutions. To the contrary, the bulk of it may reside among the industries of the region. However, the university is still a critical catalyst, because it continuously furnishes new talent, including expert talent in the very fields most relevant to the region's core activity. Moreover, the university can upgrade the abilities of people already involved in that activity; it can offer consulting strength; and it can serve as an exchange point for experts from industry, who otherwise have limited access to open intellectual environments.

When I say, in my second point, that the university must have social importance and public credibility, I mean that people in the broader society of the region must have confidence in the institution and must see it as centrally important to the welfare of the region. They must regard it as a place for educating the most talented of their young people, and they must perceive it as a place where the issues of the society can and will be addressed and where solutions will be found. A university with strength in these public connections has the power to affect events in its region and the power to make things happen. Just as important, it commands the confidence that it must have to gain the public and private investment essential to the very creation and sustenance of programmes that give rise to the knowledge advantage.

As I outlined the role of the University of Texas at Austin in our state, my purpose was to illustrate how well the university is situated with regard to social importance and public credibility. For decades, it has held the leading position among Texas universities in these respects, and that position has been critical to its work on behalf of economic development, not only in the Austin region, but throughout the state.

Third in my list of conditions was that the region must be attractive to talented people. Folks who can enable and drive extraordinary economic development have choices about where to live and work, and they will migrate to the most attractive. Physical beauty and recreational advantages are among their considerations, and both are high among the reasons for the success of Silicon Valley, San Diego, the Research Triangle and Austin. Good transportation is absolutely essential, and, in the U.S., that means convenient access to an airport that offers non-stop service to a significant spectrum of cities. Affordability is a secondary consideration. Of course, the university can do nothing about any of these things, but they do affect in a strong way whether extraordinary growth is really possible.

The absence of real advantages in this sphere is probably the main reason for the lack of examples of such development around the truly great universities located in the smaller "college towns" of America. Many of these towns are quite healthy economically, precisely because of the effect of the local university, and many have experienced modest to good recent development rooted in their university's intellectual strengths. But my focus here is on extraordinary development, and college towns just do not have the assets required for that.

Universities do have a strong influence on one important aspect of liveability, namely, the cultural milieu. Creative people like to be around universities, because the intellectual atmosphere is lively, and cultural opportunities are more plentiful than in the larger society. The attractiveness of the environment created by the three universities of the Research Triangle is a big part of the success in North Carolina, and the same can be said of Austin. For decades, Austin has been known as a place that harbors a great range of creative people. Favourite T-shirts and bumper stickers in the Austin area even admonish the community to "Keep Austin Weird". While Austin is widely known as a technology centre, it is a multi-dimensional place with all political and cultural viewpoints expressed, with an appreciation for education and intellectual activity, with a strong environmental tradition, with an especially varied live-music scene. Austin also has a professional symphony orchestra and professional opera and ballet companies operating at a quite high standard. The combination is very unusual for a city of Austin's size. There are also strong elements in the visual arts and drama. Finally, Austin is even the home of Lance Armstrong, recently the winner for the seventh time in the Tour de France. Much of Austin's atmosphere and activity flows from the youth and intellectual liveliness of the University of Texas at Austin, and these things are powerful assets of the community.

My fourth and last condition for extraordinary growth was that the university leadership must be well engaged with the business and political leadership of the region, and all parties must be interested in fostering economic development. Economic development rarely happens in this era just because intellectual conditions are right. It is fostered by collaborations among civic leaders, including the leadership of universities. In the case of Austin, I noted above how such collaboration was essential to attracting MCC and Sematech. Without the public confidence emphasized just a moment ago, the required collaboration could not have happened. But also required was entrée to top-level leadership of the state. The strength of U.T. Austin's governing board in the life of Texas helps to sustain the essential connections. In the Austin area and in Texas at large, collaboration of this kind continues to be important, as the region seeks to persuade firms to locate new facilities, or to upgrade established ones, in our region.

One final point: land is a special asset of a university that can be important in collaborative regional economic development. Stanford's use of its extensive landholdings in support of knowledge-based corporate development is a very large part of the Silicon Valley story. The commitment of university land and facilities to MCC and Sematech was likewise critical to the Austin story.

CLOSING COMMENTS

Of course, there are many specific lessons about the impact of universities on regional development, of which we have been able to examine only a few here. Perhaps my main message is to suggest the importance of the interaction between a university and its surrounding society. That interaction is what leads to social energy, leverage on capital, and political help with removal of barriers — all critical for amplifying the university's benefits in the larger society. I have focused here on American stories, because I know them well, but there are others that could be cited from around the globe. And there surely will be more in years to come.

In the world before us, ideas and know-how, developed talent, and a well-educated workforce are more essential to regional economic well-being over the long term than access to capital and materials. The great research university has become the single most powerful and persistent source of regional wealth and social strength, because it builds the basis for adaptation in a continuously changing social environment. The society that discovers this truth and invests on the basis of it will own a good share of the future.

REFERENCES

Bureau of Business Research in the U.T. McCombs School of Business. (Source of statistics about the economic impact of the University of Texas at Austin on the city and state).

Faulkner, Larry R. (2004). "Knowledge is Power: The Role of the University of Texas in Regional Economic Development", speech presented at the Second Chinese-Foreign University Presidents Forum, August 9, 2004, Beijing. http://www.utexas.edu/president/speeches/china_08092004.html. (Many of the ideas in this presentation and some of the language were expressed in this speech).

Florida, Richard (2002). *The Rise of the Creative Class*, Basic Books, New York.

Perryman (2004). 21st Annual Perryman Economic Outlook Conference, December 2004. (Source for statistics on Austin's gross regional product.)

U.S. Census Bureau figures (1960 and 2004). (Consulted for Austin population figures.)

U.T. Office of Institutional Research. (Source of information for comparisons about U.T.'s employment figures and budget from 1960-2005).

CHAPTER 18

Challenges in University-Industry Collaborations

Wayne C. Johnson [1]

INTRODUCTION

During the past decade, much has changed in the way people interact. The emergence of a pervasive, global communications infrastructure has made it both possible and convenient to engage in conversation and dialogue with others at the furthest corners of the earth. Human knowledge continues to advance and doubles at a rate of every seven years. And social problems also seem to grow in scope and complexity, evidencing whole new categories of issues that continually challenge the accumulated wisdom and the infrastructure and capabilities that have been developed throughout the modern world.

These forces have also visited upon the industry and university sectors. In the past ten years, industry has been subjected to very significant challenges and shifts in its operating paradigms as it has attempted to bring new innovative products and services to market, to provide employment and growth for its employees, and deliver value to its shareowners. In this time period an entire "era" has come and gone (the dot-com rise and, subsequently, the bubble burst), and many of the hard-earned lessons learned from these types of ventures have already been put to work in the new business models that are part of the ongoing march of progress. Universities too have experienced their own challenges and changes as they work to get ahead of world evolution, and to provide the insight, thought leadership and research that can point the way

1 The author would like to acknowledge, with gratitude, the assistance of Mr. Lou Witkin, of HP's University Relations Worldwide, and Mr. Ron Crough, of Vosara, Inc, in the preparation of this chapter.

into a compelling, opportunity-filled, more promising future than the one humankind has experienced so far.

The efforts of Vannevar Bush (Bush, 1945), the national focus on science and technological advancement, a relatively abundant investment strategy, and the set of initiatives that were created by government over the past five decades, created an impressive, extended renaissance of unparalleled technological development, significant contributions to society, advancement of knowledge, a thriving environment for companies and economic prosperity for the nation. It provided us with the foundation for a virtuous partnership-based ecosystem between universities, industry and government.

This arrangement seemed to have stood the test of time, until very recently. Cracks have begun to emerge in this foundation, and it now appears that future success and accomplishment can no longer be assured, given the challenges and shifts we are witnessing in these present spaces. It's somewhat ironic that while recent infrastructure developments have enabled us to collaborate and engage with each other more easily than at any other time in history, changes in our thinking, attitudes, beliefs and motivations have simultaneously placed obstacles in the way that have to be overcome.

THE COLLABORATIVE FUTURE

Researchers throughout the world are more and more discovering like-minded colleagues who are interested in their work, and who can add to it and advance it through unique insights and contributions. Companies now realize that products and services are not delivered to customers in isolation, but rather through the richness of an ecosystem of players who add value beyond what was imagined in the original product concept. Governments are interacting more with each other as they work to address present needs and link the efforts of others into their new planned initiatives and programmes. The first expression of interconnection and engagement is well underway as people recognize the opportunity to be harvested from engaging with others of like kind in distant corners of the globe, with whom they can naturally and easily synergize perspectives, problems and plans.

The second development in interaction and engagement is not so far along. How does one engage with different and diverse-minded individuals, organizations and institutions across the globe? What happens when people and systems come together that hold different philosophies, value systems, beliefs, and criteria? How can they productively engage with and collaborate with each other in interesting and virtuous ways in order to discover additional insight and contribution beyond what was previously possible? How can academia, for example, engage on a broad scale with industry? How can governments utilize and link with these two societal resources to accomplish great things? How can all three come together in significant ways and complex arrangements in order to meet some of the challenges that are faced by all of humankind?

Collaborative engagement will be the norm in the knowledge and information exchange wave (Johnson, this book). Industry brings to such collaborations the understanding of how research advances can be applied and provides inspiration to the university researchers' quest for fundamental understanding (Stokes, 1997). Yet we have not figured out all the ways of successfully and easily collaborating on a broad scale. In order to understand this area, we will now examine some recent developments in the university-industry relationship space, with government as a backdrop to that work. We will explore some of the factors and forces motivating the shifts and changes in each of these areas with a view to understanding some of the unhealthy overlaps that have been created as a result.

ECOSYSTEM TRANSFORMATION

There are three broad categories of factors and forces contributing to the transformation that we are experiencing in the university-industry relationship space. These will be discussed in the following sections, from the perspective of those affecting —

- University mission, context, and environment;
- Industry mission, context, and environment;
- Government purpose, directions, and agendas.

Factors & Forces Affecting University Mission, Context and Environment

A number of factors and forces contribute to the university community's motivations, directions, operating parameters and ongoing ability to successfully navigate the road ahead. Some of the ones relevant to our discussion around collaboration are:

- Building and equipment asset bases continue to age, and are in need of renewal, upgrade, replacement and/or revitalization;
- Governments, both federal and state, continue to reduce funding in science and technology, particularly in the physical sciences area;
- The rise in entrepreneurial successes and the dot-com era create expectations of large paybacks from brilliant "new ideas". Much of the focus is drawn to what is possible, and little attention is given to the large number of company failures that don't materialize success;
- Professors and small research teams gain increased motivation to build start-up companies in order to profit from their new ideas;

- Bayh-Dole legislation is passed, and its interpretation leads to an increased desire in controlling who gets the rights to commercialize technology;
- The "get rich" archetype gains momentum from a small number of impressive data-points (both universities and research teams);
- Universities (as institutions) are encouraged and asked to participate in economic development outcomes by local and regional government interests;
- Focus and emphasis shift from educating students and dissemination of early-stage knowledge and information, to research, revenue generation through Intellectual Property ("IP") licensing, and downstream control of commercialization rights and parameters.

Factors & Forces Affecting Industry Purpose, Context and Environment

A number of forces and factors contribute to industry's motivations, directions, operating parameters and ongoing ability to sustain themselves into the future. Some of the ones relevant to our discussion around collaboration are:

- Companies are forced to blend new business models with "brick-&-mortar" operations, as they struggle with their internet presences and value delivery systems;
- Dot-com bubble gains momentum, then bursts;
- The internet takes root as the information infrastructure of choice, and activities accelerate (in both durations and timeframes) as information moves freely and easily between companies and across international borders (Friedman, 2005);
- Business becomes more "real-time" in almost every dimension;
- The increased competitiveness and real-time information flows erode margins and shorten product lifetimes, thereby putting downward pressure on goods and services pricing;
- Disintermediation becomes the norm, as companies rewrite the rules of their distribution and value delivery networks;
- Globalization grows and continues to accelerate, as companies move more and more jobs (and job categories) to capable, lower cost economies (Friedman, 2005);
- Consolidation, cutting costs and the lowering expense structures become the order of the day;
- In the absence of strategic relationship interests and outcomes, funding to universities decreases (considered philanthropy);
- The newest emerging paradigm requires companies to excel at both innovation and reducing costs simultaneously. Previously, these two

situations were perceived to be in conflict, and a single organization was either clearly in a growth/investment mode, or clearly in a consolidation mode.

Factors & Forces Affecting Government Purpose, Directions and Agendas

A number of forces and factors contribute to governmental motivations, directions, operating parameters and ongoing ability to create sustainable environments. Some of the ones relevant to our discussion around collaboration are:

- Government continues to struggle with high spending deficits, due to a variety of factors;
- Reductions in science and technology investment are offset by increased focus on bio-tech, pharma and homeland security;
- Recession takes place (2000-2003), recovery is slow, and economists disagree as to whether latest numbers show growth and recovery, or "stag-flation";
- Economic development becomes a motivating factor in many government actions and decisions, at the federal, state and local levels;
- Loss of jobs (globalization, offshoring) becomes both a regional and national focus;
- The U.S. struggles to return to virtuous environment it has enjoyed in past.

A Confluence of Factors Creates "The Perfect Storm"

During the past decade, cracks have begun to emerge in what used to be a solid virtuous relationship foundation between American universities and industry. Revenue shortfalls, reductions in funding from all sources, changes in legislation, global competition and many of the factors discussed earlier have caused both companies and universities to intensify their focus on revenue generation, cost cutting and accomplishing more with less. This has precipitated an unhealthy overlap of interests in the commercialization space that had not been experienced previously on a broad scale, and left these partners of many decades puzzled and confused as they try to figure out what has been happening to the overall system. Some of the symptoms of this troubling situation are:

- Universities increase focus on downstream commercialization through IP patenting and licensing as a vehicle to enhance revenue;
- Universities increase their role in economic development under pressure from various governmental interests;

- Companies increase focus, consolidate activities, execute cost-cutting strategies and increase efficiencies in order to deal with the competitive forces and pressure on cost-structures;
- Companies participate in globalization and increase offshoring activity in an attempt to cut costs and preserve competitiveness, be sustainable and maintain healthy levels of profitability;
- Patent trolling becomes more pervasive, as many players (both companies and universities) attempt to extract revenue from the successful commercialization of technology after the investments have been made and the risks overcome.

The net effect of all this is that many more players are now attempting to occupy positions within the same space, with overlapping interests, while trying to work together more intimately and more intensely than ever before:

- The commercialization space becomes very crowded as many more companies enter the fray due to internet-enabled global competition;
- New categories of players (universities), who before had focused much of their interests on early-stage research, have become interested in participating in the commercialization space, as a vehicle to generate revenue;
- Intellectual property (IP) patenting and licensing issues become a major barrier in the ability to negotiate joint research contexts and gain agreement on collaborative research efforts, joint ventures, cooperative R & D, and a host of other mutually beneficial arrangements.

THE EMERGENCE OF 'IP' AS A LOCUS OF DIFFICULTY

After some reflection and examination of the situation, one question continues to persist: "How is it that universities and companies are recently experiencing great difficulty in working with each other, while company-to-company relationships haven't seemed to have suffered from the same problems, over this same time period?"

Companies, despite their drive for growth and their competitive nature, for the most part have developed reasonably successful models for working together over the decades. Perhaps it's the many years of failed experiences, the talented staffs and the savvy business managers who were developed through these experiences that enable the situation. Perhaps it's the commonality of the shared value system. In any event, there exists a rich set of models and relationship structures, together with a body of knowledge and expertise, by which one company can engage with another, even when the two are in direct competition. To list a few of these inter-company engagement models there are technology exchanges, joint developments, contracted system —

sub-system developments, procurement relationships, those who may develop testbeds and prototypes, companies who will perform services for each other (such as testing, verification, quality assurance, etc.), and many, many more.

Concrete Outcomes vs. 'Delayed Binding'

When the range of these inter-company engagement structures were examined, they all seemed to have one thing in common — they were founded on an exchange of something *tangible and concrete*. The outcome and the reason "why" two companies were working together was known at the onset of the relationship development activity, and the object(s) of exchange were specific, known and able to be negotiated in a tangible way. For example, some of the types of outcomes and exchanges on which companies can work together are — acquiring software or hardware from one another, executing a joint product development, acquiring technology, procuring a completed component, sub-system or system, contracting for a product element or an entire product to be developed, securing a prototype or testbed which embodies a particular concept or capability, instantiating an algorithm, conducting a simulation, building a model, producing an analysis or report of some system element, and so on.

When the array of successful inter-company engagements was further examined, it was determined that many of the process models were developed first around the exchange of *tangible outcomes*, and then the secondary discussion could take place around who gets to own it, who pays for it, who gets to replicate or leverage it, who gets to license or sub-license it, etc. The point is that the "it" was known and mutually understood, before all of the ownership structures around the "it" were dealt with. The object(s) of the exchange set a direction and context for all of the other conversations to take place. And the negotiations around ownership were anchored in an understanding of what specifically was being considered as the object of the partnership arrangement or relationship structure.

When looked at the company-university interactions, the situation was quite different. "IP" was talked about as if it were a tangible object. Yet there seemed to be little precise understanding of what the "it" — the output of the collaboration — was. At the onset of the interaction, the intent was to create a joint research context, to collaborate in some area of mutual interest, and IP was a *proxy* for something to be determined in the future, which presumably had value. This deferral of reference or "delayed binding" made the ownership and licensing discussions intangible and indirect, and an order of magnitude more complex. The fact that we were even discussing the ownership rights to something that might be created in future is rather ethereal. Since it was neither guaranteed that IP would necessarily be created, nor was it assured that it would have a value that both sides could agree on (if it had any value at all), agreements as to what value transfer should occur to which party, also became difficult to converge. Couple this with the fact that some parts of the law require that the fair-market-value of the IP not be determined or given away "up-front" (essentially before it is created), and we have all the forces necessary in the system to provide for a very complex negotiation of arrangements.

Furthermore, once having begun the IP negotiations, the issues seemed to take on a life of their own as teams of people from each side attempted to plan for and negotiate every eventuality, "in case" something valuable might come out of the joint collaborative activity. The discussions very quickly became hypothetical, ungrounded, and oriented around the *ownership rights* of something, as well as around *responsibility for* and *risk avoidance of* it, should the "it" become problematic. Many of these "IP" discussions became focused further up the food chain, closer to the ideas and concepts development, instead of being focused further down the food chain, closer to implementation. The negotiations also seemed to take on an emotional aspect, as the participants became very attached to their own ideas and the perception of an over-estimated value that they might have later. If we contrast this with the typical "matter of fact" business negotiations that usually take place around specific deliverables in most inter-company negotiations, it is easy to understand why the negotiations stall and become difficult to converge.

Model Differences and 'Intent'

Yet there was still something deeper going on throughout these interactions. There was a difference in how each partner approached the area of "intent". Universities were negotiating, not with an intent to commercialize their work (as most companies do in typical inter-company technology exchanges), but with a view to who should hold the rights to commercialize the work and which other players may be blocked from doing so. This is not a situation in which there are equal players with a common intent to move forward (as there are in many inter-company negotiations.) This situation is more like a model in which there's a late "assert play" involving payment for the continued rights to be able to ship product. Because of the inherent inequality of partners, and the difference in their intents (one is trying to move forward with something, the other is trying to receive compensation for not blocking it), these conversations inherently contain the seeds of distrust.

The underlying difference of intents, together with the undercurrents of distrust that are embedded therein, represent a somewhat contaminated model. They cause what would otherwise be a rational conversation between two potential partners to encounter difficulty rather quickly, and either end in difficulty or not converge to conclusion. At the root of it is both a slightly contaminated and somewhat contemptuous model — "We're not able to commercialize this, but if any of our *ideas* are contained therein, we will assert control over which parties get which rights to use it, and which parties will be blocked in their attempts to do the same." The conversation thus necessarily involves blocking positions and negative future potential, instead of two partners moving forward together in a useful way. In the negotiations phase, it's not a win-win situation that is being worked toward, but a compromise at best, and some might even liken it as being similar to "bad faith" negotiations. Even when the IP negotiations are successful, frequently none of the participants like the outcome or feel that it was a win, worthy of their time and attention.

Criteria and Value Systems

An important set of criteria that companies optimize around is *design freedom*. Companies need to have, as much as possible, the freedom and ability to commercialize their ideas and concepts in order to survive, to be sustainable, to provide employment, and to provide value to their customers and to society. They will naturally move away from any relationship or partnership structure that seeks to limit or erode design freedom in their current or future product development efforts. They must do this as a matter of survival.

Furthermore, companies know how to preserve design freedom in a competitive arena. The rules of competitive engagement have been around for decades, are supported by law, and provide both restrictions and remedies for "anti-competitive" behaviour, all the while supporting a system which seeks to provide a mostly level playing field for new and established entrants, and all who participate.

Universities, on the other hand, optimize around *academic freedom and open inquiry* in the context of their education mission. They will naturally tend to avoid any attempts to limit their thinking or be constrained in the areas they investigate, as they conduct their research and educate students in the pursuit of their academic mission.

These two value systems are usually compatible with each other when universities pursue early-stage, pre-competitive research interests, and companies focus their time and efforts in the later-stage commercialization and application of technology to problems and opportunities of interest. Of late, these two philosophies and value systems have been made to intersect in the commercialization space, as the focus and intensity of IP negotiation around ownership and licensing rights have been taken to an all-time high.

At this time, we haven't yet developed the necessary knowledge and experience to successfully blend the preservation of design freedom, with the desire for open inquiry, in the commercialization space. The symptoms of this become apparent when trying to conclude IP negotiations while setting up a collaborative arrangement in an area of interest. The challenges and frustrations that many people experience in this negotiation process are simply not worthy of the time and effort expended.

Cross-Licensing & Technology Transfer

An interesting aspect of the inter-company engagement model is around patent cross-licensing. Consider, for example, that many large companies in the IT space have broad cross-licensing arrangements with each other, *even including their competitors*. They know that sooner or later, deep down inside their large organizations, some ambitious groups will spring up, who will want to exact a pound of flesh from a competitor who is on the way to market with a product that they can block or assert rights over.

Senior organizational leaders know that this is bound to happen in a competitive space. They know that a common failure mode of high-level strategy is to be focused on competitors, and to lose track of the customers, innovation and of value creation. Accordingly, they will usually want to have most of their company's efforts focused on creating value for customers, and they will optimize their internal systems to do so. They accomplish this by setting policy which makes product rights and claims "trolling" a non-opportunity from the outset. Rather than investing large amounts of negative energy blocking each others products from getting to market, companies usually favour some form of broad cross-licensing arrangement. Implicitly, they want the competitive arena to be the marketplace, where value is delivered to customers, and not based upon who has the best attorneys or who can synthesize the best blocking positions from their past work efforts through their current patent portfolio. Simply stated, they want the focus to be in the right area to ensure the long-term survival and competitive advantage of the company. Notwithstanding the discussion of assert rights and patent trolls, long-term successful companies are not built by extracting payment from others détente in blocking their efforts to bring products to market.

Companies also do not view patents and licensing as the vehicles of technology transfer. Technology access and transfer are treated as a separate business activity, worthy of first-class attention and focus. Their preference is also not to "buy" patents from each other, but to trade them within an overall cross-licensing strategy. If there are significant differences in the value of each portfolio, then some compensation will usually change hands. But the cross-licensing strategy is more like an "ante" — something that others must have to play in the game. As this strategy builds out, other companies are then encouraged to show up with "roughly equivalent patent portfolios" in order to play in the space.

Universities view this quite differently. They believe that "patents" are indicators of a technology that is "sitting on the shelf", ready to be sold, transferred and used. They see these licensable ideas as highly valuable, and will withhold use rights depending on how many companies may be interested in the work. From their point of view, the more companies that are interested, the higher the value of the ideas must be.

Yet companies know that these technologies which are being offered for licensing are not working, maintained and operable somewhere within the university environment. At best, there may be demonstration vehicles and prototypes for the concepts embodied; a jumble of lab equipment that works well in controlled experiments may or may not translate to a reliable, affordable product (Mitchell, 2005). In contrast, when two companies are engaging in significant and substantial technology transfer, those technologies have usually been reduced to practice and used across a variety of products. There are people, resources, equipment, processes and competencies associated with them. When they are transferred or otherwise made available, the receiving company (licensee) is usually provided access to this entire range of assets for use in applying the technologies to commercial applications. Companies see the value of technology acquisition and transfer as being quite independent of patents. While they will trade patents as bargaining chips, they will invest substantial time, human capital and equipment in making a technology transfer real with another industrial partner.

CONCLUSION

Given these inherent philosophical, value and model differences, it's not surprising that companies and universities experience difficulty in concluding IP agreements around the commercialization of ideas and concepts, in the course of trying to work together collaboratively. If the difficulty were just limited to one area, the situation would not be so worrisome. Unfortunately, a single IP negotiation turned sour between a company and a university usually damages the relationship, and has lasting effects that carry over to other areas of interaction.

At the present time, we are caught in the middle of a grand "sticking point" — possibly an inflection or transition to greater opportunity. The future holds significant promise for those who can collaborate and work with others to advance concepts and ideas. However, the area of sponsored research agreements brings industry and universities unnaturally together, in a space for which there is not yet a body of practice and experience for how to work successfully with each other. The proxy for the yet-to-be-determined solution set is the IP negotiations surrounding the collaboration.

How does one resolve the two different energies — the desire to move forward with the intent to commercialize, and the intent to protect and dole out "rights" in order to extract maximum value? How can a company and an institution have a "good relationship" at one level, when their organizations are in conflict over blocking IP positions? The researchers desire to work together and collaborate. The institutions and companies want to have good relationships and to be members of an innovation ecosystem that works well, with government, for the benefit to society and for the greater good. These model differences represent uncharted territory that we are presently grappling with. Perhaps a good first step is to recognize this, gain additional perspective and understand the situation from the higher level of philosophical orientation, values and criteria.

REFERENCES

Bush, Vannevar. (1945). *Science, the Endless Frontier, A Report to the President on a Program for Postwar Scientific Research*, Office of Scientific Research and Development (reprinted by the National Science Foundation, Washington D.C., 1990).

Friedman, Thomas L. (2005). *The World is Flat*. Farrar, Strauss, and Giroux, New York.

Johnson, Wayne. (2004). "Globalization of Research and Development in a Federated World", Weber & Duderstadt (eds), *Reinventing the Research University*, Glion IV Colloquium, Economica, Paris, pp. 159-175.

Johnson, Wayne. (this book). "The Collaboration Imperative", in Weber & Duderstadt (eds), *Universities and Business: Partnering for the Knowledge Economy*, Economica, London.

Mitchell, Lesa. (2005). "Moving Innovations to Market, Why the U.S. Technology Transfer System is Clogged — and How We Hope to Help Open the Pipeline". Ewing Marion Kauffman Foundation, Kansas City, MO., http://web.kauffman.org/items.cfm?itemID=503

Schramm, Carl. (2004). "Accelerating Technology Transfer and Commercialization" Kauffman Foundation IP Commercialization and Research Spinouts Conference, Boston MA. http://www.kauffman.org/pdf/IPCommercRev.111504b.pdf

Stokes, Donald E. (1997). *Pasteur's Quadrant, Basic Science and Technological Innovation*. R. R. Donnelley and Sons, Harrisonburg, VA.

CHAPTER 19

Effective Knowledge Transfer: From Research Universities to Industry

Thomas Connelly

INTRODUCTION

The model for industrial research has changed. The era of large, independent industrial research laboratories, operating in isolation, has largely passed. This trend started a decade ago and continues apace. It is the consequence of several forces that continue to gain momentum. And even as industry looks increasingly outside its own laboratories for new technologies, changes within the universities make them more receptive to industry partnership.

In the U.S., the Bayh Dole Act in 1980 launched a fundamental change in the position of public universities concerning applied research, and the licensing of consequential intellectual property. In the European Union, Janez Potocnik, Commissioner for Science and Research, has spelled out a new direction for E.U.-sponsored research, emphasizing "simplification" in the Seventh Framework Programme for 2007 to 2013. One goal of this simplification is enhanced university-industry collaboration. The U.K.'s 2003 Lambert Review (H.M. Treasury, 2003) outlined new approaches needed for university–industry interactions in that country. Japan, through its Ministry of Education, has liberalized the terms on which its universities engage in work with industry, offering professors more freedom in undertaking compensated work outside their university appointments.

Thus, the largest economies of the world are driving changes in the way that their universities work with industry. Tighter budgets for government-sponsored research are another factor driving universities toward more industry-funded research.

Since the end of the Cold War, the U.S. national laboratories have explored new technologies and sought new missions. Federal legislation enacted in the late 1980s opened the door for technical transfer offices at the national laboratories. Collaboration with industry is now more attractive to government labs in the U.S. and elsewhere.

Another important trend for industry has been the development of a vibrant world of technology-driven start-up companies, funded by venture capital markets. This has created new options for researchers in industry and different risk/reward profiles for their careers. Ideas and technology generated in the start-up companies form another basis for collaboration. Thus, large-budget research companies look not just to universities and government labs, but also to the world of start-ups as sources of technologies and new businesses. Small cap companies have emerged across a broad range of industries and technologies, ranging from biotech to software to electronic materials. Frequently technologies of start-up companies have had their origins in universities or in larger companies, or even in government laboratories.

Within industry, pressures from cost competitiveness and global innovation intensify. Companies seek ways to improve R & D productivity, to reduce costs of R & D infrastructure and to bring products to market faster. External research partnerships have become the preferred means.

EVOLUTION FOR UNIVERSITY-INDUSTRY COLLABORATION

Structures have emerged in both universities and industry to deal with these trends. Research universities have established technology transfer offices, to facilitate their interactions with industry. Companies have formed groups to deal with in-licensing from universities. Companies have set up venturing organizations to tap technologies from start-up companies. Venture capitalists are looking for large cap companies as investors, or advisors, in part to develop some "built-in" exit options for their ventures. Everyone is forming and populating "advisory groups" to track and to learn from research approaches in the other sectors. All of this is a far cry from the past practices of university-industry relations.

During most of the last century, industrial financial support to universities had a large philanthropic component. Outright grants were provided by industry to endow chairs and to construct university buildings. Research sponsorship was often provided to obtain preferential access for recruiting purposes. The sponsored research was conducted in areas of general interests to companies, but with a focus on fundamentals, model systems or "precompetitive" technology.

Industrial researchers have always followed academic contributions to the scientific literature, and valued the development of fundamental knowledge.

at the heart of academic research. However, the strongest historic link between universities and industry focused on knowledge transfer, not through the literature, but more directly, in the form of human capital. Universities were, and remain, the source of trained talent to populate industrial research laboratories. These incoming researchers normally maintained their contacts at their universities. University professors not only trained potential industrial researchers, but also had skills and insights that were useful in industrial research, and thus served as consultants.

Only very occasionally, in the old model, was there work in the academic labs of direct interest to industry. One of the early DuPont successes dates back to 1925 with the recognition of the work of Professor Nieuwland at the University of Notre Dame. Professor Nieuwland's chemistry became the basis for chloroprene monomer synthesis, practised commercially for nearly 40 years. Acquisition of Professor Nieuwland's technology occurred just two years before DuPont attracted, in 1927, a young instructor from Harvard University, Wallace Carothers, to join the DuPont Company. This was university-industry knowledge transfer of the other sort.

OPEN INNOVATION

The new industrial research model positions universities directly in industry's value creation strategy. University research no longer is used only to inform the research in industry; it can contribute directly to it. University-industry collaboration is only one option in an array of external research partnerships that industry is now pursuing.

Other options make use of web-based sources. A number of web-enabled marketplaces for technologies are now operating. All seek to bring together technology seekers and technology sources. Yet2, NineSigma and Innocentive are three leading examples. While they have nuanced differences in their business models, all of them seek to match technology providers with technology needs. All recognize that there is a global market for technology, with a myriad of providers and users. All recognize that potential sources of solutions are globally dispersed.

"Open Innovation" is a term that has been applied to this new model of research. Professor Henry Chesbrough's book (2003) by that title explains that technology development now relies on a combination of in-house capabilities, and accession of critical technologies from external sources. Speed and productivity are recognized as the principle drivers of open innovation.

Open innovation is a global pursuit. The development of science is more and more widespread. Newly industrial nations are training a larger and larger fraction of the world's scientists and engineers. Information technology allows us to access ideas instantly from around the world.

EXAMPLES FOR UNIVERSITY-INDUSTRY COLLABORATION

Leading industrial research companies may pursue dozens or even hundreds of university-sponsored research programmes. Certainly the pharmaceutical industry will partner with universities in a different way than the microelectronics or software industries. Nonetheless, virtually every industry is now intent on development of strong university-industry partnerships.

These partnerships can take on various forms: from very specific to very broad. Below, are a few current examples from the DuPont Company's experiences.

Hamburg University

Professor Detlef Geffken, Institute of Pharmacy of Hamburg University developed a research lead for an agricultural chemical, a molecule with interesting fungicidal properties. Having come to the attention of DuPont in 1989 DuPont licensed Professor Geffken's lead compound and elaborated this lead through the synthesis of more than 700 related molecules. This work resulted in a highly successful commercial fungicide under the brand, Famoxate® Collaboration with Professor Geffken's laboratory has continued, but this has not extended beyond this single laboratory.

University of North Carolina-North Carolina State University

Professor Joseph DeSimone holds joint appointments in chemistry and chemical engineering at the University of North Carolina and North Carolina State University. Professor DeSimone is also director of the National Science Foundation Science and Technology Center for Environmentally Responsible Solvents and Processes. DuPont has collaborated with Professor DeSimone since he received a DuPont Young Professor Award more than a decade ago. Among Professor DeSimone's research interests is the use of supercritical CO_2 as a medium for a number of reactions. This technology offers environmental advantages compared to conventional technologies, solvents or surfactants that are used to conduct certain types of chemistry. DuPont had a strong interest in this work, and struck a partnership to develop the technology for use of supercritical CO_2 to polymerize certain fluoropolymers products. Extensive licensing arrangements were concluded with Professor DeSimone. The supercritical CO_2 technology was further developed and scaled up in DuPont laboratories. With the support of the government of the State of North Carolina, we successfully commercialized that technology in North Carolina. Professor DeSimone's students have been hired by DuPont, and we continue to collaborate broadly with his Center.

In a separate collaboration at the University of North Carolina, Professor Maurice Brookhart had developed a family of late transition metal catalysts for single-site polymerization of polyolefins. DuPont entered into a licensing agreement for the initial patents, hired one of Professor Brookhart's group members, expanded the research in DuPont laboratories, and supported the continuing research in Professor Brookhart's labs.

DuPont-MIT Alliance

DuPont MIT Alliance (DMA), started in 2000, represents a new level of commitment in an industry-university partnership. The largest alliance of its kind, it has served as a model for other collaborations. The initial focus of DMA was industrial biotechnology, and the intent was to jumpstart DuPont's entry into this exciting new field. This initial scope allowed plenty of room for innovation in areas such as biopolymers, biosensors, bio-surfaces and biomedical materials. DMA did not target a single professor or a single department. Rather it involved the full scope of MIT. More than 15 MIT academic departments and centres have participated in dozens of research projects.

Initially, work was of a more fundamental nature. As the research teams have gained more experience in working together, the level of openness has increased. Projects are proposed by MIT or DuPont. More and more projects are jointly proposed.

Recognition of the education role of DMA is reflected in the fact that a significant portion of the funding has been set aside for education purposes. First-year graduate student funding was a key financial need for MIT. DuPont supports DuPont Presidential Scholars. More than 100 students have been supported so far.

Another educational dimension of DMA is the offering of tailored short courses by MIT faculty on subjects of DuPont's choosing. These courses have ranged from highly specialized presentation on narrow research subjects to an overview of biotechnology designed for DuPont corporate leaders.

Recently, the DMA has entered a new phase, and will be continued for a second five years. The scope has been expanded beyond the original focus on bio-based materials. New technology areas such as nanotechnology, flat-panel displays and microcircuit materials are now included.

Current university-industry collaborations tend to be focused in a company's home country, close to its internal research base. This pattern is just beginning to change, but globalization of university-industry is occurring. For example, U.S. research universities are engaging in collaborations with companies headquartered in other regions.

LEARNING FROM UNIVERSITY-INDUSTRY COLLABORATION

Obstacles to university-industry collaborations are numerous, but the above-outlined factors provide a potent driving force for even more collaborations in the future. The universities and companies that will be most successful in collaboration will be those who succeed in overcoming the historic and cultural barriers that exist on both sides.

Overcoming Barriers to University-Industry Collaboration

Knowledge transfer remains at the heart of university-industry collaborations. Individual faculty members, programmes or departments with expertise and accomplishments in a given field are a powerful magnet for industry seeking technologies. Nonetheless, more collaborations are problematic than successful, so that steps must be taken to improve the likelihood of success.

This begins with a clear understanding of the objectives of both parties for the collaboration: industry must recognize the research and education missions of the university, thus the needs for continuity of funding for students, for topics that are compatible with the university's research mission, and for the ability to publish results of the research. Universities must recognize that which is important to industry: the ability to exploit a technology in exclusivity and the imposition deadlines, milestones and redirects. Unrealistic expectations by either side can derail collaborations.

Universities must have a disposition that supports industry collaborations as appropriate to the university mission. Many universities lack adequate staffing or experience in technology transfer. This often slows the development of partnerships. Universities or professors can have unrealistic expectations in the valuation of technology and IP rights, or fail to consider the cost associated with launching a technology, post-discovery, and its impact on valuation. In the case of state-supported institutions, similar unrealistic expectation can arise from government–local/regional investment, or job-creation, or other constraints on exploitation are barriers that are sometimes imposed.

Industry, for its part, must be open to a collaborative approach. "Not-invented-here" attitudes defeat any attempt at open innovation. It is also important that industry recognize the mission of the university, and select or adapt the subject collaboration to that mission. Universities are not contract research operations, nor outsourcing vehicles.

The most significant barriers to effective university-industry collaboration are mutual, rather than originating on one side or the other. The key to successful collaborations is the commitment of effort, beyond the financial support. Below are some best practices in university-industry collaborations:

- Selection of appropriate projects of genuine interest and importance to both the university and the company.
- Realistic expectations.
- Clear understanding of intellectual property, or other rights associated with the work to be undertaken.

- Defined responsibilities and assigned accountable persons in both organizations.
- Frequent (ideally weekly) contact between researchers from both sides, using teleconferences, visits or co-location of the team.
- Regular assessment of project performance vs. expectations.
- Continuity of project staffing and predictability in financial support.
- Involvement and visible support from leadership in both the university and the company.

Benefits of University-Industry Collaboration

For the university, industry represents a development partner and a commercial outlet for early-stage university research. As a partner, and holder of intellectual property, the university stands to share in financial benefits of research.

Collaboration also offers to universities an access to industrial experience, resources and know-how to support research on such subjects as pilot facilities, scale-up, health and safety management, patent strategy and marketing. Collaboration is also helpful to the education mission of the university, offering students practical training in contact with the industrial research setting.

University partnerships bring industry an access to world-class expertise and access to students, who are potential future employees. Joint work with universities also represents a stimulus to an industrial research organization. The flow of new concepts and the intellectual rigor of academic research complements the need to "get to an answer" in industry. Universities may also present a cost-effective alternative to in-house research, for more speculative research projects. Universities are also sources of in-licensed technologies that cut time as well as cost on development of projects.

Finally, it must be recognized that today there is neither a shortage of top-flight research universities, nor a shortage of able industrial research partners. Both universities and companies must acknowledge that what they offer to the other is generally not in short supply. This realization should promote a spirit of reasonableness during the negotiation phase, and throughout the conduct of the collaboration. This is already understood by leading universities and companies, alike. Thus, one should expect to see continuing strong growth in university-industry collaborations, and these collaborations will be increasingly boundary-less and global in nature.

REFERENCES

Chesbrough, H. W. (2003). *Open Innovation: The Imperative for Creating and Profiting from Technology*, Harvard Business School Publishing, Boston.

European Industrial Research Management Association. (2004). Working Group No 63 Report: Technology Access for Open Innovation. Paris.

H.M. Treasury. (2003). *Lambert Review of Business-University Collaboration*. H.M. Stationery Office, London.

Hounshell, D. A. & Smith, J. K. (1988). *Science and Corporate Strategy*. Cambridge University Press, Cambridge.

Innocentive. www.innocentive.com

Ninesigma. www.ninesigma.com

Yet2. www.yet2.com

PART V

•••••••••••••

Human Capital

CHAPTER 20

Declining Demand among Students for Science and Engineering?

Georg Winckler and Martin Fieder

Leading industrial as well as developing countries have identified research and innovation as the driving forces for future economic development. As a consequence, policies aim at increasing not only research budgets, but also the number and quality of scientists and engineers. In this context the education of scientists and engineers is of increasing importance.

In 2000 the E.U. announced the Lisbon goal: to become the world's leading knowledge driven economy. A major step towards this goal is "the 3% objective" (3% of the GPD for research and development) in 2010. Related to this objective is the need for about 700,000 additional scientists in the public and in the private sector in the E.U. by 2010, about 50% of them at Ph.D. level. This number is derived from a comparison of the number of researchers per 1,000 members of the workforce between Europe and other parts of the world. In the E.U.-15 this number is 5.7, and 3.5 for the ten new member states. In Japan there are 9.1 researchers per 1,000 members of the workforce, and 8.1 in the U.S.

To achieve the objective of a leading knowledge economy, the role of European universities has to be strengthened. In the past, universities were perceived merely as sums of individual researchers or research groups, as conglomerations of individual departments or just as accumulations of study programmes. The Lisbon goal, however, implies that European universities emerge as strong institutions which are the main actors in creating and transmitting knowledge (Winckler, 2004).

GENERAL ENROLMENT — AND GRADUATION RATES

In several European countries (Austria, Finland, France, Germany, the Netherlands, Spain, U.K.) overall enrolment rates in post secondary education have risen generally, but differ significantly from country to country. The lowest rates have Austria and France with about 30% of an age-group enrolled in post secondary education; the highest enrolment rate has Finland with 77% (Germany: 35%; the Netherlands: 53%; Spain: 50%; the U.K.: 47% [OECD, 2004]; the data for Austria and Germany also include the sector of vocational training). These numbers indicate clearly that there are substantial differences between European countries, and between the U.S. and Europe. The low participation rates in higher education in Austria are particularly surprising because, until 2001, no tuition fees were charged and restrictions on access to higher education were introduced only recently — July 2005 — in a few fields, e.g., medicine.

Concerning overall participation rates in tertiary education, Europe is clearly lacking and is behind the U.S. (52% net entry rate in the U.S.) The low participation numbers in higher education in Europe may be explained by a high investment in vocational training at the upper secondary level. This is especially the case for Germany and Austria. If countries invest too much in vocational education instead of in higher education, they may run the risk of losing innovative power: vocational education enables workers to operate established technologies very productively, whereas general education enables workers to develop and adapt new technologies more easily (Krueger, 2004).

Increasing participation rates of the age-group in higher education might be a way to attract more students for fields of science and engineering. This seems to be a promising policy, especially in countries with low participation rates. Generally enhancing the accessibility of higher education — that is, the ability of people from all social and economic backgrounds to enter higher education — remains an important issue for future policy making. The "massification" of higher education should not be perceived negatively, since massification might be the very foundation of the modern knowledge economy (Usher & Cervenan, 2005).

ENROLMENT RATES IN THE SCIENCES AND ENGINEERING

The overall percentage of graduations in the sciences and engineering differ among OECD countries; graduation rates vary also with respect to the fields of study (OECD, 2004): in Korea, Germany, Finland, France, the U.K., Austria, Spain, Italy, Australia, the U.S. and Poland, from 14.9% in engineering and manufacturing to 1% in mathematics and statistics. Korea, Germany and

Finland are leading the pack. In contrast, the U.S. has a relatively low per-centage of graduations in science and engineering (Table 1). One reason for the differences might be the existence of polytechnics in a particular country and the size of this sector.

Table 1: Percentages of graduations in the sciences and engineering of OECD countries (OECD, 2004). Vocational education in Germany and Austria are partially included.

OECD Countries	Engineering, manufacturing, construction % of total Graduations 2002	Life sciences % of total Graduations 2002	Physical sciences % of total Graduations 2002	Mathematics and statistics % of total Graduations 2002	Computing % of total Graduations 2002	Total
Korea	27.4	2.1	3.5	1.9	3.5	**38.4**
Germany	17.6	3.4	5.0	1.7	3.3	**30.9**
Finland	21.6	1.4	2.0	0.6	3.4	**29.0**
France	12.5	5.8	4.9	2.5	3.0	**28.7**
U.K.	10.1	6.2	4.8	1.4	5.7	**28.1**
Austria	18.0	3.6	3.0	0.7	2.7	**28.0**
Spain	14.3	2.5	3.1	1.2	3.2	**24.3**
Italy	15.2	3.3	1.6	2.0	0.7	**22.8**
Australia	7.7	3.3	2.3	0.5	7.9	**21.6**
U.S.	6.3	3.7	1.4	0.9	3.4	**15.73**
Poland	7.3	0.7	1.2	0.6	1.0	**10.8**
Average	**14.9**	**3.4**	**3.0**	**1.3**	**3.4**	**25.3**

Enrolment rates in science and engineering seem to be cyclical (Bhatta-charjee, 2004). Despite a recent modest increase of the enrolment rates in the U.S., the 1993 peak has not been reached since.

INCREASE IN NUMBER OF RESEARCHERS AND THE EVOLUTION OF RESEARCH TEAMS

If Europe wants to increase the number of graduations in order to raise the total number of researchers, care has to be taken to ensure that the rise in number of researchers is in line with the "absorbing" capacity of the overall research system. Growth that is too fast may lead to inefficiencies in the use of resources. The absorbing performance of a research system is especially determined by the formation and composition of research teams: the size of research teams should be large enough to enable specialization and the division of labour (Katzenbach & Smith, 1993); it may spur creativity, but may also promote conflicts and miscommunications (Larson et al., 1996). Due to these reasons, the evolution of research teams takes time and depends on parameters like team size, fraction of newcomers and the tendency of incumbents to repeat previous collaborations (Guimerà et al., 2005).

CURRICULUM DEVELOPMENT

Universities play a major role in educating future scientists. Therefore, it is of great importance to make the curricula in science, medicine and technology more attractive to students and to increase thereby the number of graduates in these fields. Traditionally the courses offered in science and technology are too much weighted towards the "knowledge domain" (Barnett, 2004). What is needed is that learning is based on the discovery of new knowledge to inspire a passion for discovery.

The attractiveness of curricula will be increased by focusing on making students familiar with the range of methods (including mathematical and statistical tools) currently used in physics, chemistry, molecular biology or other fields. Sufficient methodological competence is one of the most important prerequisites for working as a scientist. Acquiring methodological skills will usually take a long (and sometimes difficult) time. In addition, science and engineering students acquire the substance of knowledge mostly during "field work", guided by experienced scientists. This kind of "knowledge transfer" is highly relevant for the training of future scientists. The design of science curricula should take into account the fact that guidance in research by experienced scientists is necessary.

Due to these reasons, especially in Europe, a new understanding of the "design" of science and technology curricula should emerge. The Bologna Process provides a unique chance to do so. Despite excellent general scientific education of students, early participation of students in research projects should be offered. Project management and other transferable skills should also be part of the curricula from the very beginning (Gago, 2004).

Interdisciplinary education is of special importance for the sciences, as often problems in the sciences can only be solved by intensified collaboration among disciplines (National Academy of Sciences, 2005). Concerning undergraduate and graduate interdisciplinary education, the academy gives some recommendations:

- Interdisciplinary work should be regular in order to strengthen experimental knowledge;
- For undergraduates to gain deeper interdisciplinary insights, they need to work with faculty members who offer expertise both in their

home discipline and in working together with scientists or scholars from other disciplines;

- Most important for a student is to take a broad range of courses and develop a solid background at least in one discipline. To instigate a broader horizon of students, universities should not offer curricula which are so packed with obligatory examinations that it is nearly impossible for students to take any courses outside their primary field.

WOMEN STUDYING SCIENCE

Overall the proportion of female students enrolled in higher education has been increasing since the 1970s (currently 50 to 60%). Despite this high overall enrolment, it is important to increase the number of women studying sciences and engineering if more scientists and engineers are needed in the future. Yet women opt less frequently for a science curriculum, especially one in the "hard sciences" and engineering when mathematics is an important prerequisite. As mathematics is less important in the life sciences, a high percentage of women have opted for the life sciences (e.g., out of all students enrolled in engineering, only 20% are women, in the "hard sciences" 40% are women, yet in the life sciences the figure is 65%; [Ayalon, 2003]). The reasons might be manifold and may include social influences as well as other more contested factors. Differences between the sexes in mathematical problem-solving remain ambiguous (Walsh, 1999; Green, 1999). As this theme is usually discussed ideologically and emotionally (see, for example, the discussion about the remarks made by Lawrence Summer, president of Harvard University [Dillon, 2005]), for the sake and the importance of the issue, an honest and less ideological discussion needs to take place.

The E.U. is increasing efforts to raise the proportion of women researchers in the sciences: according to the working document "Women and Science: Excellence and Innovation — Gender Equality in Science", €5.7 million will be earmarked for women and science in 2005-2006, bringing the total in the Sixth Framework Programme to around €20 million. A series of gender monitoring studies, designed to monitor progress in gender equality and relevance awareness in the Sixth Framework Programme are currently being launched, as well as an expert group "Women in Science and Technology". The expert group involves the participation of many prominent representatives of European industry with the goal of developing an integrated approach to the cultural change involved within companies in this respect (EU — News from Science and Society in Europe, May 2005). If programmes are turned into action, the "family career conflict" faced especially by female scientists should be considered (Watkins et al., 1998).

PUBLIC UNDERSTANDING OF SCIENCE

To make a curriculum in science and technology more attractive, public awareness of the importance of science and technology has to be raised among school children. Among other initiatives the establishment of "children's universities" contributes to a high visibility of research from school childhood onwards. The number of universities engaging in such activities has sharply increased, e.g., the University of Vienna has organized a "Children's University" every year since 2003, with more than 2,000 children attending in the summer of 2005.

The example of U.S. high schools dedicated to science demonstrates that an intensified science and technology education leads to trained graduates who have an excellent foundation for further studies. These schools offer opportunities especially for women (Kendall, 2005). Universities and research organisations should provide opportunities to prominent scientists to communicate complex scientific subjects to the public (Schiermeier, 2005).

THE DEMOGRAPHIC DEVELOPMENT

In many western industrial societies, the current demographic trends hamper the evolution of innovative knowledge societies. There are two possible reasons: (1) It is well known that, especially in the hard sciences, many discoveries and innovations are done by scientists in their early years (Zuckermann, 1979); (2) A society with a majority of older people may not be driven as strongly towards future goals and visions as is the case in societies with a majority of young people. Among other points, these two reasons might explain the recent success of fast-growing economies, such as China and India.

A SCIENTIST'S CAREER

Most scientists are less interested in earning high salaries, but rather are ethically or emotionally attached to their work. Hence, it is important to specify the role, responsibilities and entitlements of scientists as well as of employers accordingly. The nature of the relationship between scientists and employers or funders should be conducive to successful scientific performance, for example by granting freedom of research. In March 2005, the E.U. Commission launched a European Charter for Researchers and a Code of Conduct for the Recruitment of Researchers (*Journal of the European Commission*, 2005) in order to contribute to the attractiveness and sustainability of a trans-European labour market for researchers.

GOALS AND VISIONS

The interest of young people in science and engineering will increase if goals and visions are challenging and attractive. It is up to the people responsible for the development of research to communicate empathy for research to the public. Focusing solely on the goal of increasing economic growth rates or merely stressing the importance of research for well-being might be too technocratic: broad visions for research strategies should be developed. As outlined by the Center of Cultural Studies & Analysis (2004) in the paper "American Perception of Space Exploration", the overall vision should include the following key features:

- Visions must reflect the larger culture in which they must operate;
- Visions are contextual. If the context changes, the meaning of the visions changes;
- Visions depend on the belief that the future should be better than the past;
- A cultural belief that everything can and should be improved;
- An ethic that celebrates and rewards inventors and innovation;
- Business interests that promote the vision of a "better" world in which their products play a key role;
- A driving external force or event that makes the vision the optimal and necessary choice.

CREATIVITY AS A DRIVING FORCE

The most important point may also be the most incomprehensible: creativity. We must try to attract the most creative and unconventional thinkers into our research systems. As Herbert Simon (Simon, 1983), winner of the Nobel Prize in Economics, explained creativity:

- The disposition to accept uncertain problem definitions and to structure them;
- To engage over a longer period of time with one problem;
- To acquire relevant and potentially relevant background knowledge.

Creativity and innovation have been the driving force in the evolution of Homo sapiens from the beginning, with the invention of first tools, art and technology, up to now. More scientists and engineers should inspire more creativity and innovation in our world.

REFERENCES

Center for Cultural Studies & Analysis. (2004). *American Perception of Space Exploration.* Presentation 21 April, 2004, Washington D.C.; available online: http://www.hq.nasa.gov/office/hqlibrary/documents/o55201537.pdf

Ayalon, H. (2003). "Women and Men Go to University: Mathematical Background and Gender Differences in Choice of Field in Higher Education". *Sex Roles,* 48, pp. 277-290.

Barnett, R., Parry, G. & Coate, K. (2004). "Conceptualising Curriculum Change". *The RoutledgeFalmer Reader in Higher Education,* Ed. Tight, M., RoutledgeFalmer, London & New York, pp. 140-154.

Bhattacharjee, Y. (2004). "Weak Economy, Higher Stipends Send More to Graduate School". *Science* 305, pp. 173.

Dillon, S. (2005). "Harvard Chief Defends His Talk on Women". *The New York Times,* 18 Jan 2005, p. 16.

EU — *News from Science and Society in Europe. (2005).* Quarterly newsletter, Issue n° 2, May 2005.

Gago, J. M. (2004). *"Europe needs more Scientists",* Report to the EC conference: "Increasing Human Resources for Sciences and Technology in Europe", Brussels, 2 April 2004.

Green, B. A., De Backer, T. K., Rav-Indran, B. & Krows, J. (1999). "Goals, Values, and Beliefs as Predictors of Achievement and Effort in High School Mathematics Classes". *Sex Roles,* 40, pp. 421-458.

Guimerà, R., Uzzi, B., Spiro, J. & Nunes-Amaral, L. A. (2005). "Team Assembly Mechanisms Determine Collaboration Network Structure and Team Performance". *Science,* 308, pp. 697-702.

Journal of the European Commission. (2005). Recommendation on the European Charter for Researchers and on a Code of Conduct for the Recruitment of Researchers. European Commission, Brussels. (L75/67, 11 March, 2005).

Katzenbach, J. R. & Smith, D. K. (1999). *The Wisdom of Teams: Creating the High-Performance Organization.* HarperCollins, London.

Kendall, P. (2005). "Hothouse High". *Nature* 235, pp. 874-875.

Krueger, D. (2004). "US-Europe Growth Differences: The Role of Education". *32, Volkswirtschaftliche Tagung der Oesterreichischen Nationalbank,* Vienna, pp. 37-49.

Larson, J. R., Christensen, C., Abbott, A. S. & Franz, T. M. (1996). "Diagnosing groups: charting the flow of information in medical decision-making teams". *Journal of Personality and Social Psychology,* 71, pp. 315-350.

National Academy of Sciences, (2005). *Facilitating Interdisciplinary Research.* National Academies Press, Washington D.C.

OECD (2004). *Education at a Glance 2004.* OECD, Paris.

Schiermeier, Q. (2005). "The philosopher of photons". *Nature,* 234, p. 1066.

Simon, H. A. (1983). "Discovery, invention, and developement: human creative thinking". Proceedings of the National Academy of Sciences of the United States of America, 80, pp. 4569–4571.

Usher, A. & Cervenan, A. (2005). *Global Higher Education Rankings. Affordability and Accessibility in Comparative Perspective.* The Educational Policy Institute, Washington D.C.

Walsh, M., Hickey, C. & Duffy, J. (1999). "Influence of Item Content and Stereotype Situation on Gender Differences in Mathematical Problem Solving". *Sex Roles*, 41, pp. 219–240.

Watkins, R. M., Herrin, M. & McDonald, L. R. (1998). "The juxtaposition of career and family: a dilemma for professional women". *AWL J.* 1, Winter; available online: http://www.advancingwomen.com/awl/winter98/awlv2_watkins5.html

Winckler, G. (2004). "The Contribution of Universities to a Knowledge-Based Economy". *32, Volkswirtschaftliche Tagung der Oesterreichischen National Bank*, Vienna, pp. 51-55.

Zuckermann, H. (1979). *Scientific Elite. Nobel Laureates in the United States*. MacMillan Publications, London.

CHAPTER 21

Declining Interest
in Engineering Studies at a Time
of Increased Business Need

Wayne C. Johnson and Russel C. Jones

INTRODUCTION

The numbers of students studying engineering have declined in recent years, both in the United States and in Western European countries. Many factors have contributed to this decline — including the difficulty of the curriculum, the attractiveness of alternate paths to good technical jobs, and the lack of attractiveness of projected employment paths for engineering graduates. This decline has occurred at a time when the employers of engineers face new challenges due to globalization, offshore outsourcing and the need to "move up the food chain" in innovation and technical expertise in order to remain competitive — thus creating a demand for more highly qualified engineering graduates. Much of what needs to be done to make engineering more attractive to bright students is well known — but educational institutions, employers of engineers, and government policy-makers have been slow to move aggressively to address the issues effectively. The authors attempt to describe "what can be done" in a comprehensive way.

PIPELINE ISSUES

The number of engineering graduates at the bachelor's level in the U.S. peaked at around 80,000 per year in the mid-1980s, then declined to about 65,000 per year until the end of the century (Engineering Workforce Commission, 2004). The number of graduates is increasing again, but not yet keeping pace with employers' needs. To put these numbers in global perspective, it is of interest to note that China currently has 3.7 million engineering students in its pipeline.

There are many reasons for the decline of student interest in engineering:

- *The curriculum is difficult* — Much difficult study and hard work are included in the current undergraduate curriculum in engineering, and that is built on top of strenuous prior preparation requirements in the secondary education years. Engineering curricula typically start with two years of intense mathematics and science — including calculus, probability and statistics, modern physics, chemistry and biology — often taught by service department faculty members who do not put this preparatory work in the context of engineering applications. This is typically followed by challenging engineering science courses, taught by engineering faculty members — but often research-oriented doctoral graduates with little applied engineering experience to bring into the classroom for motivation.

- *The curriculum is densely packed and inflexible* — Even though the number of credit hours required for graduation in engineering has drifted downward as other parts of the university head for only 120 credit hours for graduation, the actual time required for engineering students to complete degree requirements remains much higher than for other fields. The four-year bachelor's degree programmes in engineering schools are typically highly lock-stepped, with prerequisites offering little flexibility for individualized programmes or broadening experiences — such as a semester abroad. Engineering students who miss a required step in the proper order often must take an additional semester or year to complete their studies — at considerable extra expense and loss due to postponed employment.

- *Other paths to good jobs are easier* — High school students looking at various options for university level study often compare engineering to alternate paths — such as computer science — where the curriculum is less formidable, and where jobs at compensation levels similar to engineering jobs are readily available.

- *Engineers treated as commodities by employers* — In the current employment environment, engineers are often treated as commodities by employers. They are likely to be laid off when the quarterly balance sheet is not positive, or when new graduates with sharper technical skills are available at lower cost, or when their function can be off-shored at lower cost to the company. This leads to employment patterns that include multiple positions with different employers, but often involving lateral moves at best. Previous patterns of upward mobility throughout a progressing career are often lacking (Jones & Oberst, 2003).

- *Traditional entry level jobs are being offshored* — The types of jobs that fresh engineering graduates have filled until recently — support positions in technical operations of large employers of engineers — are now often being outsourced to offshore locations where good technical talent is available at much lower cost. This can result in fewer job opportunities for bachelor level engineering graduates, and lower salary offers (Oberst & Jones, 2004).

- *Media reports indicate instability* — The offshoring of technical jobs, as reported often in the media, transmits an aura of instability in the engineering profession — including the spectre of unemployment. Potential engineering students and their families see such reports, and are often influenced away from engineering study and employment.

Another area of concern in the engineering education pipeline is the lack of diversity in the student population — both women and minority students (National Science Foundation, 2003a, 2003b & 2004). Women students typically make up less than 20% of engineering classes, and minority engineering student populations typically fall well below the percentage of Black or Hispanic people in the community from which students are drawn. These populations often leave the potential engineering student pipeline even before high school — often opting not to take the math and science courses that would be needed to make them eligible to enter an engineering programme at the college level. In addition to the factors listed above, women are often turned off by engineering due to stereotyped images of engineers as nerdy white males.

A very major concern in the U.S. today is the size and composition of the doctoral pipeline in engineering (National Science Foundation, 2003c). In the dot-com boom years, jobs were so lucrative for engineering bachelor's graduates that few went on to graduate study — particularly through a doctoral degree. Universities responded by attracting increased numbers of foreign graduate students to fill research and teaching assistant positions — and eventually faculty ranks. In some fields today, well over half of the engineering faculty are foreign born. In the post 9/11 era, the flow of foreign graduate students to U.S. engineering graduate schools has slowed substantially — due to visa and security problems. In addition, developing countries such as China and India have developed their own good-quality graduate engineering programmes, allowing students from those countries to stay at home for study — and countries such as Australia are aggressively seeking students who would previously have sought U.S. graduate educations.

Some observers in the U.S. do not believe that there is a problem with declining engineering enrolments. They argue that market forces will keep the supply and demand in balance. While that dynamic may have been at least somewhat true in the past, it is drastically altered in the rapidly globalizing workforce environment — where offshoring and mechanisms such as H-1B visas give employers options other than increasing salaries to attract U.S. engineering graduates to their jobs. The authors of this paper believe that the flow of engineering graduates should be kept at a high level — both to meet the needs of employers who traditionally hire engineering graduates, but also to supply the growing number of fields where the quantitative skills and problem-solving abilities of engineering graduates are increasingly valued.

BUSINESS NEEDS

In an increasingly global environment for businesses and for professional practice, engineers who will be employed by industry need to be much broader than graduates of previous generations. And they will need to be credentialed in ways that are recognized across national borders, and available in sufficient quality and quantity to meet the expanding need of employers seeking graduates with superior quantitative and problem solving skills (National Academy of Engineering, 2004).

Globalization impacts

The globalization of business requires university graduates with an international perspective and with at least some international experience (Jones & Oberst, 1999). While that is typical of engineering graduates in Western Europe, it is not typical of engineering graduates in the United States. Just over 5,000 U.S. engineering students studied abroad in 2002-03, just 2.9% of all U.S. students studying abroad that year (Institute of International Education, 2004). Well less than 10% of all engineering graduates in the U.S. have *any* international experience when they graduate from their university programmes. Several universities do require international experience for their engineering graduates, and many others are instituting programmes to provide such experience — but the total activity in this area remains well behind the power curve.

In addition to well qualified graduates from U.S. engineering programmes, U.S.-based companies need qualified engineering graduates in developing countries in sufficient numbers to allow direct foreign investment in such countries (Jones & Oberst, 2000). The days of being able to send business and technical personnel from the North to staff operations in the South are over; an indigenous pool of technical personnel must be available to staff the operations of multinational companies, in order to be politically acceptable to developing nations (InterAcademy Council, 2004). To address this issue, many companies — in their enlightened self-interest — are involved in stimulating and supporting capacity building efforts in developing countries. Hewlett-Packard, for example, is heavily involved in an "Engineering for the Americas" capacity-building effort being mounted through the Organization of American States and the World Federation of Engineering Organizations.

Graduates of engineering programmes today need significant "soft skills" in addition to technical expertise, if they are to be effective for their business employers. With strong input from industry advisors, the U.S. Accreditation Board for Engineering and Technology (ABET, 2000) since 2000 has required the following outcomes of engineering education programmes:

"Engineering programs must demonstrate that their graduates have:

a) an ability to apply knowledge of mathematics, science and engineering;

b) an ability to design and conduct experiments, as well as to analyze and interpret data;

c) an ability to design a system, component, or process to meet desired needs;

d) an ability to function on multi-disciplinary teams;

e) an ability to identify, formulate and solve engineering problems;

f) an understanding of professional and ethical responsibility;

g) an ability to communicate effectively;

h) the broad education necessary to understand the impact of engineering solutions in a global and societal context;

i) a recognition of the need for, and an ability to engage in lifelong learning;

j) a knowledge of contemporary issues;

k) an ability to use the techniques, skills, and modern engineering tools necessary for engineering practice."

Engineering schools must show, through outcomes assessment, that these attributes have been acquired by their graduates.

Offshoring impacts

Business needs native engineers who can help to lead their organizations up the food chain as routine activities and jobs are outsourced offshore. These native engineers need to be able to work effectively with international colleagues, having appropriate sensitivity to cultural differences. They also must be able to work in teams that are geographically separated, utilizing high-tech tools that make such distributed teamwork effective.

Quantitative needs

Business requires a sufficient quantity of engineering graduates to meet its employment needs — with appropriate high quality and appropriate diversity in gender and ethnicity. Broadly educated bachelor's level graduates continue to be needed, but increasingly master's level graduates are needed to lead engineering practice up the food chain. Doctoral level graduates are needed — particularly in U.S. domestic operations — to provide innovation and to utilize research and development in applications in order to keep competitive new products and services coming.

Additional qualitative needs

Beyond the basic quality needs cited above, industry needs engineers who are lifelong learners, able to keep up with technological advances in this rapidly developing world. And engineering graduates for companies must increasingly be interdisciplinary in education and approach, to keep abreast of and take advantage of the convergences in this bio-, nano-, info-technology world.

WHAT CAN BE DONE IN EDUCATION?

Engineering education in the United States is perhaps the most studied and discussed intellectual endeavour in the country. But for all the study, pilot projects, reformation attempts and discussion, it is among the slowest to adopt systemic change.

Many suggestions are relevant to improving engineering education in the United States — and perhaps other portions of the world — to make it more relevant to the needs of business in the increasingly globalized workspace (National Academy of Engineering, 2005):

Undergraduate engineering education

- Make the curriculum more user-friendly (e.g., bring design down into the freshman year in order to motivate students for math and science immersion; concentrate on how to learn rather than trying to cover everything in an intense four-year curriculum; substitute active learning for formal lectures; etc.)
- Focus curricula on its relevance to the solution of society's problems, to provide motivation for the hard work involved (e.g., environmental, health and infrastructure needs; and the needs of developing countries);
- Prepare students for international practice by promoting study abroad and other international exposure opportunities (e.g., engineers without borders experiences);

- Make undergraduate engineering *education* at universities a priority equal to *research* (as the Coalition program of the U.S. National Science Foundation once did);
- Take advantage of the flexibility offered by ABET's Criteria 2000 to offer programmes that produce more broadly educated, internationally oriented, entrepreneurially stimulated engineering graduates;
- Embrace continuous improvement of engineering education programmes, not just periodic change in anticipation of the next accreditation visit;
- Promote systemic change, across the whole of the national engineering education system, based on successful scattered innovations.

Graduate engineering education

- Promote practice-oriented master's degree programmes, in addition to research oriented ones (e.g., the current Body of Knowledge effort by the American Society of Civil Engineers):
- Persuade ABET to drop its prohibition against dual-level accreditation, so that schools can seek accreditation of master's degree programmes in the same fields that they currently have accredited at the bachelor's level, in order to promote innovation in integrated bachelor's-master's programmes;
- Expand relevant continuing education opportunities, to facilitate lifelong learning by graduates;
- Teach prospective engineering faculty members how to teach, as a part of their graduate education experience.

One major beneficial thrust for the improvement of engineering education programmes at all levels would be providing more opportunities for engineering faculty to get international experience by going abroad for research, educational and industrial experience.

What can be done in business?

Business leaders must interact with educators and government policy-makers in order to assure that technical employees of appropriate quality and quantity are available for employment. In the current environment, the impacts of globalization and offshoring require particular attention in business-university-government interactions.

Offshoring impacts

- Employers of engineers should be encouraged to develop rational, forward-looking approaches to determining what technical work to out-

source offshore and what to retain in-house — considering issues such as innovation management, intellectual property security, strategic manpower deployment, etc., in addition to short-term financial advantages;
- Business leaders and universities should collaborate on revising the educational preparation of engineering students to prepare them to help companies move up the food chain as routine work is offshored;
- Recognizing that a significant number of current engineers will become unemployed, and possibly unemployable, due to offshoring of their jobs, business leaders should work with universities and government officials to develop and fund appropriate retraining programmes.

University-Industry interactions

- Business and university leaders should work together to close gaps between engineering education and the advanced state-of-the-art in practice;
- Where there are gaps between industrial developments and the abilities of universities to appropriately prepare graduates in rapidly moving fields, businesses should offer faculty development programmes (e.g., such as the programmes in quality management offered some years ago);
- Industry should continue to provide funding to universities for relevant research and development efforts;
- Opportunities for faculty members to spend time in industry should be encouraged by both businesses and by universities.

What can be done at the policy level?

Many of the recommendations and suggestions listed above would be facilitated by policy level decisions in the United States (Jones, 2004). Following are several suggestions:

- Encourage relevant legislative action to develop rational visa policies, in collaboration with business and professional society leaders;
- Provide financial aid to attract native students into the Ph.D. pipeline, tied to the national imperative to compete in the global marketplace (like the National Defense Education Act, initiated after Sputnik);
- Make creative use of funds from H-1B and similar visa grants to stimulate native students to fill industry's needs;
- Expand pre-college efforts at attracting women and under-represented minorities into the engineering education pipeline;

• Enhance the public understanding of engineering and its contributions to society.

CONCLUSION

The decline of interest of bright students for the study of engineering is the result of many factors — difficulty and lack of flexibility of the curriculum, their perception of the current employment environment where engineers appear to be treated as commodities, and reports of offshoring of many technical jobs. The need for a steady supply of engineering graduates well prepared to work effectively in the global marketplace is undiminished, however. University, business and government leaders must take coordinated action to assure the flow of well qualified engineering graduates in appropriate numbers in order to assure national competitiveness.

REFERENCES

Accreditation Board for Engineering and Technology — ABET. (2000). *Criteria for Engineering Programs — 2000* (and annually). Baltimore, Maryland.

Engineering Workforce Commission. (2004). *Engineering and Technology Degrees — 2004* (and annually), American Association of Engineering Societies, Washington D.C.

Institute of International Education. (2004). *Open Doors — 2004* (and annually). New York.

InterAcademy Council. (2004). *Inventing a Better Future: A Strategy for Building Worldwide Capacities in Science and Technology*, Amsterdam.

Jones, R. C. & Oberst, B. S. (2003). "Are US Engineers Being Treated as Commodities?" *European Journal of Engineering Education*, Vol. 3, no. 28, pp. 395-402.

Jones, R. C. & Oberst, B. S. (2000). "International trends in engineering accreditation and quality assurance," in Michel, J. (ed) *The many facets of international education of engineers*, Société européenne pour la formation des ingénieurs (SEFI), Annual Meeting Proceedings, Paris.

Jones, R. C. & Oberst, B. S. (1999). "Education for International Practice," *Engineering Education: Rediscovering the Centre*, Société européenne pour la formation des ingénieurs (SEFI), Conference Proceedings, Copenhagen.

Jones, R. C. (2004). "Cross-Border Engineering Practice", *Proceedings of 2004 Annual Meeting*, American Society for Engineering Education, Washington D.C.

National Academy of Engineering. (2004). *The Engineer of 2020: Visions of Engineering in the New Century*, Washington D.C.

National Academy of Engineering. (2005). *Educating the Engineer of 2020: Adapting Engineering Education to the New Century*, Washington D.C.

National Science Foundation. (2004). *Science and Engineering Educators — 2004* (and annually), Washington D.C.

National Science Foundation. (2003a). *Science and Engineering Infrastructure for the 21st Century*, Washington, D.C.

National Science Foundation. (2003b). *Broadening Participation in Science and Engineering Research and Education*, Washington D.C.

National Science Foundation. (2003c). *The Science and Engineering Workforce: Realizing America's Potential*, Washington D.C.

Oberst, B. S. & Jones, R. C. (2004). "Canaries in the mineshaft: engineers in the global workplace", *Proceedings of 2004 Annual Meeting*, American Society for Engineering Education, Washington D.C.

CHAPTER 22

A Mosaic of Problems

Wm. A. Wulf

I would like to talk about a predominantly U.S. issue — or better, a mosaic of issues — that concern me. Taken separately, or viewed from "up close", each of these issues is not a crisis — and hence doesn't get a lot of attention. Viewed from a distance, however, I think they collectively form a mosaic that paints a very disturbing pattern.

You all know the storied procedure for boiling a frog. "They say" that if you drop a frog in boiling water, it will jump out — but, if you put a frog in cool water and heat it very slowly, the frog won't jump out and you will boil it. The theory is that each increment in temperature is not enough to make the frog react. I don't know if this is true, but it is a great story and fits my purpose.

My fear is that the U.S. is getting boiled — that incremental decisions are being made that aren't by themselves "big enough" to raise a warning about the deeper, fundamental problem evident in the mosaic as a whole.

I have a longer list, but let me mention a few of these issues.

IN THE WAKE OF 9/11

Below are a "cluster" of points in the mosaic that manifest themselves as reactions to 9/11. Let's acknowledge that 9/11 really did change things! It is entirely appropriate to rethink our "balance point" with respect to a number of things such as immigration and export controls. In particular the nature of the adversary has changed. The Soviet Union was both a "rational actor" and exquisitely "research capable"; terrorist cells are neither. Thus, we wanted the Soviets to know enough about our capability that they didn't make miscalculations about them, and it made little sense to hide what they were perfectly capable of reproducing. The same disclosures to terrorists might be counterproductive, to say the least.

253

- *Visas:* Much has been written about the impact of new visa policies on students, and the situation has improved — as of this writing, the average time to process visas for students is less than two weeks. I continue to be concerned, however, that, while the average time has shortened, the distribution has a long tail — that is, there are still some students that wait a year or more. Moreover, some very senior scholars, including a Nobel laureate, are experiencing the same sort of lengthy, demeaning treatment. It is these latter cases, not the average processing time, that are reported in the international press, with the result that the image of the U.S. being a welcoming "land of opportunity" has changed to exactly the opposite.
- *Deemed exports:* Export controls originated in the U.S. in the 1980s, and were originally intended as an economic tool against the perceived Japanese "threat". They have now become tools for national security, and are intended to keep critical weapons technology out of the hands of potential adversaries. Export of controlled technology requires a special "export license" from either the Department of Commerce or the Department of State. Disclosure of information about a controlled technology to a foreign national in the U.S. has been "deemed" to be an export of the technology itself, and thus requires an export licence as well. Reports of the Inspectors General of the Department of Commerce and several other agencies have suggested that the implementation of the rules governing deemed exports has been too lax, and suggested tightening them in several ways. The university community is concerned that a literal interpretation of the I.G.s' suggestions would essentially preclude involving foreign graduate students in research and would require an impossibly complex system to enforce. Given that 55% of the Ph.D. students in engineering in the U.S. are foreign-born, the effect could be catastrophic.
- *Sensitive But Unclassified (S.B.U.) Information:* You may not have as much experience with this — but it has become the bane of National Academies' existence. On one hand, this is a good example of an issue that needed to be re-balanced after 9/11. There are things not covered by traditional classification that it is clear would be better kept from a less research-capable adversary. But, unlike traditional classification where there are precise laws, limited authority to classify, mandatory declassification after a period of time, and a philosophy to "build high fences around small places", the counterparts do not exist in the S.B.U. domain. There are no laws, there is no common definition, there are no limits on who can declare something to be S.B.U., etc. In at least some cases it appears as though S.B.U. is being used to suppress criticism.

TOWARDS A BETTER QUALITY OF LIFE

There is another cluster of tiles in my mosaic that has to do with disinvestment in the future. Prosperity and security require that we forego some current consumption in order to ensure a better quality of life in the future. Quite aside from the notoriously poor individual savings rate in the U.S., I think we are failing to invest collectively as well.

- Demise of corporate R & D: I probably don't need to elaborate this point for this audience, but let me briefly remind you that some of the most fundamental results in the last century came from corporate laboratories: Bell Labs, GE Research, etc. While vestiges of these laboratories still exist, they now have a much shorter time horizon, and a product development focus. As Jim Duderstadt notes in his paper for this Colloquium, the U.S. system for accomplishing research evolved after WWII as a self-reinforcing triangle of industry, academia and government — one side of that triangle is now missing, and the resulting structure is much less stable. Some would say that this is the result of the short time horizon of the stock market, and undoubtedly to some extent it is. But I think it is also a failure to account for research as an investment rather than as an expense — and thus, in effect, to say it has no lasting value.

- The state of physical science and engineering research funding: I probably don't need to elaborate this either, but let me note that while there have been huge increases in the support for the life sciences, most physical science and engineering funding has been flat or even declining. This seems especially ironic since so many of the medical devices and procedures that we enjoy come from developments in the physical sciences and engineering: endoscopic surgery, smart pacemakers, dialysis machines, etc.

- The view of higher education as a "private good": historically the U.S. has viewed higher education as a "public good". That is, we took the view that a more educated citizenry was a benefit to the country as a whole — not just to the individual so educated: (a) that is why we supported universal K-12 education; (b) that is why in the 1860s we created the land grant colleges; (c) that is why a system of superior State universities was created and generously supported, and scholarships were given to needy students; (d) that is why we passed the "GI Bill" after WWII, and the National Defense Education Act in the 1950s.

  Now, however, we see disappearing state support from the state universities, soaring tuition to replace that support, and we give loans rather than scholarships — all indications that we now view higher education as a private good, that is, of value only to the individual student.

- The number and percentage of physical science and engineering undergrads: human capital — an educated and innovative workforce — is the most precious resource a country has.

  Yet, the number of engineering undergraduates in the U.S. peaked in the mid-1980s, then declined 25% during the 1990s. The number seems to have rebounded recently — but not to 1985 levels, and only to something like a fourth of the numbers from each of China and India.

  Perhaps even more troubling is that the percentage of undergraduates studying engineering in the U.S. is the second lowest among developed countries, between 4-5% in the U.S. vs. 12% in most of Europe, and more than 40% in China.

I have a much longer list, for example:

- A failure to really act on the energy issue;
- A failure to really act on greenhouse gas emissions;

but it would be too depressing to recite the whole list.

The mosaic, the pattern, I see in all these is one of short-term thinking and lack of long-term investment:

- It's a pattern of preserving the status quo rather than reaching for the next big goal.
- It's a pattern that presumes we in the U.S. are entitled to a better quality of life than others, and we just need to circle the wagons to defend that entitlement.
- It's a pattern that that does not balance the danger in things like foreign students with the good that comes to the U.S. from: (a) immigrants like Einstein, Teller and Fermi, without whom the Germans might have had the bomb before we did; (b) students who return to their home country and are our best ambassadors; (c) economic benefits of open trade, and the increased security that comes with a better quality of life in developing countries; (d) increased quality of life in the U.S. from sharing scientific results and thus "moving faster" in new technologies; and (e) funding the underpinnings of our understanding of nature, and a generally educated citizenry.

Universities are all about long-term investment — investment in people and investment in new knowledge. To the extent that this pattern is real and reflects a trend in the attitude of U.S. society, the implications for universities as we have known them are not good!

The 2001 Hart-Rudman Commission, which proposed the Department of Homeland Security, said: "… the inadequacies of our system of research and education pose a greater threat to U.S. national security over the next quarter century than any potential conventional war that we might imagine." (Road Map for National Security, 2001).

The report was written before 9/11; had it been written afterwards, I am sure "conventional war" at the end of the quote would have been changed to include terrorism.

Yet, as a country we seem to be taking decision after decision that trades an appearance of near-term security for long-term damage to our system of research and education. The more I look, the more I see such problems — individually sub-critical, but collectively painting a disturbing larger pattern.

If you see the same pattern that I do, then the obvious question is "what should we do about it?" I am sure that I don't have all the answers, but let me suggest a few and then ask you to suggest more.

I fear that some of what we have been doing about, for example, student visas, sounds like special pleading — for example the message in some university statements seems to be "our enrolment will fall, and we'll get less revenue". That may get attention from some members of Congress — just like any constituent gets attention — but not the kind of serious attention that this mosaic of issues deserves.

Let me remind you of Vannevar Bush's *Science the Endless Frontier* (1945) — the report that is largely responsible for the pattern of federally funded, university-based research in the U.S. Recall that before WWII there was essentially no federal funding of university-based research. During the war, university scientists and engineers were critical to the war effort — they produced radar, precise bomb sights, the atomic bomb, etc. After the war, President Roosevelt asked Vannevar Bush how we could be sure that, in the event of another war, there would be the people to do this again. Bush wrote *Science the Endless Frontier* in response to this, and in it he argued:

- The way to ensure the supply of people was to fund research at universities;
- The researchers themselves, not government, should decide what research is done; and
- That, in return, researchers would insure national security, prosperity and health.

Mostly we have delivered on that promise — but I increasingly hear our community talking as though science and engineering research was an end in itself. It's not. It is to create educated people, and to deliver societal goals like security, prosperity and health. Simultaneously I hear policy makers referring to the research community as (just) another special interest group. So, my first answer to "what to do?" is be sure that we couch our arguments properly, and particularly to tie them to the nation's goals, not our own.

My second answer is that, the Academy being the Academy, we will be doing a report, or possibly a series of reports. But one, or even several, reports from the Academy are not going to change a national malaise. Lots of people need to be talking about this mosaic of issues and the pattern they create — that's why I am talking to you. I would like you to go back to your faculties and start a conversation. We need you to write op-eds. We need you to talk to your political representatives.

Let me take a detour for a minute: at its August meeting each year the National Academy of Engineering Council has reviewed our strategic plan. The Strategic Plan's Purpose begins with the words: "To promote the technological health of the nation…"

As you know, the Academies operate under an 1863 Charter from the U.S. Congress that calls on us to provide advice to the government on issues of science and technology. That's a passive role… if and when asked, we provide advice to the government. The Strategic Plan's Purpose, however, does not say "wait till asked", it does not say "only provide advice" and it does not limit our target audience to the government. Rather, it is a much broader and more proactive mandate.

A question arose in the Council's discussion of the Purpose, namely will engineers "stand up"? That is, are engineers, both individually and collectively, willing to provide the leadership needed — willing to take a stand? When it was first asked, I thought it was a "no brainer" — of course we would! On reflection, I am not so sure: (1) the culture of engineering is to be unassuming; (2) the culture of engineering rewards technical achievement, not leadership (how often have you heard "she isn't an engineer any longer, she is a manager"); (3) the culture of engineering proscribes that we advise only with respect to technical matters (how often have you heard, "that's a political question, we have nothing to contribute".)

Don't misunderstand me. I believe we should "stand up", but we're going to have to ask ourselves some tough questions about our culture, what we value and how we "stand up" and preserve what we value. But, to come back to the question of what we need to do in the face of this mosaic, I believe that what we need most is for all of us to "stand up".

CONCLUDING THOUGHTS

I have taken a distinctly U.S. and distinctly engineering perspective in these remarks because that is what I know best. There are some, I know, who would be delighted to see the downfall of the American hegemony, especially its most recent manifestation. Being an American, I cannot be unbiased about this, but I sincerely believe that is not in the best interest of the world if the mosaic of issues suggested here are ignored. Nor do I think that the rest of the developed world is immune to the underlying causes of the mosaic I have tried to depict here. We have a shared problem!

REFERENCES

Bush, V. (1945). *Science, the Endless Frontier, Report to the President on a Program for Postwar Scientific Research* (Office of Scientific Research and Development, July 1945), http://www1.umn.edu/scitech/assign/vb/VBush1945.html
"Road Map for National Security: Imperative for Change" (2001). The United States Commission on National Security/21st Century. http://govinfo.library.unt.edu/nssg/PhaseIIIFR.pdf>http://govinfo.library.unt.edu/nssg/PhaseIIIFR.pdf

C H A P T E R

Best Practices
in Knowledge Transfer

Charles M. Vest

INTRODUCTION

The United States operates as an innovation system — a loosely coupled interaction among universities, industry and government that generates new knowledge and technologies through basic research, primarily in universities, and educates young men and women to take such knowledge and technologies and move them into the marketplace as new products, processes or services. The core of this system derives from the report, *Science, the Endless Frontier*, issued at the end of World War II (Bush, 1945). The Bush Model made public and private research universities the primary research infrastructure of the nation. By funding university research projects, selected on the basis of merit review, the government's money does double duty: it procures new knowledge and it educates the next generation of researchers, engineers, doctors and business leaders.

MIT, as we know it today, epitomizes this approach and shows that over time, it can be very effective. In 1997, a report by the economics department of BankBoston, *MIT: The Impact of Innovation* (MIT, 1997) determined that there were over 4,000 extant companies founded or co-founded by MIT graduates or faculty, employing 1.1 million people worldwide, and receiving annual sales of $232 billion. MIT has also contributed to education beyond its own campus in two primary ways. First, educational knowledge and information have been transferred through the work of men and women who earned their doctoral degrees at MIT and then joined universities around the world as faculty members, taking with them MIT course notes, pedagogical approaches and the integration of research and teaching, all of which they modified, adopted and expanded to fit their own teaching contexts and objectives. Second, educational knowledge and pedagogy were promulgated through numerous textbooks.

But today the world expects a much faster pace, more goal-oriented research and education, better understood pathways to economic advancement, and recognition of the globalization of just about everything. Things are not only faster, they are more complex as boundaries between traditional disciplines must be penetrated or eliminated, and as the distinction between basic and applied research is frequently fuzzy or non-existent.

Establishing policies and mechanisms to meet these changing objectives is complicated because the stakeholders have varied objectives. Simply put, young people are usually attracted to science and engineering through curiosity, awe of nature, and excitement about fundamental unknowns; researchers advance their fields through fire in the belly and obsessive concentration on challenging puzzles; legislators believe that tax dollars for universities should produce jobs; and companies want faster and faster innovation that directly drives profits.

All of these considerations suggest that at minimum we must experiment with new models of knowledge transfer (and production). Yet we must do so with care, because the fact remains that the model derived from the Bush report has had astounding success, driving more than 50% of U.S. economic growth during the past 60 years.

The following sections are brief outlines of three large experiments in new modes of knowledge transfer involving MIT. The first, Knowledge Integration Communities developed by the Cambridge-MIT Institute, is intended to positively influence the competitiveness of an entire nation. The second, the DuPont-MIT Alliance, is intended to both advance science and technology and to create strong synergy between MIT and individual science-driven corporations. The third, MIT OpenCourseWare, is an initiative to promulgate educational materials and knowledge rapidly, freely and openly using the power of the internet and World Wide Web.

THE CAMBRIDGE-MIT INSTITUTE AND KNOWLEDGE INTEGRATION COMMUNITIES

The Cambridge-MIT Institute (CMI), an alliance of Cambridge University and MIT, is a bold and unique initiative funded by the U.K. government, initially for six years. The mission of CMI is to enhance the competitiveness, productivity, and entrepreneurship of the U.K. It is to do so by improving the effectiveness of knowledge exchange between universities and industry; educating leaders; creating new ideas; developing programmes for change in universities, industry and government; and building networks of participants beyond the two universities.

I note parenthetically that CMI has preferred the term knowledge *exchange* to knowledge *transfer*, because the latter connotes a one-directional handoff rather than a two-way exchange.

One explicit goal of CMI is to study the innovation process in a broad national context. Indeed, as part of CMI's work, Crawley and Greenwald (2004) have recently proposed a framework for national science, technology and innovation, based upon CMI experience, and especially on disciplined interviews of leaders in government, industry and universities on both sides of the Atlantic. Their national knowledge system consists of pathways through four stages: Discovery, Development, Deployment and Delivery.

To understand the motivation for forming Knowledge Integration Communities for CMI research projects, it is useful to draw on one of Crawley and Greenwald's observations: as products or services move from the deployment to the delivery stage, traditional economic market forces are in play and bring strong feedback and efficiency to the process. On the other hand, the movement of ideas from Discovery to Development usually has no market forces to bring either feedback or efficiency to the process. Presumably this process will always be inefficient; however, in the spirit of *Pasteur's Quadrant*, useful feedback can be had, and some efficiency improvement can be gained. The formation of Knowledge Integration Communities (KICs) for CMI research projects is an attempt to enhance feedback and efficiency — and to do so in a manner that elicits enthusiasm among the academic researchers who do the creative work. In other words, CMI research is intended to generate fundamental new ideas which can be developed with a consideration of use and an eye toward needs of industry.

Enhancing the effectiveness of knowledge exchange is the primary driving force in the CMI model. Knowledge exchange should link Research, Education and Industry, and CMI is positioned as a common platform for this exchange. The exchange occurs through Knowledge Integration in *Research*, through *Education* for innovation and leadership, and through engagement of *Industry*. As spelled out in detail by Acworth and Ghose (2004), KICs are the primary mechanism for knowledge exchange among stakeholders during the conception and execution of CMI research projects.

The stakeholders who comprise a KIC typically include academic researchers, industry participants from large and small companies, government policymakers, special interest groups such as regional development authorities, and educators from a variety of institutions who come together to pursue a common science, technology and social end goal. Although this broad involvement runs counter to many academic instincts, it appears to be working rather well because considerable thought and effort have been put into the process and because the concept itself arose out of careful discussion and iterative planning among the stakeholders.

CMI research projects are intended to discover knowledge and create technologies that have a potential for developing or advancing important, science- and technology-based industries. It is instructive to note that the current CMI KICs are Silent Aircraft (strategies and technologies to dramatically reduce noise beyond airports); Next Generation Drug Discovery (eliminating bottlenecks in drug discovery); Pervasive Computing (human-centred computing and the U.K. role in developing this emerging technology); Communications Innovation (developing roadmaps for U.K. global communications industries in collaboration with B.T.); Competitiveness and Education (a centre for executive education, benchmarking and assessment); and Quantum Computing (developing future computing and encryption technologies). These are "hot", exciting topics that provide excellent platforms for serious academic research.

A typical set of KIC participants are those in the Silent Aircraft Initiative in which representatives of Rolls Royce, British Airways, the British Airports Authority and regional airport operators join university researchers. The research component of a typical KIC is comprised of 4 to 6 individual research projects. The governing philosophy is to fund a modest number of large, interrelated projects, rather than a large number of small, unconnected ones. Actual research proposals are solicited from faculty of Cambridge and MIT by publishing broad themes suggested by the KIC. Specific ideas to be pursued are therefore developed by the researchers and are peer reviewed. Each KIC has a designated manager who maintains the multiple relationships and communication. The work of each KIC is formally reviewed every six months.

CMI's Knowledge Integration Communities are works in progress. More years of experience will be required to rigorously evaluate their effectiveness. Indeed, the hope and intent are that KICs develop into long-term, self-sustaining activities.

Louis Pasteur famously observed: "Chance favours the prepared mind." I consider that the goal of Knowledge Integration Communities is to support excellent fundamental research, but also to create a collective prepared mind of multiple stakeholders.

THE DUPONT-MIT ALLIANCE

The DuPont-MIT Alliance (DMA) similarly creates a collective prepared mind, but it is a more focused relationship and mechanism for knowledge transfer/exchange between MIT and a single corporation. It builds on strengths of both organizations and has established a strong synergy associated with fundamental strategic goals of DuPont and MIT at this point in time.

DuPont is a 200-year-old company with world-class R & D capabilities in areas such as polymer chemistry and engineering. It has had three distinct periods over its long history. In its first century, DuPont was focused on explosives. In its second century, it became a global company based on chemicals, energy and materials. As it has entered its third century, its strategy is to become a dynamic, science-based company that, as noted in the DuPont Vision Statement (2005), creates "sustainable solutions essential to a safer, healthier life for people everywhere".

DuPont has a specific interest in developing bio-based materials that can be produced with small environmental footprints. This interest is at the core of the first five years of DMA. MIT wants to do world-class interdisciplinary research in this area that has strong scientific and technological content, to advance both research and education, and to encourage industry development of our technologies, and value informed industrial input and feedback to much of our research. DMA is an experiment for both partners, and, to date, both partners regard it as a success. Of course, it has evolved and improved over time, and will continue to do so. What follows are some of the details that those involved think has made this a successful partnership and mechanism for knowledge transfer/exchange.

DMA supports research and education that is proposed *bottom up* by MIT faculty within broad thematic boundaries set by the sponsor. DuPont is engaged in both the evaluation of proposals and informs the conduct of the research through continuous, professional dialogue. In addition to funding research projects, DMA includes a Fellows Program and supports a variety of courses, workshops and tutorials at both DuPont and MIT.

During its first five years, DMA has supported 33 research projects, of which 19 are currently active. These have engaged 58 MIT faculty across 15 academic departments and centres. Projects have been fundamental, long-range and pre-competitive, but of clear interest to DuPont. White papers, 3 to 5 pages long, including skeletal budgets were solicited from the entire MIT faculty. Approximately 25% of the projects described in these white papers have been selected, based on quality and relevance to the DMA mission, and their authors were encouraged to submit full proposals. Approximately 85% of these proposals were funded after a rigorous review by faculty colleagues and, independently, by leading DuPont researchers. Large, multi-investigator, highly structured projects have flourished, along with smaller, more speculative, single-investigator seed grants. At the current time there are 58 graduate students and post-doctoral researchers. Agreements regarding intellectual property are favourable from DuPont's perspective, but are well within the bounds of MIT's normal policies.

A sense of the intellectual breadth and depth of DMA can be gained by considering some typical projects:

- Next-generation advances in metabolic engineering, including genome-wide analysis and modelling for the production of chemicals and intermediates from renewable bio-feedstocks;

- Early-stage research to develop a novel biopolymer-based nervous system implant that could replace non-functional brain tissue following traumatic brain injury;
- Development of a device for tissue-like culturing of liver cells, designed to provide early assessment of the toxicity of new pharmaceuticals; and
- Creation of a material inspired by the naturally water-repellent surface of the lotus leaf, with potential applications like self-cleaning fabrics and bacteria-resistant plumbing.

DMA also has a strong educational mission; indeed, a major sum is invested annually in education programmes in bio-based materials. These range from a one-day short course on biotechnology for senior DuPont executives, including the CEO, to a number of two-day short courses for engineers and managers, a lecture series, and several 2- to 3-hour tutorials on specialized topics.

DMA supports fellowships for first-year MIT graduate students. To date there have been 112 DMA Fellows. In addition to engagement with DMA projects and faculty, there is an annual Fellows visit to key DuPont research facilities. Needless to say, the Fellows programme is highly valued by MIT students and faculty, and creates a wealth of contact with DuPont.

Over time, increasing trust has been built, and through the ongoing work of the research teams and their interaction with their DuPont liaisons, DMA has become more tightly aligned with DuPont's business strategies and interests. But this has occurred in a transparent and academically acceptable manner. DMA will move forward with somewhat more clearly defined goals.

There are many characteristics of this alliance that have led to its general success as an innovative mechanism for knowledge transfer. DMA has critical mass, a good balance of academic goals and intellectual flexibility with business interests, and a continual flow of information and professional interaction. Education is recognized and supported. Perhaps the most important glue for this effort, however, is the trust developed by serious and continual engagement of first-rate engineers and scientists from the sponsor with the faculty and students.

MIT OPENCOURSEWARE

My final example of knowledge transfer, drawn from Vest (2005), concerns sharing educational materials through MIT's OpenCourseWare initiative. In 2002, with generous financial support from the Mellon and Hewlett Foundations, MIT pledged to make available on the web, free of charge to teachers and learners everywhere, the substantially complete teaching materials from virtually all of the approximately 2,000 subjects taught on the

MIT campus. For most subjects, these materials include a syllabus, course calendar, well-formatted and detailed lecture notes, exams, problem sets and solutions, lab and project plans, and, in a few cases, video lectures. The materials have been cleared for third-party intellectual property and are available to users under a creative commons license so that they can be used, distributed and modified for non-commercial purposes. This is a new, open form of publication and knowledge transfer. It is neither teaching nor the offering of courses or degrees. It is an exercise in openness, a catalyst for change and an adventure.

It is an adventure because it is a free-flowing, empowering and potentially democratizing force, so we do not know in advance the uses to which it will be put. Currently, materials for 1,100 courses are mounted. The OCW site — which typically has 20,000 unique visits per day — has 43% of its traffic from North America, 20% from East Asia, 16% from Western Europe, and the remaining 20% of the users are distributed across Latin America, Eastern Europe, the Middle East, the Pacific Region, and Sub-Saharan Africa. International usage is growing rapidly. Roughly 15% of OCW users are educators, and almost half of their usage is directly for course and curriculum development. One third are students complementing a subject they are taking at another college or university, or simply expanding their personal knowledge. Almost half are self-learners.

An Arizona high school teacher motivates and supervises group study of MIT OCW computer science materials within his after-school artificial intelligence club. A group of then-unemployed programmers in Silicon Valley used MIT OCW materials to master advanced computer languages, upgrading their skills when the job market became very tight. An educator at Al-Mansour University College in Baghdad is utilizing MIT OCW Aeronautics and Astronautics course material in his air traffic control research. The computer science department of a university in Legon, Ghana, is updating its entire curriculum and is using MIT OCW materials to help benchmark and revise their courses. An underground university based largely on MIT OCW educates young men and women who, because of their religion, are forbidden to attend one country's universities. Heavy use is made of OCW by almost 70% of the students on our own MIT campus to review courses they have taken in the past, to reinforce the classes they are currently taking and to explore other areas of study.

OpenCourseWare seems counter-intuitive in a market-driven world, but it represents the intellectual generosity that faculties of great American universities have demonstrated in many ways over the years. In an innovative way, it expresses a belief that education can be advanced around the world by constantly widening access to information and pedagogical organization and by inspiring others to participate.

MIT OCW is starting to catalyse other participants in a movement to deploy and use well organized open course materials. Universia, a network of 840 universities in Spain, Portugal and Latin America has translated into Spanish the materials from almost 100 MIT OCW courses and made them available on their website. The People's Republic of China has established CORE (China Open Resources for Education), a network of 100 universities with more than 10 million users. CORE's goal is to enhance the quality of higher education in China by translating MIT OCW and other course materials into Chinese, and also by sharing Chinese courses globally. Rai University in India has established a very substantial activity called Rai Courseware. Japan and France have OCW efforts underway.

In the U.S., the University of Michigan, Utah State University, the Johns Hopkins University School of Public Health and Tufts University's Health Sciences and Fletcher School of Diplomacy all have established OCW efforts. Here I use the term OCW to denote substantial, comprehensive, carefully managed, easily accessed, searchable, web-based collections of teaching materials for entire courses presented in a common format.

In this emerging open course ware movement, it is not only the teaching materials that are shared. We have also implemented and actively encouraged the sharing with other institutions of software, "know how" and other tools developed by MIT OCW.

Day-to-day communication and data transfer among scholars and researchers are now totally dominated by internet communications. Large, accessible scholarly archives like JSTOR and ARTSTOR are growing and heavily subscribed. There is an enormous potential impact of Google's new programme to provide free access to the content of several of the most important university libraries in the U.S. and the U.K. The use of OpenCourseWare is developing in the U.S., Asia and Europe. I believe that openness and sharing of intellectual resources and teaching materials — not closely controlled point-to-point distance education — are the most important emerging ethos of global higher education.

In my view, a global *Meta University* is arising that will accurately characterize higher education globally a decade or two hence. Like the computer operating system Linux, knowledge creation and teaching at each university will be elevated by the efforts of a multitude of individuals and groups all over the world. It will rapidly adapt to the changing learning styles of students who have grown up in a computationally rich environment. The biggest potential winners are in developing nations.

REFERENCES

Acworth, Edward & Ghose, Siddhartha (2004). *Knowledge Integration Communities.* The Cambridge-MIT Institute, http:/www.Cambridge-mit.org.

Bush, V. (1945). *Science, the Endless frontier, A Report to the President on a Program for Postwar Scientific Research. Office of Scientific Research and Development;* reprinted by the National Science Foundation, Washington D.C., 1990.

Crawley, Edward F. & Greenwald, Suzanne B. (2004). *Creating a Long Term National Science, Technology, and Innovation Framework: A Perspective Based on Experience.* Paper ID # A078, Massachusetts Institute of Technology, Cambridge, MA.

DuPont Vision Statement (2005). http://www2.dupont.com/Our_Company/en_US/ glance/vision/index.html.

MIT (1997). *MIT: The Impact of Innovation,* BankBoston, Boston, MA. Available through the MIT Website http://web.mit.edu/newsoffice/founders.

Stokes, Donald E. (1997). *Pasteur's Quadrant.* The Brookings Institution Press, Washington D.C.

Vest, Charles M. (2005). Openness and Globalization in Higher Education — The Age of the Internet, Terrorism, and Opportunity. Clark Kerr Lecture in Higher Education, University of California at Santa Barbara.

PART VI

•••••••••••••

Summary

CHAPTER 24

Universities and business — a view from a food company

Peter Brabeck-Letmathe [1]

This paper is about how Nestlé is changing, and how this change might affect our relations with universities. The subject merits, most certainly, an in-depth and prolonged discussion, but this paper will confine itself to just a few aspects.

The ongoing changes at Nestlé are quite profound. In addition to continuous benchmarking, cost reduction and product improvement (both renovation and innovation), we are in the midst of important step changes in three major spheres, namely:

- Adapting our strategic focus to changing product demand;
- Altering the way our people work and cooperate, both within the company and with the outside world; and
- Developing our internal structures and systems, in particular the flow of knowledge (this project is called GLOBE, an acronym for our search for Global Business Excellence in the Nestlé Group).

A few details on the first sphere: We can distinguish between several phases in the demand for food products, which evolve in different markets over time and as people move up the income ladder:

- Initially, food is required to meet subsistence needs — people take what they can get. One of our roles is thus to make products available over time and across a region using our know-how and technology. An example of this relates to dehydration: in the north of India, for

1 Dinner speech on the occasion of the 5th Glion Colloquium, delivered on 20 June 2005 at IMD, Lausanne.

instance, we produce a range of milk products. As milk intake is subject to seasonal fluctuations, we must be able to stock the products to allow us to respond to continuous consumer demand. And with summer temperatures of 40°C and more, the only way to preserve this produce and ensure that it reaches consumers in the big cities in a timely and safe way is through dehydration — the production of milk powder.

- Over time, and with rising incomes, a market develops for products with higher value-added; products, for instance, that offer convenience and pleasure. We meet this changing demand with a diverse range of products, and we provide them in any form (multi-portion or single portion, for example), anywhere and at any time. This allows consumers to choose what they want when they want.

- In the next stage of development of the market, people begin to see nutrition as a door opener to broader well-being and fulfilment. In response to this, we will provide research-based knowledge and solutions, active ingredients and components which ultimately allow people to *design* what they want.

We expect that one of the outcomes of this development will be that food markets become even more complex and diversified, and possibly also more volatile.

Nestlé is responding to the challenge of changing consumer preferences. We are moving from being a "respected and trustworthy *food* company" to being a "respected and trustworthy *food, nutrition, health and wellness* company". As a first step, and in order to reinforce our competitive advantage in nutrition, we have decided to create an autonomous global business organization for nutrition within the Group. The nutrition market has its own characteristics. It is based on high-level research and development, and requires supporting clinical trials, while the consumer's primary motivation for a purchase lies in the nutritional content of the product itself. Our own main focus today is on infant nutrition, health-care nutrition and performance nutrition, and this new organization, Nestlé Nutrition, will be responsible for this part of our business. It will deliver superior business performance by offering consumers trusted, science-based nutrition products and services.

In parallel, thinking further ahead, we have started to ask how, more broadly, we can contribute to consumers' well-being and fulfilment.

In the second sphere: we are altering the way our people work together by:

- moving from a hierarchical structure to flat, highly interlinked networks;

- reassigning management responsibilities and accountability at the major operational levels (profit and loss responsibilities for business executive managers);

- working in clusters around concepts, rather than according to hierarchical structures; and
- opening up to ideas and other inputs from the outside world.

Our principal objectives here are to reinforce the motivation of our staff and to increase their efficiency. Specifically, we want to become more flexible, we want to turn size into strength and enhance our ability to exploit scale, while compromising neither our proximity to the consumer nor our speed of execution. To use a nautical metaphor, instead of being a big tanker, we want to become a fleet of smaller, agile ships. This means abandoning the paradigm that dictates that only focus and streamlining can lead to efficiency. Instead, we are looking for ways to combine complexity and efficiency in constructive ways.

In the third sphere: the two changes just outlined obviously require reform of our internal structures and systems. This is the main purpose of project GLOBE. It aims to create a better, more coherent and relevant flow of information and knowledge on a day-to-day basis. Furthermore, it is designed to ensure a more systematic system of knowledge exchange in order to spread best practices across the global Nestlé network.

These transformations are a response to changing markets and technologies, but they also reflect a vision for Nestlé's development into the middle of the 21st century.

Changes are being introduced in all three spheres simultaneously, despite the inherent complexity of the undertaking. We considered using a more sequential approach, but as research has shown (Pettigrew, 2000), this is unlikely to work for systemic reasons: the three areas are interdependent, and the changes are designed to create a new overall mindset. Furthermore, I am convinced that the necessary transformations can be achieved more rapidly if they are implemented in all three spheres simultaneously.

These changes inevitably alter our existing comprehensive, complex and constructive relations with universities. Let me mention just two aspects:

- The qualifications in the graduates we want to hire are constantly changing, and they are sometimes different from those attained through university education.
- We wish to deepen our research cooperation with universities and to find new forms of partnerships.

So, what kind of graduates do we need to implement the changes at Nestlé? Our general requirements are very much business-oriented. We do not seek intellectual skills for their own sake. The best candidates will certainly have a good stock of basic knowledge, but they will also have the ability to solve unforeseen and unforeseeable problems, and to adapt to changing circumstances.

Clearly we need universities to expand scientific knowledge — and therefore to prepare selected students for doing research. But curricula should not be structured in a way that prepares students principally for academic careers (the type which, of course, their professors know best).

We want to hire graduates with high-quality education, as well as practical know-how and an understanding of business realities. At Nestlé we hire not only people who have studied management, but we also look for nutritionists, biologists, medical doctors, etc.

Recently, I had a long discussion with Professor Ulrich Gäbler, President of the University of Basel, about the training of medical doctors in Europe. He has some excellent ideas, which I think are relevant for other sectors of education, too. He described the existing, rather rigid curriculum that comprises at least seven years of basic training. Prof. Gäbler argued that a more modular education could be appropriate. He envisages a three-year bachelor degree for medical students, which could also incorporate a degree of specialization. This would provide the necessary knowledge base for general practitioners, public health officials or medical technicians. For example, at Nestlé we employ a number of doctors as nutrition specialists. Their role is to inform medical practitioners about our clinical nutrition and more sophisticated infant-nutrition products. These employees need a good academic base, but not the full seven years of training medical doctors receive today.

Further modules of university training could then be offered to those who actually need higher qualifications, or those who are planning a career in advanced research. Those would be the people we would hire for our research activities.

Prof. Gäbler provides another excellent illustration of the markets' changing focus and the rigidity of the university system. Demand is shifting from curative to preventive medicine and medical support for a person's lifestyle (beyond cosmetic surgery). The focus of university education, however, remains (for historical reasons) curative medicine; there is practically no training relating to issues of "well-being" or, for example, nutrition. As he says, both the profession and universities are struggling to accept the idea that there is a market for health care and that consumer demand is changing. They are therefore finding it difficult to adapt to these changes.

My third point is on research and development within Nestlé and the links we necessarily maintain with the academic world. We have our own global research set-up; every year, we invest around 1.4 billion Swiss francs in the development of new processes and products, innovation, renovation and improvement.

And we have excellent, rapidly expanding cooperation with universities. In order to illustrate this, I will mention just one example which is still in an exploratory phase. It shows how cooperation with universities may become an integral part of Nestlé's shifting strategic focus.

As I mentioned earlier, we are broadening our focus from only food and beverages to include nutrition, wellness and ultimately well-being. We have been building up the necessary links with universities for quite some time. For example, the Nestlé Nutrition Council, a group of international experts which advises Nestlé on nutrition and health issues, goes back 25 years. Our Research Centre near Lausanne built on the contacts and experience of the council to launch another initiative, organizing the first International Nutrition Symposium which brought together scientific leaders from a cross-section of disciplines and around the world. Over three days, they addressed key issues central to human well-being and diet. Participants included three Nobel laureates in medicine and physiology. One of them, Günter Blobel (1999 Nobel Laureate), a long-time member of our Nutrition Council, was also elected Member of the Nestlé S.A. Board of Directors in 2005. Our links with the science community have therefore been institutionalized at the highest corporate level.

And we go beyond general discussions, looking constantly for new opportunities. In a recent conversation, Professor Patrick Aebischer, chairman of the Swiss Federal Institute of Technology in Lausanne (EPFL), mentioned his new Research Centre for Degenerative Neurological Disorders. At first glance, this appears to have little to do with food. However, early research suggests that Resveratrol, a substance found in red wine, can slow degradation of the brain (caused by conditions such as Parkinson's and Alzheimer's). We have been aware of this substance for a long time and we know how to combine it, and other substances, with food so they can be easily ingested. We are now looking into ways to cooperate in this area and combine our respective expertise. It is part of our overall perception of well-being, which includes the prevention or early treatment of conditions through food choice, instead of relying on heavy medication after the damage is done.

Our overall approach is not just about preventing harm, but also contributing to well-being in a very broad sense. Let me illustrate the wide range of potential areas of interest with two further quotes: "The hedonic psychology of the future as we imagine it will analyse the full range of evaluative experience, from sensory pleasure to creative excitement, from fleeting anxiety… to joy." (Kahnemann, 1999); and: "Future synergies among nanotechnology, biotechnology, information technology and cognitive science can dramatically improve the human condition." (American Council for the United Nations University, 2005). Needless to say, we will not be able to cover all these areas — nor even try — but we will have to remain open to all these developments.

I will now take a quick look at universities as businesses. Not unlike companies, universities have started to focus on providing value for money, efficient services, etc. And, like companies, they have to handle changing supply and demand. U.S. universities have taken this approach for a long time; now it is slowly coming to Europe, and I believe Swiss universities are quite well positioned. They have started to accept that they are facing growing competition and are adapting their structures to the dynamics of markets. Students are also exposed to more business thinking in its original, pure form through, for example, EPFL initiatives to encourage start-ups by graduates.

Universities have to adapt not only to growing numbers of students and changing demand for graduate qualifications from corporate employers and end-consumers of services, but, more importantly, to a growing supply of knowledge.

We are experiencing an exponential growth in knowledge. Estimates suggest that by the time a child born in 2005 leaves university in 22 to 25 years, worldwide knowledge will have increased fivefold. By the time he/she reaches 50, the volume of worldwide knowledge will be 30 times greater than today. This increasing volume will be matched by a growing variety of uses for knowledge. [2]

The knowledge generated will not only be scientific, and confined to journals, but will consist of a broad base of relevant information.

These growth rates in the main "product" of universities — knowledge — are meant as illustrations. This growth far outstrips average growth rates in industry. Like companies, universities will have to accelerate their processes of change, and like Nestlé, you will probably have to change in several major spheres simultaneously.

It might be interesting to come back to this point that I have only briefly discussed — and see whether there really are some commonalities in the way Nestlé and universities are changing and, indeed, will have to change.

Finally, in closing, one last point. Specifically, I wish to say a few words on IMD, host of the event. What they are doing represents in practical terms some of what I have outlined above.

- IMD has been entrepreneurial right from the beginning;
- IMD provides a modular approach to education, and it constantly adjusts its curricula to its customers, i.e. it is also able to respond to fundamentally changing business needs and other shifts in markets; and
- IMD cooperates closely and successfully with Nestlé and many other firms in conducting highly relevant research.

Given their specific situation, the IMD model cannot simply be transferred to other universities, but this approach may be used as a source of ideas to stimulate further change in our university system. Nestlé is determined to participate in the process as a constructive partner and "customer".

---

2 The volume of data worldwide is growing even faster, it only takes five years to grow 30 times, according to the Gartner Group.

REFERENCES

American Council for the United Nations University. (2005). *State of the Future*, Report http://www.acunu.org/millennium/sof2005.html.

Gäbler, U. (2004). *Hochschulmedizin, wohin?*, Rektoratsrede, Basel.

Kahneman, D. (1999). "Preface" in Diener, E. Kahneman, D. & Schwarz, N. (editors), *Well-Being: The Foundations of Hedonic Psychology*, Russell Sage Foundation, New York, p. ix.

Pettigrew, A. (2000). "Change of structures, processes and focus/limits of a company" in Pettigrew, A. & Fenton, E. (eds), *The Innovating Organisation*, Sage, London.

CHAPTER 25

University-Business
Partnerships
for a Knowledge Society

James J. Duderstadt and Luc E. Weber

The Glion V Colloquium brought together university and corporate leaders from Europe and the United States to discuss how higher education and the business sector could collaborate more effectively to achieve and sustain economic growth, social cohesion, and well-being in an ever more competitive global, knowledge-driven economy. As in past Glion meetings, the discussions involved both round-table discussions of papers prepared in advance and presented by the participants, as well as informal discussions throughout the three-day meeting in Glion above Montreux, Switzerland. The papers presented at the meeting have been included in this book. This final chapter is intended both to provide a sense of the broader discussions and to identify several of the most important themes and conclusions of the meeting.

The working sessions were organized around several topics: an overview of the implications of a knowledge-intensive global economy for business, higher education and government; the changing nature of the creation and transfer of knowledge from research universities to industry and thence society; the differing perspectives of university-business relationships as seen both by universities and the business community in Europe and America; the increasingly critical role played by advanced education in producing human capital, particularly in key fields such as science and engineering; and the importance of the social sciences and humanities in achieving social cohesion in increasingly multicultural and multi-ethnic societies, while promoting sustainable development. Although the papers included in this book have been organized

281

around these subjects, as were the working sessions, in this summary it seems more appropriate to adopt an organization based on the key themes that arose from the working sessions and other discussions throughout the meeting:

- The challenges of a global, knowledge-driven economy;
- The differing perspectives of business, universities and governments in Europe and America;
- More fundamental concerns;
- The need for new paradigms;
- The implications for higher education;
- The implications for university-business relationships.

THE CHALLENGES OF A GLOBAL, KNOWLEDGE-DRIVEN ECONOMY

We live in a time of great change, an increasingly global society, knitted together by pervasive communications and transportation technologies and driven by the exponential growth of new knowledge. A global, knowledge-driven economy places a new premium on education and workforce skills and education, challenging both ageing populations in Europe, North America, and parts of Asia, and the youth-dominated populations of the developing world. Social cohesion remains an ideal in many countries that continue to be challenged by ethnic, religious and regional disputes, while the great disparity in wealth and power around the globe creates new geopolitical tensions through conflict and terrorism. Further population growth and economic development threaten global sustainability through the depletion of natural resources such as petroleum and the impact of human activities on climate.

More fundamentally, we are evolving rapidly into a post-industrial, knowledge-based society, a shift in culture and technology as profound as the shift that took place a century ago when our agrarian societies evolved into industrial nations (Drucker, 1993). A radically new system for creating wealth has evolved that depends upon advanced education, research and innovation, and hence upon knowledge-intensive organizations such as research universities, corporate R & D laboratories and national research agencies.

The implications for discovery-based learning institutions such as the research university are particularly profound. The knowledge economy is demanding new types of learners and creators. Globalization requires thoughtful, interdependent and globally identified citizens. New technologies are changing modes of learning, collaboration and expression. And widespread social and political unrest compels educational institutions to think more concertedly about their responsibility in promoting individual and civic development, democratic values and social cohesion. Institutional and pedagogical innovations are needed to confront these dynamics and ensure that the canonical activities of universities — research, teaching and engagement — remain rich, relevant and accessible.

Both developed and developing nations are investing heavily in education and research, restructuring their economies to create high-skill, high-pay jobs in knowledge-intensive areas such as new technologies, professional services, trade and health care. From San Diego to Dublin, Helsinki to Bangalore, there is a growing recognition throughout the world that prosperity and social well-being in a global, knowledge-driven economy require significant public investment in knowledge resources. That is, regions must create and sustain a highly educated and innovative workforce, supported through policies and investments in cutting-edge technology, a knowledge infrastructure and human capital development. Moreover, social challenges such as the healthcare costs of ageing populations, social diversity and retirement pensions will require comparable investments in the social sciences and humanities. Nations both large and small, developed and developing, are beginning to reap the benefits of such investments aimed at stimulating and exploiting technological innovation, creating serious competitive challenges to American and European industry and business both in the conventional marketplace (e.g., Toyota) and through new paradigms such as the global sourcing of knowledge-intensive services (e.g. Bangalore).

These imperatives of the knowledge economy provide the context for the discussion of university-business relationships, since the intensifying nature of global competition and importance of technological innovation will demand significant changes in the way research is prioritized, funded, conducted and transferred to society, perhaps shifting university emphasis towards use-driven basic research and innovation; the way we educate and employ professionals such as scientists and engineers; policies and legal structures in areas such as intellectual property; strategies to maximize contributions from institutions and workforce development (e.g., universities, corporate R & D laboratories, government agencies); and in the very nature of social institutions such as corporations, governments, NGOs and universities and the ways in which these interact with one another.

The increasing social needs of an ageing population and a slowdown in economic growth, coupled with the increasing competitiveness of rapidly growing Asian economies, have stimulated a number of European nations to adopt the Lisbon Agenda (2000) "to become the most competitive and dynamic knowledge-based economy with more and better jobs and social cohesion" by "mobilizing the brainpower of Europe". While this establishes major investments in higher education and research as priorities, with the goal of bringing Europe up to the level of the United States by 2010, there are serious concerns that such an ambitious objective may be inconsistent with the low economic growth of national economies (*The Economist*, 2005). Furthermore it will likely require major structural changes in how European universities are organized, governed and financed.

While the long-standing partnership among research universities, business and government in the United States continues to maintain global leadership in measures such as the percentage of GDP invested in R & D, the number and productivity of researchers, and the volume of high-tech production and exports, there are several worrisome trends: the decline in federal funding for basic research, the imbalance in the national research portfolio, with roughly two-thirds of university research now in the biomedical sciences; the erosion of basic research in both corporate R & D laboratories and federal agencies; the increasing complexity of intellectual property policies; and an inadequate supply of scientists and engineers in the wake of the changing immigration policies in the aftermath of the terrorist attacks of 2001. Of particular concern is achieving adequate investment in the new knowledge (research), human capital (education), and infrastructure (institutions, laboratories, networks) and policies (tax, intellectual property) necessary to sustain America's leadership in technological innovation, now challenged by corporate practices such as global sourcing of R & D, innovation and design to rapidly emerging economies in Asia.

Yet there is an additional caution here: universities have a broader public purpose than merely responding to the economic needs of society. Universities defend and propagate our cultural and intellectual heritage; they are the source of leaders of our governments, commerce and professions; and they provide through educational opportunity the skills necessary to enable social well-being and justice. They are complex social institutions characterized by great diversity, reflecting their adaptation to regional needs and challenges. While the current imperatives of the global economy have stimulated governments to encourage more competition among universities through market forces, there may be instances in which this market orientation does not align well with broader social needs.

A global knowledge-driven economy is challenging all of the assumptions and practices of the past — geopolitical, economic, information and disciplinary. It is becoming apparent in both Europe and America that our current partnerships, programmes and policies for the conduct of research and advanced education must be transformed to better serve the knowledge economy. This, then, provides the challenge, within a context of issues such as the balance between public vs. private investments, competition vs. cooperation, and public policy vs. market forces.

EUROPE AND AMERICAN PERSPECTIVES

There are many similarities between the European and American perspectives of the challenges and opportunities presented by a global, knowledge-driven economy. Both European and American companies recognize that they can no longer rely solely upon internally conducted R & D, both because of shareholder pressures and the increasing pace of technological change. Instead companies must establish networks of research partnerships in both the public and private sectors. Corporate leaders see relationships with research universities as critical in providing access to key sources of basic research and advanced. Yet there are growing concerns about the difficulty in establishing and sustaining these relationships.

The concern most frequently expressed by American companies is the difficulty in negotiating intellectual property rights with universities, which now seek to capture the considerable value of the intellectual property generated by campus-based research and attempt to defend their ownership and access to potential licensing income with complex contracts and litigation. Since many companies view intellectual property ownership and access as a defensive measure to protect proprietary knowledge rather than generate new revenues (although the pharmaceutical industry is an exception), they are frustrated by the time and expense it takes to negotiate research relationships with universities. Some companies have become so frustrated that they have now shifted their attention to universities in nations with less aggressive intellectual property objectives (e.g., China, Taiwan, India).

Business leaders noted that there has been considerable success in negotiating company-to-company relationships in sharing technology even with competitors, in part because there was a body of practice to rely upon, in contrast to company-to-university relationships, in which industry felt that the anarchy characterizing higher education meant that each negotiation began by trying to reinvent the wheel. Several industrial participants suggested that the private sector would simply not tolerate interminable discussions about intellectual property issues that showed little promise of early resolution. They urged European universities not to emulate the American practice and instead to develop a more positive and structured approach to these issues, e.g., through the intellectual property guidelines developed — among others — by the European Research Management Association (EIRMA) (2004) and the European University Association (EUA).

But university leaders also expressed frustration with the current relationships with business. As one university leader noted, many companies have downsized or eliminated corporate R & D and are now turning to research universities to fill the void. Of course, part of the challenge here is that the highly directed research sought by industry frequently does not align well either with university capabilities or faculty interests. But there is also a cultural issue, since rather than approaching this relationship as the procurement of needed technology and human capital, many companies view their support instead as more philanthropic than as a strategic quid pro quo relationship with a critical supplier. All too frequently companies suggest that their corporate taxes already have paid for the university infrastructure and personnel necessary to conduct the research, although even a superficial analysis of the financing of higher education quickly reveals the fallacy in this perspective.

There seems to be a growing awareness that, beyond the inevitable frustrations with particular issues such as intellectual property rights and full economic recovery of research costs, there were deeper issues that related to the strategic nature of the relationship to both the company and the university. The most successful examples of industry-university relationships seemed to arise when companies had a carefully designed strategy for managing their relationship with universities, perhaps through separate subsidiaries much as they manage business-to-business technology alliances. Similarly, universities need to perceive true value-added in the relationship, particularly in an era in which they were expected to generate most of the support for their teaching, research and service activities from the marketplace. As we will note later, this is particularly true in the United States, where many universities have concluded that their maximum contribution to society — and benefit to the institution — is through the spin-off of new ventures that rely heavily upon intellectual property ownership to attract private investment capital. This is a much deeper issue, since it suggests that at least some universities see their mission more as creating new industry than supporting existing industry.

Governments also have their own perspectives of these relationships. In both Europe and the United States there has been a gradual erosion in public support of universities — at least on a per student basis — associated both with the desire to provide higher education opportunities to an increasing fraction of the population (massification) and because of the shifting priorities of ageing populations (health care, security, tax relief). Yet, simultaneously, there has been growing awareness in recent years that a global, knowledge-driven economy demands enhanced capacity in research, innovation and in advanced education. The challenge is how to achieve this.

Many national and regional governments continue to view public support of higher education and research not as an investment, but rather as an expenditure competing with other current needs (e.g., health care, retirement pensions). Politicians continue to call for universities to do more with less through restructuring and enhanced productivity, suggesting that perhaps stimulating more competition among institutions will stimulate both quality and capacity even in the absence of additional investments. They suggest that by challenging faculty privileges (tenure, academic freedom) or restructuring universities (mission differentiation, competition for resources), higher education can be made far more responsive and efficient. While it is certainly true that cost-containment and accountability are important issues, it is also the case that in many nations, particularly in Europe, universities can rightly counter-argue that the main problem for them is that they are over-regulated and under-funded. On average, the total investment on higher education and research in Europe is roughly 4% of GDP, compared to 6% of GDP in the United States. It is unlikely that efficiency alone could close this funding gap that has been key to the faster development of American higher education and research over the last 20 to 30 years.

European university leaders expressed many concerns about the financial vulnerability of their institutions, still primarily dependent on tax support without appreciable student fees or gift income, relatively small, and insufficiently entrepreneurial compared to the massive research universities in America, with relatively weak governance incapable of driving major changes or exerting strong leadership. This situation was made even more difficult by the necessity of extending education to an appreciable fraction of the workforce in European nations, an imperative of the global economy. The current model for financing higher education in Europe, almost entirely dependent upon public tax support, is simply incapable of sustaining massification while achieving world-class quality. Currently the investment in higher education in European countries ranges from 0.9% to 1.8% of GDP, of which only approximately 10% comes from private sources (e.g., student fees). In sharp contrast, the United States spends roughly 2.5% of GDP on higher education, of which over two-thirds comes from private support, including student fees, private gifts, and income-generating activities (e.g., the licensing of intellectual property). Since tax revenues are already stretched thin sustaining Europe's strong social programmes, it seems unlikely that the E.U. and other developed European nations will be able to provide the advanced educational opportunities required by a knowledge-driven economy without appreciable changes in tax policies (to encourage private philanthropy) and student/family expectations (to accept significantly higher student fees).

In Europe, the goal of the Lisbon agenda to increase the level of spending in research to 3% of GDP, with two-thirds being invested by the private sector, would depend on increasing by 70% the number of researchers to 700,000, which is simply not manageable without a strong influx of scientists from other countries in East and central Europe, Asia and Latin America. Since most of the research in E.U. countries is done in the northwest region of Europe whose origin is around Vienna, this very fact would have dramatic consequences on the less developed countries in eastern, central and southern Europe.

Yet, while perhaps more generously supported from public and private sources, numerous recent studies have concluded that even the current United States research and higher education portfolio has neither the magnitude nor the balance of investment necessary to address the nation's key priorities — national security, public health, environmental sustainability, or economic competitiveness (Council on Competitiveness, 2004; National Academies, 2005). Even in the highly competitive American higher education enterprise, there is a growing concern about whether the universities have sufficient agility, capacity and quality to serve the needs of their regions or the nation itself as they face an increasingly competitive global economy.

There were also serious concerns expressed, particularly by the American participants, about the availability of graduates in knowledge-intensive areas such as science and engineering. Eroding student interest in science and mathematics and the weakness of K-12 education have led to a situation in which engineering students comprise less than 5% of American college graduates, compared to 12% in Europe and over 50% in some Asian countries. The United States has traditionally been able to compensate for this domestic shortfall by using its high quality universities to attract talented students in science and engineering from other countries. However in the wake of 9/11, a tightening of immigration policies, coupled with the increasing efforts of other nations to compete for foreign university students, has threatened this supply.

MORE FUNDAMENTAL ISSUES

There are important similarities between Europe and America as they strive to compete in the global economy. Although both European nations and American states have largely taken higher education for granted for the past several decades, allowing an erosion in public support per student as other social needs, such as health care and retirement pensions, were given higher priorities, today there is a growing recognition that a substantial reinvestment in research and advanced education is necessary for economic prosperity and security in a knowledge economy. In Europe, such initiatives are both pan-European like the European Higher Education Area (e.g., the Bologna process) or at the level of the European Commission (e.g., the Lisbon agenda), with initiatives such as the European Research Area (better integration of National and European research policies and the project of the European Research Council), with a target of increasing R & D to 3% of GDP by 2010. In contrast, the United States response to the challenge of the global knowledge economy thus far is dominated more by rhetoric than commitment at either the federal or the state level.

The Lisbon agenda tends to use as a benchmark the United States investments in higher education and research, while the Bologna process and ERC tend to emulate characteristics of the American research universities (e.g., standardizing university degrees upon the bachelors, masters, and Ph.D., while basing the envisaged European Research Council research programmes on competitive, peer-reviewed grants much like the U.S. National Science Foundation). Ironically, the United States today is not looking back over its shoulder to Europe, but rather looking ahead at the competitive threat posed by the explosion of high-quality research and education in science and engineering in Asia, particularly China and India.

There are several important differences in the approaches taken by European and American universities towards knowledge transfer from campus laboratories into society and their relationships with industry. European universities continue to embrace a linear model of knowledge transfer, from basic research to applied research and development and finally into products and services. Hence their greatest academic strengths are in the more mature disciplines such as physics, chemistry and mathematics. American universities are restructuring themselves to adapt to a highly non-linear model of knowledge flow, increasingly characteristic of technology-driven economic development. Both universities and funding agencies are blurring the distinction between basic and applied research, building the multi-, inter- and cross-disciplinary programmes necessitated by technologies such as information-, bio- and nano-technology that evolve at exponential pace (e.g., Moore's Law). While European universities and industry strive to build enduring collaborative research networks in response to national or E.U. objectives and according to their own specific comparative advantage, market-driven research universities in the United States tend to focus instead on regional technology-driven economic development through spin-off and start-up companies, giving highest priority to building new industries in cutting-edge technology (info-bio-nano) rather than sustaining older industries (e.g., manufacturing). While Europe attempts to build the university, national and EU structures and policies to produce the research and advanced education required by a knowledge economy, the anarchy of the American marketplace prefers more of a "just do it" philosophy.

The American participants reviewed the history of several of the more prominent stories of technology-driven economic development in the United States: Route 128, the Research Triangle, San Diego and Austin). It was suggested that just as "all politics is local", "all economic development is regional". In each case, the trigger event was the phenomenal success of a start-up company spun off from faculty research, which created the wealth (and the wealthy entrepreneurs) that was ploughed back as venture capital into the next round of start-ups, e.g., Digital Equipment Corporation in Boston, SAS in North Carolina, Qualcomm in San Diego, and Dell Computers in San Diego. There were notable differences, of course. The Austin economic miracle involved a partnership between the University of Texas and state government, along with public funding, to attract key research organizations (the Microelectronics and Computer Corporation); San Diego relied primarily on private capital; Stanford and Austin both made a strategic asset of their substantial land holdings. There are early signs that similar strategies of new high-tech business development are beginning to appear in Europe around several leading research institutes and universities such as the Fraunhofer Institutes and the Swiss Federal Institute of Technology.

Yet at the core of all of these efforts are world-class research universities that serve as magnets to attract top talent, along with the high quality of life characterizing their surrounding communities that kept talent in the region. These universities were characterized both by focused excellence, as well as intellectual breadth that allowed them to span many fields, engaging in both basic and applied research of the highest quality. In each case, university, industry and government leadership were well aligned and capable of working together at the highest level. Each situation began with a "big hit" that then provided both the role model and the venture capital stream for subsequent start-ups.

There is one more key feature of these success stories that may explain much of the frustration occurring today in university-business relations. In each case, ownership of key intellectual property was critical to attracting the necessary private capital for successful start-ups. Both universities and faculty entrepreneurs were aggressive in capturing and retaining intellectual property rights. In the United States, research universities have embraced a sophisti-cated, non-linear model of knowledge transfer, where they increasingly view their primary missions — not to mention their greatest rewards — as creating new industries rather than supporting old companies. Put another way, Amer-ican universities see their greatest value to society and their greatest institu-tional payoff in Schumpeter's "creative destruction", building the new indus-tries that will eventually devour the old. Hence it is not surprising that established companies seeking cooperative relationships are increasing frus-trated by the priorities American universities give to spin-offs and start-ups requiring aggressive negotiations to retain the intellectual property rights nec-essary to attract private investment. Although some companies have adopted a near-term strategy of off-shoring their R & D activities to nations with less aggressive intellectual property demands, over the longer term this will deprive them of access to many of the world's leading research universities.

More cynically, one might even question the strategy that many established companies have adopted to dismantle their own internal capacity for R & D and instead outsource R & D through cooperative relationships with research universities. Rather than welcoming them with open arms, many American universities are negotiating with them just as other companies would, insisting on beneficial intellectual property rights and adequate support of research costs. Cooperative arrangements with universities will have to have sufficient benefits to compete with spin-off activities, either through direct financial support of the university by industry or through indirect support through industry's ability to influence government policies for investing in R & D and higher education. This brave, new world of peer-to-peer university-industry relationships has been a shock to many companies that have long viewed support of higher education as philanthropy rather than a quid pro quo strategic technology alliance!

In contrast, as we could expect from the small size of most countries, European universities are less focused on regional economic development and more aligned with national policy, seeking cooperative relationships with established industry and less inclined to be aggressive in negotiating intellectual property rights. To some degree the lower number of start-up companies may be due to the more limited autonomy and agility of government-funded European research universities, thereby inhibiting risk-taking and entrepreneurial activities, as well as due to the limited availability of venture capital. Concern was also expressed that such autonomy might be further eroded by the decreasing trust in higher education institutions as well as due to E.U. integration, particularly if it introduces additional layers of bureaucracy.

While differences in university funding, governance and leadership are certainly factors in explaining the contrasts between university-business relationships in Europe and the United States, of far more importance are more fundamental perspectives of mission. The E.U. and national strategies are to build strong partnerships and collaborative networks to sustain existing industry, relying on a more traditional linear model of technology transfer, albeit with higher transactions costs. The contrasting U.S. strategy is to take advantage of market efficiencies by building competitive environments and providing universities with the autonomy and agility to create new companies and new industries through non-linear models of technology transfer.

THE NEED FOR NEW PARADIGMS

Much of the discussion at the Glion V sessions concerned the exploration of new paradigms for both higher education and its interaction with industry and broader society. It was noted that the organization of faculty within the university was changing, as communications and transportation technologies have enabled scholars to form global research communities, largely decoupled from universities. To some degree the faculty exhibits an uncertainty principle similar to that of quantum physics, since the more one attempts to determine their location, the less one is able to influence their calendar. Faculty loyalty long ago shifted from the university to disciplines, and now it is shifting again to problem areas. Discussions raised some important questions, for example, what is the best way to organize faculty expertise? What should the relation between the university and the faculty member be? What is the true value-added of a university?

The Fraunhofer Institutes provide an interesting example of the changing nature of technology transfer, innovation and economic impact. The traditional linear model began with attracting the best faculty to a research university, providing them with adequate resources, preferably through competitive grants, and then disseminating the results of research widely. However beyond the fact that this model does not scale easily and can take years, if not decades, to build institutional capacity, simply hiring the best people does not always work since experts are highly mobile. Furthermore, first-class research does not necessarily imply innovation. A variation on the traditional approach is to hire top talent and focus major investments only in highly specialized areas, relying on networking with other top programmes to broaden capacity. But this model can be inherently unstable, since while it builds strength in building spires of excellence, these may not yield the necessary ingredients for innovation in a rapidly evolving knowledge economy.

The experience of the Fraunhofer Institutes suggests an alternative approach of financing cooperative projects to create clusters, with an emphasis upon financing new ventures and promoting innovative markets through tax breaks and the active management of intellectual property. More broadly, while the benefits of innovation are widely recognized, it is hard to achieve an innovative economy. Success requires years of effort and a visible plan, acceptable to both the pubic and private sectors, which matches local strengths and achieves commitment for the long haul. While high-quality research universities are important, they should avoid technology determinism and instead bring not only basic and applied research, but also stimulate financial acumen and enlightened public policies.

Ireland and Finland provide vivid demonstrations of how effective public policies and targeted investments can create an environment in which innovation can flourish. Ireland's efforts to bootstrap to build a prosperous knowledge economy are particularly interesting. It involved an investment in human capital (e.g., universal secondary education in the 1960s and postsecondary education in the 1990s), tax policies that lowered taxes on corporate earnings, and social policies such as a national healthcare system that minimized cost to business. Today Ireland continues to invest heavily in knowledge generation through increasing university R & D (already at a greater per capita amount that the United States and allocated using international peer review) and stimulating corporate R & D through favourable tax treatment. The combination of a highly educated workforce, investment in R & D, attractive tax policies and supportive social policies has both attracted and created high-tech industry, while transforming the nation into one of Europe's most prosperous.

Although difficult to predict, it was also likely that the paradigm of the university itself was changing. It was noted that fundamental changes in higher education had occurred in the United States roughly every 50 years, from the colonial colleges of 1800 to the land-grant public universities in 1850 to graduate and professional education in 1900, to the federally supported research university in 1950. It was suggested that the next stage might be the "meta-university", in which rapidly evolving information and communications technologies, coupled with "open source/open content" philosophies, provide a platform for global universities. Ongoing experiments, such as MIT's Open CourseWare, DSpace, and Open Knowledge Initiative projects, the SAKAI Middleware Project, and Google's project to digitize and distribute online the massive holdings of several of the world's leading libraries, suggest that the future of the university is unpredictable indeed.

Hence many participants believed that it was foolhardy to constrain university evolution through detailed planning. Instead it was best to create a competitive environment, a level playing field where quality was rewarded, and in which the cream would rise to the top. Excellence comes about from backing potential winners, not from rescuing losers. While building capacity was an important role of government, it should not be confused with stimulating research excellence.

THE IMPLICATIONS FOR RESEARCH UNIVERSITIES

Although there are very significant differences between research universities in Europe and the United States, there is a strong commonality in the central role these institutions are expected to play — indeed, must play — in the knowledge economies sought by their regions and nations. This role of providing well educated graduates and knowledge professionals, research, innovation, and entrepreneurial energy will demand certain changes in how these critical institutions are structured, financed, governed and led.

The challenges are somewhat different in Europe than the United States. First, it has become increasingly clear that, with public tax support of higher education constrained by the burdens of generous social services and weak economic growth, further massification will only erode the support of research universities. While increasing student fees and modifying tax policies to encourage philanthropic support of higher education will be challenging, many participants saw no alternative to enhanced private support if Europe's universities are to remain competitive.

Stratification is also a challenge to higher education, where broad distribution of resources leads to the illusion that the E.U. has 1,000 quality research universities, with the result being that only a handful are truly world-class. Too many universities are chasing the same institutional mission as world-class research universities, where their small size and modest resource base makes this clearly impossible. There needs to be a greater transparency, realism and differentiation by mission.

Another major challenge has to do with the relative absence of comprehensive research universities in Europe with a critical mass in most disciplines, spanning the full spectrum of academic and professional disciplines and missions, as hundreds do in the United States and an increasing number strive to do in Asia. The increasingly non-linear paradigms of knowledge transfer, in which not only do disciplines interact in surprising ways, but there is extensive overlap between basic and applied research and development — and hence academic disciplines and professional education (e.g., basic life sciences and clinical practice in medicine or quantum physics and electrical engineering), demand universities of sufficient intellectual breadth and capacity. This may be one of the reasons that, although many European universities are renowned for leadership in selected areas of basic research, they are less well known for innovation or entrepreneurial activities. Although the limited intellectual span of most European universities can be addressed to some degree through the formation of collaborative alliances, in the longer run it is likely that only through the merger of many existing institutions will Europe be able to create large comprehensive universities that are competitive on a global level.

A third challenge is creating a competitive environment that encourages the evolution of world-class institutions. Clearly this is an objective of the envisaged European Research Council, which aims to implement a peer review system that recognizes excellence and focuses resources accordingly. World-class research universities arise from a resource allocation and reward system based on absolute excellence, as determined by peer review on a global level. Yet shifting from an egalitarian to a more elitist system that builds and sustains a small number of world-class research universities, likely excluding some E.U. nations entirely, will encounter political difficulties, just as it has among the have-not states in the United States. Some participants were concerned that seeking to recognize a relatively small number of research universities could lead to a policy of ossification rather than a development and recognition of research potential. Striking the right balance between focusing resources to build truly world-class research universities, while building broader research capacity in higher education, will be a public policy challenge. To these challenges to European universities must be added the burdens of long-standing traditions of governance and management, combined with relatively powerless leadership that is currently unable to provide the autonomy and agility to compete effectively in the global marketplace for talent, resources and reputation.

American universities are also facing major challenges that will demand significant changes in structure and policy if they are to play the role they must in a knowledge society. Participants suggested a mosaic of concerns that, when viewed more broadly, suggests a national trend toward short-term thinking and preserving the status quo. Recent modifications in immigration poli-cies, export controls and restrictions on so-called "sensitive, but unclassified" information in the wake of 9/11 are seriously hindering both access to foreign students and faculty and international cooperation, long key to the quality of American research universities (Committee on Science, Engineering, and Public Policy, 2005). Federal research policy, increasingly distorted by the massive increase in the funding of biomedical research demanded by an ageing population, and now seriously constrained by the budget deficits arising from ill-considered tax cuts and the build-up of national defence, threaten the research capacity of U.S. universities. In this climate, researchers are becom-ing increasingly risk-adverse, in an effort to secure and sustain research grant support. Furthermore, in some fields, such as biomedical research, a feudal cul-ture has evolved in which young investigators are held in a subservient and underpaid postdoctoral role for a decade or more, effectively as the migrant worker population sustaining the research enterprise until well into their pro-fessional careers.

The highly competitive nature of higher education in America, where uni-versities compete for the best faculty, the best students, resources from public and private sources, athletic supremacy and reputation, has created an envi-ronment that demands excellence. However it has also created an intensely Darwinian, "winner-take-all" ecosystem in which the strongest and wealthiest institutions have become predators, raiding the best faculty and students of the less generously supported and more constrained public universities and manipulating federal research and financial policies to sustain a system in which the rich get richer and the poor get devoured. More serious is a national climate in which higher education is increasingly seen as more a personal ben-efit than a public good benefiting all of society, which, in turn, leads both pol-iticians and the public at large to view its support as just another expenditure rather than an investment in the future. Today in the face of limited resources and more pressing social priorities, the century-long expansion of public sup-port of higher education has slowed to a halt and actually has been declining for the past two decades. While there may be no perceived crisis in the indi-vidual elements of this mosaic of concerns, the larger pattern is quite disturb-ing, and certainly threatening to the nation's efforts to adapt to a hyper-com-petitive global knowledge economy.

THE IMPLICATIONS FOR UNIVERSITY-BUSINESS RELATIONSHIPS

There is no single model for successful university-business relationships. Local circumstances can often dictate the nature of this interaction. For example, in those regions where the primary goal is high-tech economic development through spin-offs and start-up companies from university research activities (e.g., North Carolina's Research Triangle or California's Silicon Valley), university ownership of intellectual property becomes very important. This can frustrate the efforts of established industry to build research partnerships, since the result-ing negotiations can be complex, time-consuming and dominated by lawyers.

To be sure, there are other regions — and nations — where such intellectual property rights are not so critical, and traditional research partnerships are easily negotiated. Yet a business strategy of building R & D networks that avoid con-tentious intellectual property negotiations, perhaps even off-shoring these to developing nations such as India and China, could well be self-defeating in the long run, since it would deprive companies of access to the leading research pro-grammes. Furthermore, it is likely that most regions — and institutions — will emulate the success of the American spin-off-start-up entrepots and eventually become more aggressive in intellectual property negotiations.

An additional challenge will be the changing nature of the university itself. As innovation and entrepreneurial activity become more significant priorities for academe, stimulated both by the increasingly non-linear nature of knowl-edge creation and transfer, as well as by the needs of a knowledge economy, universities are likely to strive for a different mix of basic and applied research and development (Council on Competitiveness, 2004). Of course, this is not a new phenomenon, as evidenced by the agricultural experiment stations cre-ated by the American land-grant university movement and later the compre-hensive academic medical centres, combining basic research, medical training and clinical care. In fact, some universities may even attempt to emulate suc-cessful external efforts like the Fraunhofer Institutes in Europe or the national laboratories in the United States.

Hence it is important for industry to recognize that their university partners will increasingly resemble other business partners rather than the traditional ivory towers of academe. That is, it could well be that established companies and universities would be more successful in building research alliances according to well established business-to-business relationships, rather than traditional university-industry models. This will require a more strategic approach to university relations on the part of the business community, view-ing these as more as quid pro quo alliances providing both knowledge (basic research, technology and perhaps even innovation) and human capital (grad-uates in science, engineering, business and other high-demand fields) in return for comparable financial support and technology sharing than a phil-anthropic relationship. Universities, in turn, will be held more accountable for honouring the terms of the negotiated relationship, requiring faculty com-mitment, and accepting some degree of financial liability. Clearly (and, unfor-tunately inevitably), lawyers will continue to be an important part of this negotiation in the United States.

It is likely that new types of organizations will be necessary to create and sustain such alliances. Existing industry may find it useful to create new companies or organizations for the strategic management of such technology alliances, behaving more as start-up ventures than long-established enterprises. Universities could consider more flexible structures similar to the academic medical centre for building alliances with industry for basic and applied research and innovation such as the Discovery-Innovation Institutes recently proposed by the U.S. National Academy of Engineering.

Let there be no doubt, however. In a global, knowledge-driven economy the keys to economic success are a well educated workforce, technological capability, capital investment, and entrepreneurial zeal — a message well understood by developed and developing nations alike throughout the world that are investing in the necessary human capital and knowledge infrastructure. Key in this effort will be building strong relationships between universities, as the source of new knowledge and the well educated graduate, and industry, with the goal of adding value to the knowledge and human capital necessary to produce competitive products, processes and services to achieve profit and social prosperity in a global economy.

REFERENCES

Committee on Science, Engineering, and Public Policy. (2005). *Policy Implications of International Graduate Students and Postdoctoral Scholars in the United States.* National Academy Press, Washington D.C.

Council on Competitiveness. (2004): "Innovate America", Washington, D.C. Available online at: *http://www.compete.org/pdf/NII_Final_Report.pdf;*

Drucker, P. F. (1993). *Post-capitalist Society*, Harper Collins, New York.

European Research Management Association and others. (2004). "Responsible Partnering, Joining forces in a world of open innovation". http://www.eirma.org/f3/local_links.php?action=jump&id=796

Friedman, T. L. (2005). *The World is Flat: A Brief History of the 21st Century*, Farrar, Strauss, and Giroux, New York.

Lisbon European Council. (2000). Presidency conclusions, 23-24 March. http://ue.eu.int/ueDocs/cms_Data/docs/pressData/en/ec/00100-r1.en0.htm

National Academy of Engineering Committee to Assess the Capacity of the U.S. Engineering Research Enterprise, J. J. Duderstadt, chair. (2005). *Engineering Research and America's Future: Meeting the Challenges of a Global Economy*, National Academies Press, Washington D.C.

National Academies Committee on Prospering in the Global Economy of the 21st Century, Norman Augustine, Chair (2005). *Rising Above the Gathering Storm: Energizing and Employing America for a Brighter Economic Future*, National Academies Press, Washington D.C.

The Economist. (2005). "The state of Europe's higher education is a long term threat to its competitiveness", 8 September.

Réalisé en P.A.O. par STDI - Z. A. Route de Couterne - 53110 Lassay-les-Châteaux
N° 389859H - *Imprimé en France.* - JOUVE, 11, bd de Sébastopol, 75001 PARIS